ADVANCES IN LIBRARY ADMINISTRATION AND ORGANIZATION

ADVANCES IN LIBRARY ADMINISTRATION AND ORGANIZATION

Series Editors: Edward D. Garten and
Delmus E. Williams

Recent Volumes:

Volume 1:   Series Editors: W. Carl Jackson, Bernard
                 Kreissman and Gerard B. McCabe

Volume 2–12:   Series Editors: Bernard Kreissman and
                 Gerard B. McCabe

Volume 13–20:   Series Editors: Edward D. Garten and
                 Delmus E. Williams

Volume 21–24:   Series Editors: Edward D. Garten,
                 Delmus E. Williams and James M. Nyce

ADVANCES IN LIBRARY ADMINISTRATION AND
ORGANIZATION   VOLUME 25

ADVANCES IN LIBRARY ADMINISTRATION AND ORGANIZATION

EDITED BY

EDWARD D. GARTEN
University of Dayton Libraries, Ohio, USA

DELMUS E. WILLIAMS
University of Akron Libraries, Ohio, USA

JAMES M. NYCE
Ball State University, Muncie, Indiana, USA

SANNA TALJA
University of Tampere, Finland

ELSEVIER
JAI

Amsterdam – Boston – Heidelberg – London – New York – Oxford
Paris – San Diego – San Francisco – Singapore – Sydney – Tokyo

JAI Press is an imprint of Elsevier

JAI Press is an imprint of Elsevier
Linacre House, Jordan Hill, Oxford OX2 8DP, UK
Radarweg 29, PO Box 211, 1000 AE Amsterdam, The Netherlands
525 B Street, Suite 1900, San Diego, CA 92101-4495, USA

First edition 2007

Notice
No responsibility is assumed by the publisher for any injury and/or damage to persons
or property as a matter of products liability, negligence or otherwise, or from any use
or operation of any methods, products, instructions or ideas contained in the material
herein. Because of rapid advances in the medical sciences, in particular, independent
verification of diagnoses and drug dosages should be made

British Library Cataloguing in Publication Data
A catalogue record for this book is available from the British Library

ISBN: 978-0-7623-1411-9
ISSN: 0732-0671 (Series)

For information on all JAI Press publications
visit our website at books.elsevier.com

Printed and bound in the United Kingdom

07 08 09 10 11 10 9 8 7 6 5 4 3 2 1

Working together to grow
libraries in developing countries
www.elsevier.com | www.bookaid.org | www.sabre.org

ELSEVIER   BOOK AID
International   Sabre Foundation

CONTENTS

v

LIST OF CONTRIBUTORS

Ari-Veikko Anttiroiko	Department of Regional Studies, University of Tampere, Tampere, Finland
Eeva-Liisa Eskola	Department of Information Studies, Åbo Akademi University, Åbo, Finland
Edward D. Garten	Dayton, Ohio, United States
Turid Hedlund	Swedish School of Economics and Business Administration, Helsinki, Finland
Maija-Leena Huotari	Department of Finnish, Information Studies and Logopedics, University of Oulu, Oulu, Finland
Mirja Iivonen	Tampereen University Library, Tampere, Finland
Arja Juntunen	University of Kuopio Library, Kuopio, Finland
Vesa Kautto	Tampere, Finland
Terttu Kortelainen	Department of Finnish, Information Studies and Logopedics, University of Oulu, Oulu, Finland
Harriet Lönnqvist	Department of Information Studies, University of Tampere, Tampere, Finland
Ilkka Mäkinen	Department of Information Studies, University of Tampere, Tampere, Finland
James M. Nyce	Department of Anthropology, Ball State University, Muncie, USA
Päivi Rasinkangas	Department of Finnish, Information Studies and Logopedics, University of Oulu, Oulu, Finland

Annikki Roos   National Public Health Institute, Helsinki, Finland

Jarmo Saarti   Kuopio University Library, Kuopio, Finland

Reijo Savolainen   Department of Information Studies, University of Tampere, Finland

Sanna Talija   Department of Information Studies, University of Tampere, Tampore, Finland

Kimmo Tuominen   Library of Parliament, Helsinki, Finland

Timo Turja   Library of Parliament, Helsinki, Finland

Gunilla Widén-Wulff   Department of Information Studies, Åbo Akademi University, Tavastgatan, Åbo, Finland

Delmus Williams   University of Akron Libraries, OH, USA

PREFACE

Over the years, we the editors of ALAO have worked to internationalize the annual volume. In addition to work done in the United States, we have featured articles from Taiwan, Thailand, Australia, New Zealand, Canada, Germany, South Africa, and Great Britain, among others. It has never been our interest to simply report on events elsewhere in the world, but rather to recognize and promote the quality of the LIS literature colleagues produce who have been trained and work throughout the world. Several years ago, James M. Nyce approached us with the idea of producing a volume that would showcase Finnish research in library and information science. We jumped at the opportunity and have worked with the volume editors to develop a concept for this book. The result is the volume you have in hand.

Why did we choose to focus on Finnish LIS scholarship? Simply because the Finns offered us the opportunity to publish their work and, as we think you will agree, the work that they produced for us is first rate. In recent years, Finland has produced noteworthy research in our field, but that work has never before been pulled together in a single volume as we have done here.

But please do not take from this that this book is just about Finnish librarianship. Our charge to the editors to the volume and theirs to the volume contributors was to give us their best work on librarianship and information science independent of the location from which it came. That is not to say that there are no topics in the volume that of particular interest to the Finnish community of scholars, but rather that we tried, and we think succeeded, in getting the Finnish perspective on some universal problems related to library and information science. We hope that this kind of volume will be of interest to all of our readers. Given the success of this effort, we plan to do subsequent volumes that will also highlight international contributions to our field while continuing our search for individual articles that can be integrated into every volume that appears.

Finally, we the editors of the series would like to thank Sanna Talja and James M. Nyce for the work they have done in bringing this volume to print. We would also like to thank the individual authors who contributed

to the volume. In the end, the value of the volume rides on the quality of
their work, and we very much appreciate their efforts to make sure that the
product is worthwhile. We commend these essays to you, and, let the authors and editors impress you with their work and contributions.

Edward D. Garten
Delmus E. Williams
Editors

INTRODUCTION

This is the ALAO journal's first volume devoted to a particular nation state. Like previous ALAO volumes, this one gathers together state-of-the-art articles on topics familiar to every reader of LIS literature. Among these are how to manage tradition and innovation in public/university libraries, information and communication requirements and patterns in complex professional settings, and the library's role in supporting formal and informal learning. What sets this volume apart is that it provides an opportunity to understand how issues like these play out in a particular country, Finland, and how LIS scholars in Finland approach these topics.

The ongoing scholarly concerns, practices, and disputes within LIS in Finland are very similar to those of LIS scholars in North America. Finnish LIS scholars, like others elsewhere, have spent a fair amount of time debating the dual nature of the field, i.e., whether library science or information science should provide the dominant paradigm for doing the community's intellectual business. What intrigues us here is that given that sociocultural context of practicing LIS is different in Finland than in North America does this give LIS in Finland a distinguishable, unique character? Are familiar topics approached or framed *analytically* differently?

There is no simple "yes" or "no" answer to this question given that in Finland library science is not a monolith. The Finnish LIS community is spread across three university departments, each with their own research profiles, and across the country's public and academic libraries. The university departments each belong to different faculties.[1] This suggests that each department's agendas and intellectual trajectories may differ in significant ways from the others. The Department of Information Studies at the University of Tampere belongs to the Faculty of Information Sciences, the Department of Information Studies at Åbo Akademi University is part of the Faculty of Economics and Social Sciences, and the Department of Information Studies in the University of Oulu is within the Faculty of Humanities.

While Finnish LIS may in some aspects differ from that practiced in North America, it may not differ in significant ways from "Nordic LIS." This is because library services and socioeconomic conditions are to a high degree similar in Nordic welfare states, Sweden, Denmark, Norway, Finland, and Iceland. Further, the Nordic LIS community has a long tradition of sharing experience and knowledge between LIS institutions. This tradition of sharing experiences helps leaders, managers, and researchers in the Nordic LIS community to design and implement information services, especially those intended to further social and economic welfare. There is also within Scandinavia perhaps not unique but certainly an extremely strong tendency to delve as deeply as possible into the philosophical foundations of LIS professional and scientific knowledge.

These discussions raise fundamental issues not only about the choices of "platforms" from which to approach practical, professional issues in LIS. These discussions address such questions as how knowledge and science are constituted, whose voices are represented and whose are not. Sometimes inquiries of this kind form a kind of backdrop from which to tackle "lower order" professional or scientific problems. More often than not however, it is the very positions of knowledge production that are investigated, challenged, and tested as honestly and carefully as possible. This "deconstructive" enterprise may be interpreted negatively as shaking the foundations on which LIS is built upon, but in essence it is constructive deconstruction. It is one that can be undertaken because scholars can safely trust that there is an audience of professionals and colleagues equally willing to intellectually reflect upon and test their basic assumptions and beliefs.

This may occur in Finland and Scandinavia because of a belief that inquiries of this kind in the end advance basic knowledge and understanding. Or perhaps this reflects the fact that libraries and information service organizations are so strongly established in Nordic countries, both culturally and economically, and so deeply intertwined with the functioning of democracy, that no amount of questioning and analyzing them can shake them or divert attention and resources from them to "more urgent matters".

A core belief in Finnish LIS is that even the most practical LIS topics have a philosophical aspect to them. To give but one example, it can be argued that laboratory IR research, intentionally or not, is deficient or atheoretical in its theoretical foundations. However, this does not mean that one cannot investigate whether there might be a sound theoretical justification for "atheoretical" laboratory IR research. This was exactly what two Finnish researchers Jaana Kekäläinen and Kalervo Järvelin (2002) set out to do in one of their most cited papers.

That science plays out differently in different nation states may easily be masked by dominant paradigms of scientific thought and practice. In other words, we do not often consider how models underlying research are bound by history and culture. As pointed out by Ilkka Mäkinen in his article in this volume, it is not a coincidence that the conference series "Conceptions of Library and Information Science" and "Information Seeking in Context" originated in Finland. Further, in the Finnish LIS literature, there has been a systematic critique of existing models of information seeking and information behavior. For example, in his discussion of Dervin's Sense-Making theory, Reijo Savolainen (1993) noted that what informed this model was the "central position of individual actor[s], the importance of making things happen and moving forward, in spite of barriers faced, and reliance on individual capacities in problem solving" (p. 26). What Savolainen suggested was that the sense-making theory implicitly reflected not only a purely theoretical stance but one of the most American story of stories, the Horatio Alger story (Thomas & Nyce, 2001).

The models of information seeking and behavior LIS researchers use tend to favor either the individual (or individual minds) or social context. Finnish LIS scholars have tended to stress the fundamental socialness of human thought and action; and argue that the dualism between individual and the social is an artificial one, and one whose origins and authority needs to be critiqued and challenged. A more inclusive focus on social practices, Finnish scholars believe, may also help us to overcome another familiar dualism, that of "system-centeredness" and "human-centeredness". Whether this will eventually bring in the same kind of analysis of both technology and humans as social actors – a position strongly advanced recently by Ingwersen and Järvelin (2005) is not entirely clear at the moment. Nevertheless, this is an innovative line of thought and one well worth exploring.

NOTE

1. In Finland, like Scandinavia, universities are divided administratively and intellectually into faculties. Swedish universities for example are divided into philosophical and technical faculties. The academic staff of each faculty elects a rector (dean) who serves a set term of office. In Swedish universities, there are no other administrative units (like colleges in N. America) than faculties and departments.

REFERENCES

Ingwersen, P., & Järvelin, K. (2005). *The turn: Integration of information seeking and retrieval in context*. Heidelberg: Springer.

Kekäläinen, J., & Järvelin, K. (2002). Evaluating information retrieval systems under the chal-
    lenges of interaction and multi-dimensional dynamic relevance. Proceedings of the Co-
    LIS 4 Conference, July 2002, Seattle, USA, pp. 253–270. Available at: http://
    www.info.uta.fi/tutkimus/fire/archive.php
Mäkinen, I. From marginal to excellence: The development of the research in information
    studies in Finland. This volume.
Savolainen, R. (1993). The sense-making theory: Reviewing the interests of a user-centered
    approach to information seeking and use. Information Processing & Management, 29(1),
    13–28.
Thomas, N., & Nyce, J. (2001). Context as category: Opportunities for ethnographic analysis in
    library and information science research. The New Review of Information Behaviour
    Research, 2(November), 105–118.

James M. Nyce
Sanna Talja
Editors

MOTIVES FOR SHARING: SOCIAL NETWORKS AS INFORMATION SOURCES

Gunilla Widén-Wulff

ABSTRACT

It is clear that a lot of information acquisition happens through networks and therefore the focus in this article will lie in the relationships that bind a network together. The attempt is to map the motives as well as the group identity factors as means of exploring the reasons for sharing. The theoretical framework is brought from the social capital and group identity literature combined with the theories on information sharing in context. The aim is to see how information-sharing practices are developed in two different organisations and these theories are mirrored in the information sharing practices in an insurance company and in a biotechnology firm. The analysis of the cases shows how the group identity and the local context affect information sharing practices. The human and social processes underpin the formal structures enabling information interactions.

Advances in Library Administration and Organization, Volume 25, 1–31
© 2007 Published by Elsevier Ltd.
ISSN: 0732-0671/doi:10.1016/S0732-0671(07)25001-1

BACKGROUND

The idea that networks are an important information resource is a perspective that has received growing attention in information science in recent
years. Managing information sharing in any organisation requires knowing
the individuals, the group, and the context. Information sharing is affected
by many factors, and a number of researchers in information science have
addressed the need to understand the multiple layers in this process. Recently,
the social navigation of information behaviour has been emphasised (Forsman,
2005; Solomon, 1999; Davenport & Hall, 2002; Talja, 2002; Bruce, 2003;
Mackenzie, 2003; Hyldegård, 2004; Sonnenwald, Maglaughlin, & Whitton,
2004). A primary reason for this has been the discussions that have taken
place in many fields since 1988 relating to social capital and its role in
effective information and knowledge management in organisations (Cross &
Borgatti, 2004; Hoffman, Hoelscher, & Sherif, 2005). Also the organisational advantages given by social networks are well known (Lesser &
Prusak, 2000; Burt, 2001), as is the importance of trust in facilitating trans-
actions and collaboration (Fukuyama, 1995). However, although we know
about the significance of structures and relations that play in effective information management, there are very few empirical studies about the
mechanisms behind information sharing and there are only few empirical
studies on the topic (Huysman & de Wit, 2002).

It is clear that a lot of information acquisition happens through networks
and, therefore, the focus of this article will be the relationships that bind a
network together. The attempt is to map the motives as well as the group
identity factors as means of exploring the reasons for sharing. The theoretical framework comes from discussions of social capital and group identity combined with theories on information sharing in context. The aim is
to see how information-sharing practices are developed in two different
organisations and how these theories are mirrored in the information-sharing
practices in an insurance company and in a biotechnology firm. The
following questions are explored:

1. *What motivates individuals in an organisation to share what they know?*
2. *How are group behaviour attributes connected to knowledge sharing?*
3. *How are social networks used as an information source?*

These are important questions related to the development of the information and knowledge management field as such and in developing IM and
KM initiatives in different kinds of organisations. The ability to manage
information processes and people involved in communicative action are key

challenges of information and knowledge management today (Sinotte 2004; Widén-Wulff et al., 2005), especially in expert and service organisations such as libraries.

GROUP BEHAVIOUR ATTRIBUTES AND MOTIVES FOR SHARING

Information sharing happens in a constant mix of organisational and in-dividual motives; and factors like purpose, timing, and availability play an important role as enablers and barriers to sharing (Sonnenwald & Pierce, 2000; Solomon, 2002). In this context, every individual has their own per-ception of how to make use of their networks, and the identity becomes an important connect to this picture; both on individual and group level. Solomon (Solomon, 1999) illustrates the mix as information mosaics where context, task, and individual action preferences come together and create *patterns of information behaviour.*

The basis for understanding the information behaviour in a group or organisation is the organisational context where the *information culture* forms the communication climate (McDermott & O'Dell, 2001; Widén-Wulff, 2001; Widén-Wulff, 2003; Widén-Wulff, 2005). Further, the behav-ioural engagement in groups, *the group identity*, is important to consider in order to understand why group members engage in critical behaviours tar-geted at helping their groups (Tyler & Blader, 2001). According to Tyler & Blader (2001), the group identity is mainly built from identification, roles, and status in the group, cooperation, attitudes, and values. Information sharing is influenced by the individual and organisational factors, and it is, therefore, important to focus the communications climate and group iden-tity in relation to the personal motives which are embedded in the person's identification and status in the group or network (Choo, 1998; Hooff & Ridder, 2004).

This leads to the exploration of *individual roles* in the process of sharing. The transfer of information and knowledge between individuals depends upon people initiating and facilitating those transfers (Lang, 2004). Infor-mation exchange is a motivated process mostly initiated to do and solve work tasks. Members select what to share and with whom in order to satisfy goals (Wittenbaum, Hollingshead, & Botero, 2004). The motives are hidden in many aspects, and there are many purposes for information sharing that are connected to the individual level of the human behaviour. One very important factor in this is the trust that makes the sharing possible (Huotari

& Iivonen, 2004). Also the social and expert status in a group affects information exchange, though not always in the way we expect. Thomas-Hunt (Thomas-Hunt, Ogden, & Neale, 2003) shows that socially isolated members in a group participated more and expressed greater and more unique knowledge than did socially connected members. The strategy lay in the fact that socially isolated members wanted to underline their usefulness by focusing on the unique contribution they could make. The blend of experts and non-experts within a group is an important aspect when considering motives of information sharing.

These motives are also connected to the actual use of and *access* to information and sources. Wilson (Wilson, 2000) connects contextual variables in addition to individual variables affecting the use of information. He refers to O'Reilly (O'Reilly, 1982) who suggests that the use of information sources by organisational decision makers is not only dependent on source and information quality but is a blend of contextual and individual causes. The motives for using a source are connected to experience, roles, accessibility, and networks. The organisational structure may restrict access to quality sources. Further, organisations may have incentives affecting information interactions where members are rewarded for seeking information of a particular type and punished for using other types. Decision makers also often rely on sources deemed to be trustworthy or credible. Relationships more than knowledge are often the reason why an individual is sought as an information source (O'Reilly, 1982; McKenzie, 2003).

In summary, the motives for sharing, described above, are a blend of organisational and individual preferences. In picturing the patterns of information behaviour, we can define four important features; the information culture forming the communication climate, the group identity, individual roles, and accessibility (Table 1).

Table 1.   Building Information Behaviour Patterns.

PATTERNS OF INFORMATION BEHAVIOUR	
Information culture forming the communication climate	
Group identity	
Roles	Access
Status	Availability
Relationships	Trust
Experience	Structure
Trustworthiness	

SOCIAL NAVIGATION

Definition of Social Capital

It is said that the information behaviour patterns are anchored in the individual and organisational structures where people interact. Information seeking often takes place in collaborative settings and, therefore, the social aspects play an important role. Contextual and social factors affect group members' physical activities and their cognitive and emotional experiences with relevance to information sharing (Hyldegård, 2004). Therefore, empirical studies of information seekers within their social context focus on practices rather than on the individuals' information seeking behaviour. The analysis shift from cognitive to social elements, looking at the information seekers within their social context where connections and interactions with sources are underlined (Mackenzie, 2003; Hyldegård, 2004).

Although these aspects bring cultural and social factors into the information behaviour setting, we do lack a good method to navigate among these things. Social capital has emerged as an increasingly popular concept. It is an interesting concept in several contexts. On asocietal level, social capital refers to "... networks, norms and trust that enable participants to act together more effectively to pursue shared objectives" (Baron, Field, & Schuller, 2000). In organisational contexts, "social capital consists of the stock of active connections among people: the trust, mutual understanding, and shared values and behaviours that bind members of human networks and communities and make cooperative action possible" (Fukuyama, 1995; Cohen & Prusak, 2001, p. 4). The social capital perspective helps us, therefore, to explore the context in which information sharing takes place. It provides us with a framework for the hidden motives of information sharing, giving information behaviour its social context.

Social capital is developed from a sum of many perspectives associated with structural, communicative, and relational factors (Hazleton & Kennan, 2000). These better-known dimensions of social capital (Nahapiet & Ghoshal, 1998) help group the perspectives. The *structure dimension* affects access to other actors, individual, and corporate entities. This structure influences the two other dimensions of social capital and is necessary for the development and utilisation of social capital (Nahapiet & Ghoshal, 1998; Hazleton & Kennan, 2000). Social interaction ties (structure) are channels for information and resource flows. Through social interactions, an actor may gain access to other actors' resources (Tsai & Ghoshal, 1998). This dimension reflects the impersonal properties of the network relations, and a network tie is the fundamental structural concept, the basic element of communication networks (Upadhyayula & Kumar, 2004).

The *communicative (or cognitive) dimension* is a visible condition necessary for formation and utilisation of social capital. Communication is the mechanism whereby the available stock of social capital can be accessed and expended to further organisational goals and objectives (Hazleton & Kennan, 2000).

The *relational dimension* is concerned with expectations and obligations as central features of social capital. This dimension influences three of the conditions for exchange and combination. These are access to parties, anticipation of value through exchange, and the motivation of parties to engage in knowledge creation through exchange and combination (Nahapiet & Ghoshal, 1998; Hazleton & Kennan, 2000). Trust is the primary relational feature of social capital in Coleman's (Coleman, 1988) model and also the most studied concept of social capital (Portes, 1998). As trusting relationships develop inside a network actors build up reputations for trustworthiness. There are different levels of trustworthiness which result in different levels of resource exchanges and combinations (Tsai & Ghoshal, 1998).

From this description of social capital and its dimensions, it is obvious that there is much consensus in the literature on motives for information sharing in organisations. This article focuses mainly on the relational perspective (identity and trust) combined with structural perspectives on network ties.

SOCIAL CAPITAL IN ORGANISATIONS

While the empirical context of this study is put in corporate settings, it is important to look at research in this area. Research on social capital is well documented in corporate research driven primarily by interest in the rise of the knowledge-based organisation (Lesser, 2000). Social capital and social networks are seen as giving financial advantage. Firms benefit from social capital because it facilitates cooperation and coordination, which minimise transaction costs (PovertyNet, 2004). Social capital is the stock of shared resources which are accessed based on relationships (Tymon & Stumpf, 2003). Creation and maintenance of social capital is growing in importance whereas the turbulent business environment reduces the opportunities for individuals to build this valuable resource (Lesser, 2000). This is, therefore, the main aspect of research relating to social capital in the business organisation literature.

Information about different social networks can supplement more economically based explanations of organisational conduct, and furthermore give more precise predictions about organisational behaviour. Social capital is seen as an advantage that individuals or groups have because of their location in social structure. The weaker connections between groups are holes in the social structure of the market. These holes in social structure create a competitive advantage for an individual whose relationships span the holes. Several studies report high performance from groups with external networks that span structural holes; when top managers have boundary-spanning relationships beyond their firm and beyond their industry (Burt, 2001; Reagans & Zuckerman, 2001).

Social capital affects firms internally, promoting greater coordination among people and between units. Further, trust is the foundation for co-operation internally as well as externally between enterprises. Companies that are working together in a joint effort are able to establish deeper relationships with one another, and these can be accessed in the future for other business projects. The theoretical framework points out the importance of social capital aspects in developing a deeper understanding of information sharing in groups and organisations. Structural, communicative, and relational features are important to the discussion about information behaviour patterns. However, managing social capital explicitly is complicated while social capital formation is more a local process and involves social practices (Davenport & Snyder, 2005). In this article, we have underlined that awareness, access, willingness, and trust (Cross & Borgatti, 2004), as well as group identity (Tyler & Blader, 2001) and cultural matters (McDermott & O'Dell, 2001) are particularly important in social capital formation; Widén-Wulff (2005) develops a picture of the motives for sharing. Studying these aspects in empirical settings will contribute to a more coherent understanding of the multiple layers behind information sharing in the organisational context, and find ways of managing these processes.

FINDINGS IN TWO FINNISH ORGANISATIONS

Methods

The data for this paper were gathered during 2003–2004 from two Finnish companies, an insurance company and a biotechnology firm. Two case studies of quite different kinds of groups are examined to provide insights into information sharing as an organisational behaviour. The interviews and questionnaires addressed information seeking, information sharing, tasks undertaken in the workplace, the construction of organisational memory, and aspects of group identity. The measures for investigating the information sharing were derived from several sources. It is important to consider conditions and consequences, the social climate and information culture, and the skills, convictions, attitudes, and behaviour (Ginman, 2002; Widén-Wulff & Ginman, 2004).

The findings presented here have emerged from analysis of interview transcripts. The transcribed data were analysed using content analysis to find categories and themes. Two coding schemas were adopted: high level codes were used to describe activities and behaviours across each of the organisations ("lateral" codes), and more specific codes described aspects of individual practice ("vertical" codes). The former allowed the coder to derive a number of broad units of analysis (sources, personal networks and so on). From the latter, a number of "information profiles" (roles, responsibilities, and reporting status) were derived that were used to compare patterns of interaction with shared artefacts and colleagues. These have been used to provide the stories of the two cases below.

Material

Case A: The Claims Handlers

The persons who were interviewed work in a claims applications unit in a Finnish insurance business group offering insurance and financial service to small- and medium-sized companies and private persons. The company was established at the beginning of the 20th century and has been operating as a group of different insurance services since 2001. The company employs about 440 persons and has a nationwide service network with more than 30 offices. The claims applications unit is situated in the life insurance branch of the company and has about 30 employees.

Case B: The Biotechnology Experts

Data were gathered from a Nordic high-tech company in the dental industry that was founded in 1997. The company bases its activities on cooperative research conducted with more than 40 universities in different parts of the world and a program of continuous education and training of its partners and customers in over 20 different countries. The company operates through a well-established local partner network. The company has acquired a prominent market share in both Europe and the USA. The company invests in R&D in close cooperation with universities and opinion leaders in Finland and abroad.

THE CLAIMS HANDLERS

Subjects and Environment

The claims department for life insurances has a broad field of work: health and life insurances, savings, and benefits. The personnel are grouped according to which insurances they handle (health insurances, children's insurances, death benefits, and pre-handling). The people who were interviewed represent different areas of responsibilities in the unit. Five of the ten interviewed persons are *claims handlers*. This is the work task that is done by most of the persons in the unit. Each person is expected to handle a certain number of cases per day. There are routine tasks like checking to see if the insurance premiums have been paid, clauses, earlier diagnosis, and reimbursement decisions. More complicated cases require a broader set of information such as medical information, information from the Social Insurance Institute (SII), and customer information. In the most complicated cases, information is solicited from colleagues and claims procedures or from other experts such as company doctors, the section manager, and lawyers. Difficult cases are also always discussed in regularly scheduled claims handling meetings that are held once a week.

Three of the people interviewed are responsible for *claims procedure*. In this process, the insurance policy must be granted again based on a new decision resulting from new information about the customer's health conditions before the previous insurance was granted. There will be sanctions in premiums, or the insurance is cancelled. Claims procedure has the responsibility to assist the claims handlers with advice on what kind of additional information that is needed from the customer. Further, they determine whether the insurance decision should be changed when additional information is delivered. The main work tasks are investigations of the customers' medical conditions. This means reading a lot of different kinds of papers, documents, collaborating with the doctors in the company, and assessing whether the decisions are in line with the clauses and insurance conditions.

Only one person handles *claims administration* but an assistant was trained for these tasks at the time when the interviews were held. The administrative tasks are checking outgoing reimbursements of the day, checking savings- and investment-insurances and bookkeeping. Contact with customers about savings, and changes of benefits are managed by the administration. The work tasks include a lot of collaboration on an individual level with actuaries, lawyers, payments, and allowances. Cooperation with

Table 2. Work Tasks in the Claims Handling Group.

	Tasks	How Long in the Organisation
Person A	Claims handler	0–1 years
Person B	Claims administration (payments)	30 years
Person C	Claims procedure	11–15 years
Person D	Head user – system administration	11–15 years
Person E	Claims procedure	11–15 years
Person F	Claims handler	2–5 years
Person G	Claims handler	0–1 years
Person H	Claims handler	6–10 years
Person I	Claims procedure	11–15 years
Person J	Claims handler	11–15 years

ICT is important, because a lot of programs and databases must be maintained all the time.

The *head user* has responsibility for testing new systems, solving problems with information systems, and maintaining databases. There is one person in the unit with this work description. The person must be an experienced claims handler to be able to test the systems in which the claims are processed. The person is the link between this department and the ICT department (Table 2).

Group Behaviour Attributes

Earlier in this paper, it was concluded that the willingness to come together and collaborate and share information is rooted in the group identity, roles, and status (O'Reilly, 1982; Tyler & Blader, 2001; Thomas-Hunt et al., 2003; Wittenbaum et al., 2004). The patterns of information behaviour are shaped by the information culture, the group identity, the individual roles, and the access to information sources. In order to picture these patterns the analysis is based on questions concerning the experienced values and advantages of belonging to the group as well as attitudes towards sharing. This description will be combined with the experiences of roles and social networks in the group.

Members of the claims handler unit indicate that the foremost advantage of working in their department is the cooperative working style operating in the unit. It is seen as an advantage where many work task decisions are difficult to make on ones own, and consulting a colleague is important. They have managed to create an atmosphere where collaboration is highly valued.

Table 3. Assessment of Group Identification.

Identification	Agree	Neutral	Disagree
Tell friends about how good the workplace is	9	–	1
Same individual values as the organisation	7	3	–
Proud to work in the organisation	10	–	–
Recommend this workplace to others	10	–	–
Work important for how I feel as individual	5	4	1
Positive comments about workplace feel personal	7	1	2
Usually talk about the work in a collective form	9	1	–
$N = 10$			

Through the collaborative style of working, they have shaped a strong atmosphere and group identity. They all underline the good atmosphere and the fact that they have good friends and colleagues at work. It is their view that they work more together than do people working in other units and that they actually have a good atmosphere when the size of the unit is taken into consideration. It is also an unwritten rule that they help each other when the workload is heavy.

There is a strong common understanding about the group identity of this unit. The unit is considered to be a good work place that can be recommended to others. The people who work there feel appreciated, their ideas are valued, and it is obvious that the group members feel a strong sense of solidarity within the group. There is a fellowship in both work tasks and values, a strong agreement in how to perform the work, and feelings of pride and togetherness are distinguishing features of the group (Table 3).

It is obvious that the claims handlers like their work tasks, and consider theirs a challenging job. The handlers refer to the fact that they have to look up a lot of different kinds of information in order to make the right decisions. They also feel that they do work that nobody else does in the organisation, work that demands special knowledge and special skills.

> We feel that we do a very important job for the company and the customers. And nobody else in the company does this work; it makes us feel quite special. We have unique knowledge that does not exist in the other departments. And that contributes also to our atmosphere and identity. (Claims procedure – I)

Customer orientation is a central value, which means that all customers should get equal treatment (accuracy). This is a formal value which is communicated in the company and within the unit. Formal and informal values merge where customer orientation is assessed in a collective atmosphere.

There are of course differences in how we interpret the value of customer orientation. Some persons look more into customer benefits than others. Some are stricter and some are more flexible. These different views of the customer orientation are then always discussed in the claims handling meetings. We discuss how far a customer-oriented view can be drawn, and that we must have the similar treatment for all. These lines must be drawn, and afterwards also remembered. (Claims procedure – I)

The claims handlers see themselves as strongly connected to the group where they shape their norms and rules. The work is based on the claims handling rules which are stipulated in insurance clauses and principles. This means that rules and norms are visible features of the work processes in this group. Although the group sees itself as a unit working and deciding together, the hierarchical thinking towards the management on a higher level is visible. Decisions and rules are followed even if they are found not to be very suitable, and the decisions made by management are seldom opposed. Therefore, important values are also the facts that one's duties must be performed and that one should respect the superior. Wrong decisions are accepted by most of the members except for the oldest and most experienced members. Following norms and regulations even if they are wrong follows the same pattern; wrong regulations are accepted by all but the oldest member. To follow instructions is thought to result in an effective organisation, which then reflects on the routine-based work. Also, the fact that all strive to do their duties reflects the working style where routine is a very important part of the work.

The overall picture is that the persons feel that they benefit from mutual decisions, that the decisions are fair, and that there is a prospect that they can affect decisions. The question is obviously connected to decisions on the unit level where all employers are actively involved in decision making at the claims handling meetings. However, older members of the group are slightly more likely to affect decisions in the organisation. The attitudes of knowledge sharing and decision making show a parallel to the aspects on identity and values. The unit seems to experience involvement, and therefore, the feeling of mutual knowledge sharing is also strong and there is an interest among staffers in cooperating with and learning about the organisation outside their own unit (Table 4).

As a summary it can be said that the group identity in the claims handling group seems to have the following features:

- They believe that they perform a very unique and important job.
- They have an open communication climate and a cooperative working style.
- There is open knowledge sharing within the unit, but hierarchical communication and decision making is preferred on the organisational level.

Table 4. Attitudes to Knowledge Sharing, Decision Making, Exchange.

Attitudes	Agree	Neutral	Disagree
Benefit from mutual decisions	9	–	1
Decisions are fare	6	2	2
Decisions are followed up	8	1	1
Possibilities to affect decisions	7	2	1
Possibilities to express opinions	7	2	1
Personal opinions are considered	6	3	1
I put forward new ideas	6	4	–
Help others who have a lot of work	9	1	–
Expect favours in return	5	2	3
More effective to cooperate	9	1	–
Learn from older colleagues	10	–	–
Circulate to other units	8	2	–
$N = 10$			

- The individuals are valued.
- There is a strong feeling of belonging with good friends at work.
- Individual and group values match.
- Individual and group identity are closely connected.

Social Navigation and Networks as Sources

The social navigation is best described through the use of personal networks and individual action. The common basis for the different work tasks is processing claims from applications to reimbursements. Within the process there are persons doing general claims handling and other people with more specific assignments and expertise (procedure, administration, and systems). Although there are different kinds of tasks in the department, the staff there commonly use four groups of information and information sources (Table 5).

On a general level it can be said that there are a limited amount of sources (types) used within the claims handling unit although the work tasks and the decisions made there include a lot of detailed information. The claims handlers all underline that the work tasks demand a careful style of working. Information for claims handling is retrieved mostly from formal sources such as insurance clauses and company conditions, but validating this information and one's decisions is mainly made through the group network.

Table 5.   Main Information Sources in Claims Handling.

1. Internal Database ("Infomap")	2. Internet
Rules	Formal information
Clauses	Medical information
Principles	Customer information
Best practice	
3. Meetings	**4. Personal network**
Cases and best practice	Validation of information
General information	Access to information for special work tasks
	Best practice
	Access to knowledge about other sources

Table 6.   The Preferences of Turning to a Special Person within the Unit.

	Tasks	How Long (Years)	Personal Network Preferences
Person A	Claims handler	0–1	1. Physical location 2. Reliability 3. Expertise, experience 4. Personal
Person B	Claims administration (payments)	30	1. Expertise, experience
Person C	Committee procedure	11–15	1. Expertise, experience
Person D	Head user – system administration	11–15	1. Expertise
Person E	Committee procedure	11–15	1. Expertise
Person F	Claims handler	2–5	1. Physical location/anybody 2. Expertise
Person G	Claims handler	0–1	1. Physical location/anybody 2. Expertise
Person H	Claims handler	6–10	1. Expertise 2. Personal
Person I	Committee procedure	11–15	1. Expertise
Person J	Claims handler	11–15	1. Expertise

The reasons for interacting with people in the group are assessed from the perspective of performing work tasks. The purpose of the information interactions are concerned with validating staff members' own decisions, validating information retrieved from other sources, and asking for advice with difficult cases.

In this group, there are mainly four reasons for choosing who you turn to within the group network (Table 6).

- Physical location – turn to the nearest person
- Expertise – different persons have different areas of expertise
- Reliability – the degree of carefulness
- Personal – you learn to cooperate better with some persons

Looking at the table, it is clear that the new members of the group access the network primarily because of physical location. All of them also refer to expertise, and they acknowledged that there are individuals with different areas of expertise. However, they have not yet learned to recognise all the key people in the unit. This means that new members use the network on a broader basis.

> I have usually asked the one who is the closest or the one who is free for the moment. There are new methods and treatments that are not always mentioned in books and then it is important to complement with asking a colleague. If one person doesn't know you go to the next one – like doing exit polls. (Claims handler – G)

The older members of the unit all access the network directly on the basis of expertise, and they also consistently use the same people (strong ties) for information interaction. It is also interesting to see that there is clearly an order of precedence, a kind of rank, assigned based on knowledge and expertise.

> You know that there are some claims handlers that know especially about old conditions, those who have been here for a long time. And you ask them. Or if it is about payments you know there are a few handlers who were involved in the development of the payment system. And you ask them. In all, you learn that different persons know about different things. There are those who always have some level of knowledge – may remember or not. You turn to them if you don't get the expert. (Committee procedure – I)

The reliability assessment also shows some special patterns. New members of the group rely on written information rather than information gained from the personal network.

"... I prefer written information rather than oral information. So that I can read and motivate how I understand the text/contents" (Claims handler – F). The interpersonal network is used to validate information and access other sources of written information. Among the older members of the group the reliability assessment of the personal network is more coherent. Almost all of them refer to the experience of the persons and rank the reliability of their colleagues depending on the level of expertise or the knowledge that the person has. Besides the level of expertise and knowledge, the individual level of how persons get together is also assessed as a factor that affects network ties.

And it affects who you better cooperate with and those who you better get along with. There are many things which affect information interaction. Usually you turn to the same person, you have more collaboration with that person, and she turns often to you. You have perhaps the same way of thinking about things, you know the person better. You feel some persons are more logical, and some persons have sensible comments which also are important. (Claims handler – H)

BIOTECHNOLOGY EXPERTS

Subjects and Environment

Four experts in the biotechnology company were interviewed, and they also answered the questionnaire on group behaviour attributes. The company has 14 employees divided into six functional areas – top management, board, financial, training, marketing, sales, R&D, and communications. Every function has a responsible person and some functional areas include an assistant. This means that the organisation is very flat, and the structure of the work is often conducted in the form of different kinds of projects. The coordination of these projects, the resources, and the teams assigned to tasks are mainly developed during board meetings, which are held on a monthly basis. The project-based structure of work puts special demands on internal communication.

> We have an expert in every key area of the company's activities. This means that the organisation is very flat. We have no units, only a person responsible for his or her area. But then we gather teams for specific purposes, which is responsible for a part of the communicating or the continuing communications relating to a matter. This creates a challenge as people try to remember and be aware of the right people to involve in a particular work process. (Researcher)

Communications are also complicated by the difficulties in defining areas of responsibility. "The work is structured in a matrix, but there are also confusions about whose responsibility different matters are, which is the darker side of the flat organization." (Administration)

The *researcher's* main work tasks are research, aiming at innovations, development of products, and production. In detail this means documentation of own innovations, producing internal studies on traditional dental care compared to new forms of care. The work also includes reading research articles, market reports (both internally produced and external), and cooperation with experts in the area (dentists and other experts). The information about customers and markets is also important for this work.

Table 7. Interviewed Biotechnology Experts.

Expert Area	Years with the Company
Researcher, R&D	4 years
Communications	2 years
Administration	6 years
Training	2 years

The *communications* group is involved with both internal and external communication. The work tasks are mainly creating and maintaining the company website, writing the customer newsletter, planning the publication programme, and developing marketing material and information aimed at the patients. The general aim for the communications work tasks is internal and external awareness of developments.

The *administrative* work tasks include a wide variety of engagements. The administrative work is mainly concerned with background information for further decisions at the board level. Mainly, it is about external revision, sales prediction, and market analyses. It also includes information management issues such as office management, logistics, and service functions which means to gather, interpret, and produce information to different recipients in the organisation.

The *training* function of the company is concerned mainly with training the distributors about the products and their usability. The main contacts are with freelance trainers in the distributor's countries, and the job is to help them arrange lectures and courses. There is also a follow-up process to evaluate if the training has resulted in sale. The overall aim is to contribute to better sale. Internal training within the company is to create greater awareness about the company's activities (Table 7).

Group Behaviour Attributes

Individual motives to share information and expertise are emphasised heavily in this group. The company's success is very dependent on the fact that the experts who are employed are capable of working towards common aims. Motives of sharing are embedded in factors on both the individual and organisational levels. Here the organisational level will be described in forms of group identity and motivation.

The persons interviewed in this expert organisation emphasised the turbulent work environment belonging to a rather new field of industry. This is both an advantage and a disadvantage. The advantage is the fact that it makes the work very unique and challenging; the disadvantage is that it brings uncertainty about the future into the company. Further, the expertise-based work and team membership are valued as advantages as is the close connection to actual production.

Serving an international market with a lot of cooperation with networks abroad and being a part of an international context adds an important feature to the atmosphere. The people in this group work in close relationships where their areas of expertise must be constantly brought in line with the common interests of their collaborators. This serves to unite the employees. The uniqueness of the product is also an important ingredient in shaping a special atmosphere.

> We strongly believe in our product. There is no doubt that we wouldn't be working for a unique thing. This keeps the people alert. (Training)

> The uniqueness of the product is also nice to talk about outside the work. (Researcher)

The benefits of this atmosphere are that the employees support each other and know the other functions fairly well. The flat organisation also means that the experts are all on the same level; they are all near to production and to the results achieved. "You are really close to the different phases of the process, production, and results. You can see where things come from and where they go" (Communication).

The values of the company are closely related to customer service because "in the end, the customers pay your salary" (Researcher). The demand for high quality is underlined and "the products must be based on research facts – there is no room for mistakes" (Communication). The other values are related to a work environment where the cooperation and valuation of expertise is emphasised. The experts identify themselves quite strongly with their work organisation – they have similar values and an inspiring workplace. The people interviewed concluded that the feeling of belonging is high, and it is easy to feel appreciated in this organisation. The features of an entrepreneurial firm are important and valued (Table 8).

Everyone knows the importance of working together, and the knowledge of every expert must be transferred to others. "I must tell my expertise, knowledge to my colleague and he/she must tell me" (Communication). This also means that workers must really value each other and each other's expertise. It is also important to map how different activities are linked and how they proceed in relation to each other.

This is an organisation where innovativeness is important and rule following does not always create the best atmosphere for creative processes.

Table 8. Assessment of Identification.

Identification	Strongly Agree/Agree	Not Agree/ Disagree	Disagree/Strongly Disagree
Tell friends about how good the workplace is	2	1	1
Same individual values as the organisation	3	1	–
Proud to work in the organisation	3	1	–
Recommend this workplace to others	1	1	2
Work important for how I feel as individual	4	–	–
Positive comments about workplace feel personal	4	–	–
Usually talk about the work in a collective form	4	–	–
$N = 4$			

However, it is also noted that innovation must take place in a relevant framework where the common aims are the given framework. Rule following and top–down decision making are not emphasised in this flat organisation, and a creative environment is more important than routine-based work.

Decision making is not a very straightforward process in this organisation. The fact that the different activities must compete for the same resources affects the attitudes as to how well one's opinions are taken into consideration and of individual's prospect for affecting decision making. Decisions are often made at board level, and, when it comes to resource allocations, the decisions are made at an even higher level, by the board of directors (Table 9).

The experts are involved in this group because of their special knowledge. They are perhaps less agreeable on knowledge sharing, decision making, and exchange because they see themselves more as individuals than as a group doing the same kind of work. This also reflects the atmosphere where a creative mind is viewed more often as a resource than is evident in a routine-based work environment. However, the creativity must be directed to common goals, a fact that is a value that is emphasised within the group.

In summary, the group identity of the biotechnology experts exhibits the following features:

• Individual expertise is valued.
• There is a strong sense that theirs is a unique product and everyone works close to the actual production of that product.

Table 9. Attitudes to Knowledge Sharing, Decision Making, Exchange.

Attitudes	Strongly Agree/Agree	Not Agree/ Disagree	Disagree/Strongly Disagree
Benefit from mutual decisions	1	3	–
Decisions are fare	1	1	2
Decisions are followed up	1	3	–
Possibilities to affect decisions	3	1	–
Possibilities to express opinions before decision making	3	–	1
Opinions are considered	2	1	1
I put forward new ideas	4	–	–
Help others who have a lot of work	3	1	–
Expect favours in return	2	2	–
More effective to cooperate	4	–	–
Learn from older colleagues	4	–	–
Circulate to other units	2	1	1
$N = 10$			

- The work environment is versatile.
- The company works within an international market and the expertise needed to compete is international in scope.
- There is a strong connection between group and individual values.
- Group identity shapes individual identity.

Social Navigation and Networks as Sources

The work tasks within the expert organisation are very different from each other. Therefore, a common base for information sources used within the organisation is difficult to find. Every expert has their own information profile concerning information sources they use and these profiles depend very much on their specialised work tasks. The researcher relies mostly on primary information such as research reports and the organisation's own internal reports. The external contacts and reports are important in the innovation process when it is important to verify what is going on in the field. The internal contacts are mainly within the own department (R&D), in different kinds of work groups, and in board meetings.

The information for communication tasks is mainly retrieved from oral sources, both internal and external. The aim is to communicate everything of interest to a greater audience, and it is important to find the key projects that should be reported. This means constant interaction with the R&D, marketing, and training units. The internal sources are perhaps the most important resources for this function, particularly since they facilitate and coordinate the information provided to the external network as well.

The administration has the widest variety of sources available to them. The internal sources are important for administrative work tasks where the different areas of responsibility are connected and forwarded to the decision-making level of the company (board). Individuals working in administration have broad networks and active collaborations with all units and all employees, as well as contacts with external organisations such as insurance companies, customs, and tax collectors

Those who plan training mostly use oral sources of information. The network to the distributors is an interactive information-sharing network that is important in connecting the needs of customers and distributors with the actual developments going on within the company. It is important to have information from internal functions to be able to plan courses in a timely manner.

In summary, it can be concluded that the information sources used are varied, and it is difficult to find common sources because the nature of the experts' work are so different. The main groups consult a wider variety of sources, but these sources can be categorised as follows: internal/external and oral/written information sources. This gives a picture of the total range of information sources used and mentioned by the interviewed persons (Table 10).

Table 10. Summary of Information Sources Used in the Expert Group.

	External	Internal
Oral Persons Network	Market related contacts (suppliers, distributors, customers) Experts in the area and researchers (e.g. dentists, professors) Other experts (lawyers, insurance, tax)	Personal network Open office landscape Meetings (working groups, units, board, projects) Coffee – lunch breaks Training program for new staff "Corridor discussions"
Written	Market reports Databases/e.g. Medline Research articles	Own research/reports Company handbook Internal database (IS) Customer management program/ marketing program (software) Webb pages

There are a lot of meetings and constant discussions between the functional areas. The board meeting is the platform for making collaborative decisions, but there are also many project and team meetings going on simultaneously. There is also an attempt to organise general information events where current projects or themes are discussed. These events do not yet have a formal structure, and it is difficult to find people who know about them.

> Once a month we try to have an information event. It is not as effective as it could be, people tend to go there and listen, but not to discuss. And we have actually not allocated very much time for it. But this is an attempt to find a channel for discussion and we have tried to have different themes for these events. (Administration)

Each and every expert shapes the external network differently and another network is reached through the different persons in the company. The links are good examples of the phenomenon structural holes described by, e.g., Burt (1992, 1997). Information from the external networks is communicated through in the common projects and team efforts that the experts share within the company.

The social knowledge about who knows what, the ability to understand information, and personal factors affecting information sharing are also often talked about by the experts. These are their implicit information profiles, and they emerged quite clearly in the four interviewees. The meaning of information and knowledge sharing as a critical asset for the successful management of the company is stressed. "Information means different things depending on experience. The analysis of information is different, all the time you must remember to question – what does it mean, so what?" (Training).

Commonly, the internal network is easy to access, and who knows what is well understood. A more systematic picture of this is under construction. The company is in a process of developing a common formula to reach the right person with the right information. The formula is two dimensional where every area of expertise has defined the receiving partners of their information and the functions that should give them their information – "from whom should I receive information, to whom should I send information." Further, the content of information is analysed and important questions about priorities are being asked because time is always a limiting factor. The fact that you have a responsibility to communicate what you know is stressed in many contexts.

> Together we have worked out the surfaces of knowledge – who knows what. There is a responsibility to give information. If you don't know you have the responsibility to find out. (Communication)

Access to the company network is based on personal contacts. A range of contacts is continually used, but the reliability of the network depends on the person who gives the information. Information from colleagues is considered to be reliable and trustworthy in the main. There is a blend of assessing the information that the person gives and reliability of the person giving that information.

An interesting feature of this group is the fact that the network is also evaluated from the opposite point of view, the individual responsibility to be able to share critical information. The output of information processed is as important as the amount taken in and individuals are responsible for forwarding information to the right people. This includes an ability to understand and appreciate what each person needs.

> We have a lot of cooperation which demands a communicative ability and a willingness to share. You are able to destroy and slow down processes by the fact that you don't share. (Trainer)

> I trust in the fact that we are able to bother each other with questions and interactions. ... There is constant interacting and it is important that everyone participate enough in the information sharing. But not too much, there is no idea to sit on meetings where you cannot contribute. (Researcher)

Mutual respect is the aim, but human factors and personal reasons affect the situation in the end. In the information-sharing process, the ability to prioritise is also underlined. It is important to define the key tasks in order to communicate knowledge effectively. But there is also another aspect of sharing that underlines the importance of every expert: "We depend on each other's knowledge – do not upset the other or you remain without information!" (Communication).

DISCUSSION

What does all this tell us about the group identity, about the motives for and the willingness to share information, and about the use of social networks as information sources? The two cases cited are examples of organisations in quite different kinds of environments. The claims handlers work in a stable environment, while the biotechnology experts work in a more hectic, less predictable one. Also, the nature of the work done in these organisation represent two opposites, namely routine work in the one and entrepreneurial work in the other. The biotechnology work is under time pressure and the resulting time constraints affect information sharing styles to a certain extent. Information sharing is turbulent and therefore difficult to structure. The information profiles in this group show different patterns than those exhibited in the insurance context where network structures are clear and information sharing is more about verifying existing information than producing new knowledge. However, the analysis reveals that the information behaviour shown is also connected to many aspects that are not embedded in the work tasks or organisational environment. Both groups can be said to have an open climate where the ability to communicate is viewed as important. The reasons and motives for this are different, however. The claims handlers value a collaborative working style where they feel connected to each other and have mutual goals to handle a certain number of claims. The atmosphere that has developed is built upon these common goals, but they also depend on the fact that the people there like each other's company. They have common interests outside the work. The motives for sharing can also be partly explained by shared goals to do good in support of the customer's interests. The feeling of belonging to a group affects how group members behave towards their group (Tyler & Blader, 2001). It is not only the group synergies that are motivating factors, but also the possibilities that exist to develop a positive sense of self within the group setting. The younger members of the group are more optimistic about their capacity to affect activities in the organisation than are their older colleagues.

The experts in the biotechnology firm have a group identity that is mainly built around individual experts working to develop a unique product. They have their specialities as a strong value and goal, and this shapes both the individual and group identity. The communicative climate is open and everyone is aware of the importance of keeping their colleagues informed. However, in practice, the communications suffer from barriers such as time constraints and information overload. It has been concluded that in the information-sharing process here, the responsibility to receive information is underscored. But apart from the responsibility to seek and retrieve information, there is also a responsibility to understand information. It is important to note that everybody does not understand or have the same understanding of the different factors. The responsibility to verify information lies at the individual level, and there is not a social or collective judgement of reliability as in the claims handling department where the claims meetings function as a collective judgement of reliability. Therefore, information as a resource is defined as a group asset in the claims handling unit where the individual expertise and knowledge is brought to the group systematically. In the biotechnology firm, information is a personal asset delivered to the group or to specific members of the group. Although information is a personal resource that is shared with the other workers, the open office landscape helps the organisation shape some level of common knowledge base where everyone can see and hear what the other functions are working with. "The open office landscape means that everything is public information" (Communication).

The claims handling group has built a very clear structure of their information sources, and there are also clear communication patterns. Personal networks are easy to access because the whole department is physically located in the same corridor. However, the individuals within the group are able to utilise the collective knowledge base depending on tasks, expert status, and personal (individual) preferences. The personal networks are accessed according to role and status within the network. The claims handlers access the network on daily basis, and coffee and lunch breaks are part of the informal structure of the personal interactions. Because of the routine-based work the claims handlers also know how the work pace is structured among them and can adjust the personal interactions according to that.

The different roles in this group can be pictured as novices and experts where the novices use the network broadly while the older members and experts have specific persons to turn to. Workers also experience these roles as information retrievers and information producers. The access to the network also shows how weak and strong ties work (Granovetter, 1983). It is important to notice that the novices mainly use weak ties when they ask anybody for advice. At the same time, they contribute to a broader awareness of different problems in the group as a whole when they ask many persons about difficult cases. Those who use only specific persons (strong ties) limit the awareness to these persons. Information sharing in the biotechnology context does not have very visible structures. There is a hidden profile in the motives for sharing or not sharing information (Wittenbaum et al., 2004). In this group, the profiles reveal a pattern of how internal networks are built and the importance of trust in these connections. The reliability is judged to depend on individuals. Some persons are more thorough and detailed than others. Generally, information is perceived to be reliable from colleagues – people do not deliberately give wrong information. The work environment and time span put special demands on sharing, and it is important to be able to rely on the individuals around you when a formal structure and channels are missing. The motives for not sharing information are also mentioned where a decision not to share can have considerable impact on other activities.

While the biotechnology group lacks clear communicative structures, the aspect of trust is treated somewhat differently. Trust is based on the fact that the experts trust each other to share right information at the right time. Traditionally trust is seen to be built over time (Mayer, Davis, & Schoorman, 1995), which is not always possible in this environment. Trust is a more "hands on" feature where the experts must trust that the others share what they know. They are also forced to believe and trust the knowledge of another expert. It is embedded in the climate that there must be a level of trust between the individual experts, but it is clear that this is a fairly fragile state. When someone delivers incorrect information, the trust is quite soon questioned, and the level of trust must be re-built. Trust is, therefore, mainly built from high-quality expertise and an appreciation of the expertise of others. Personal relationships are also stressed. "Those who you interact with about work tasks, you more easily communicate with otherwise" (Training). It has been shown in previous research that personal relationship with an individual is the primary influence when managers select a source for information (Mackenzie, 2005).

Another challenge that must be faced is the need to combine information from the different activities. The training expert compares this heterogeneous group to a relay race – you have to wait for those processes that are slower, because information is not always transferred that easily. Cooperation depends on the individual's cooperative ability. What happens if the baton falls?

> A challenge in this kind of organization is to combine information from different sources all the time; be organised and think of who should know about this. You should function like a computer, prioritise tasks etc. But there are many human factors affecting this organised way of information sharing. Some people have a great ability to put up information but are not so good at sharing. This affects the feeling of whom is easy to cooperate with. You need the two-way communication. (Training)

The experts and their co-ordinator are bound together by an immediate objective – the creation of innovative products to sustain the company, and they work within tight time constraints. What is shared, or brought to the common attention of the group, is highly selective and depends on judgements about the consequences of sharing at any given juncture. There is more at stake – each specialist must trust the judgments of the others, as he or she is not competent to assess the quality of another specialist input. And specialist external sources must be filtered by the judgment of resident experts – few information sources can thus be used in common. The habits of the experts in the biotechnology group are similar to those that have been reported in accounts of interdisciplinary scientific collaboration among specialist experts in other contexts – water planning (Van House, 2003) and public administration (Drake, Steckler, & Koch, 2004). They have a

Table 11. Motives for What and to Whom to Share.

Preference	Claims Handlers	Biotechnology Experts
1	Shared goals	Shared goals
2	Structure[a]	Communicative ability
3	Personal preferences[b]	Personal preferences[b]
4	Social and expertise hierarchy	Social and expertise hierarchy
5	Communicative ability	Structure[a]

[a]Organisational factors (structure), there is a given matrix of information sharing, (in the biotechnology firm the structured strategies are under construction).
[b]You cooperate better with some persons.

contractual obligation to share, but they do not always believe that "outsider" recipients will fully understand the specialist data that has been sent to them, and, therefore, they will be highly selective in what they contribute to others.

To summarise, information sharing is a goal-directed behaviour, and it is important to think of the motives that influence what and to whom to share. There are five common motives for the two cases but they have different preferences in the two groups (Table 11).

CONCLUSIONS

Information sharing behaviour in the two cases cited is concluded to be different. Building a common knowledge base is better realised in the claims handling unit where personal knowledge and expertise is brought to the group systematically through weekly meetings and a functioning personal network structure. The group has a high level of trust within their structures and information and knowledge has become a collective resource. This group has, however better circumstances to develop the structures that are needed. The biotechnology field is a hectic environment, and the importance of communicative ability and trust is more critical. Trust has another role where information and knowledge are typically personal resources that are brought to a collective attention on demand. The individuals must trust that they get crucial information from each other whenever needed.

In conclusion, it can be said that KM and IM initiatives must be brought into line with the local context where the human and social processes underpin the formal structures enabling information sharing. In the study, it was clear that the common aims and values of the group motivate the individuals to share what they know. The groups shaped either formal or informal structures to enable the information interactions. Therefore it is clear that social networks can be seen as important information sources in groups and organisations. Also expertise, experience, communicative ability and trust are qualities that are important within the relations affecting information and knowledge sharing. These are important insights in the management of organisations and, especially, in the management of expert organisations where the individual knowledge base is important to bring into the common awareness.

Expert organisations such as libraries where both routine-based work and work tasks are performed typically by experts face an additional challenge in shaping a communicative structure that is suitable for different work environments within the same organisation. This kind of study underlines the challenges of information and knowledge management in today's organisations; the human and social aspects are stressed in combination with knowledge organisation and contents.

However, motives for sharing are associated with many more factors than are analysed within this paper. In future studies, the motives for sharing should also be connected to other factors such as structural, cognitive, and timing aspects, drawing a larger picture of social capital and information behaviour in organisations.

ACKNOWLEDGMENTS

This work has been supported by a grant from the Academy of Finland for research abroad at Napier University, Edinburgh. I also wish to thank my mentors Prof. Elisabeth Davenport, Napier University, and Prof. Mariam Ginman, Åbo Akademi University.

REFERENCES

Baron, S., Field, J., & Schuller, T. (2000). *Social capital – critical perspectives*. Oxford: Oxford University Press.

Bruce, H. (2003). A comparison of the collaborative information retrieval behaviour of two design teams. *New Review of Information Behaviour Research, 4*, 139–153.

Burt, R. S. (1992). *Structural holes*. Cambridge, MA: Harvard University Press.

Burt, R. S. (1997). The contingent value of social capital. *Administrative Science Quarterly, 42*, 339–365.

Burt, R. S. (2001). *Social capital: Theory and research*. New York: De Gruyter.

Choo, C. W. (1998). *The knowing organization: How organizations use information to construct meaning, create knowledge and make decisions.* New York: Oxford University Press.

Cohen, D., & Prusak, L. (2001). *In good company: How social capital makes organizations work.* Boston: Harvard Business School Press.

Coleman, J. (1988). Social capital in the creation of human capital. *American Journal of Sociology, 94*(Suppl.), 95–120.

Cross, R., & Borgatti, S. P. (2004). The ties that share: Relational characteristics that facilitate information seeking. In: M. Huysman & V. Wulf (Eds), *Social capital and information technology* (pp. 137–161). Cambridge, MA: MIT Press.

Davenport, E., & Hall, H. (2002). Organizational knowledge and communities of practice. *Annual Review of Information Science and Technology, 36*, 171–227.

Davenport, E., & Snyder, H. W. (2005). Managing social capital. *Annual Review of Information Science and Technology, 39*, 517–550.

Drake, D., Steckler, N., & Koch, M. (2004). Information sharing in and across government agencies. *Social Science Computer Review, 22*(1), 67–84.

Forsman, M. (2005). *Development of research networks. The case of social capital.* Åbo: Åbo Akademi University Press Doctoral dissertation. (in press).

Fukuyama, F. (1995). Social capital and the global economy. *Foreign Affairs, 74*(5), 89–103.

Ginman, M. (2002). *Health, information and social capital. Communicating health and new genetics.* Åbo: Finnish Information Studies.

Granovetter, M. (1983). The strength of weak ties: A network theory revisited. *Sociological Theory, 1*, 201–233.

Hazleton, V., & Kennan, W. (2000). Social capital: Reconceptualizing the bottom line. *Corporate Communications, 5*(2), 81–86.

Hooff, B. v. d., & Ridder, A. d. (2004). Knowledge sharing in context: The influence of organizational commitment, communication climate and CMC use on knowledge sharing. *Journal of Knowledge Management, 8*(6), 117–130.

Hoffman, J. J., Hoelscher, M. L., & Sherif, K. (2005). Social capital, knowledge management, and sustained superior performance. *Journal of Knowledge Management, 9*(3), 93–100.

Huotari, M.-L., & Iivonen, M. (2004). Managing knowledge-based organizations through trust. In: M.-L. Huotari & M. Iivonen (Eds), *Trust in knowledge management and systems in organizations* (pp. 1–29). Hershey: Idea Group.

Huysman, M., & de Wit, D. (2002). *Knowledge sharing in practice.* Dordrecht: Kluwer.

Hyldegård, J. (2004). Collaborative information behaviour – exploring Kuhlthau's Information Search Process model in a group-based educational setting. *Information Processing & Management, 42*(1), 276–298.

Lang, J. C. (2004). Social context and social capital as enablers of knowledge integration. *Journal of Knowledge Management, 8*(3), 89–105.

Lesser, E. L. (2000). Leveraging social capital in organizations. In: E. L. Lesser (Ed.), *Knowledge and social capital: Foundations and applications* (pp. 3–16). Boston: Butterworth Heinemann.

Lesser, E. L., & Prusak, L. (2000). Communities of practice, social capital and organizational knowledge. In: E. L. Lesser, M. A. Fontaine & J. A. Slusher (Eds), *Knowledge and Communities* (pp. 123–131). Boston: Butterworth Heinemann.

Mackenzie, M. L. (2003). *Information gathering revealed within the social network of line-managers.* Proceedings of the 66th Annual Meeting of the American Society for Information Science and Technology.

Mackenzie, M. L. (2005). Managers look to the social network to seek information. *Information Research: An International Electronic Journal, 10*(2).

Mayer, R. C., Davis, J. H., & Schoorman, F. D. (1995). An integrative model of organizational trust. *Academy of Management Review, 20*(3), 709–734.

McDermott, R., & O'Dell, C. (2001). Overcoming cultural barriers to knowledge sharing. *Journal of Knowledge Management, 5*(1).

McKenzie, P. J. (2003). A model of information practices in accounts of everyday-life information seeking. *Journal of Documentation, 59*(1), 19–40.

Nahapiet, J., & Ghoshal, S. (1998). Social capital, intellectual capital, and the organizational advantage. *Academy of Management Review, 23*(3), 242–266.

O'Reilly, C. A. I. (1982). Variations in decision makers' use of information sources: The impact of quality and accessibility of information. *Academy of Management Journal, 25*(4), 756–771.

Portes, A. (1998). Social capital: Its origins and applications in modern sociology. *Annual Review of Sociology, 22*, 1–25.

PovertyNet (2004). Social capital and firms. 2004.

Reagans, R., & Zuckerman, E. W. (2001). Networks, diversity, and productivity: The social capital of corporate R&D teams. *Organization Science, 12*(4), 89–95.

Sinotte, M. (2004). Exploration of the field of knowledge management for the library and information professional. *Libri, 54*, 190–198.

Solomon, P. (Ed.). (1999). *Information mosaics: patterns of action that structure.* Exploring the contexts of information behaviour. Proceedings of the 2nd International Conference on Research in Information Needs, Seeking, and Use in Different Contexts (Pages). London: Taylor Graham.

Solomon, P. (2002). Discovering information in context. *Annual Review of Information Science and Technology, 36*, 229–264.

Sonnenwald, D. H., & Pierce, L. G. (2000). Information behavior in dynamic group work contexts: Interwoven situational awareness, dense social networks and contested collaboration in command and control. *Information Processing & Management, 36*, 461–479.

Sonnenwald, D. H., Maglaughlin, K., & Whitton,, M. C. (2004). Designing to support situation awareness across distances: An example from a scientific collaboratory. *Information Processing & Management, 40*(6), 989–1011.

Talja, S. (2002). Information sharing in academic communities: Types and levels of collaboration in information seeking and use. *New Review of Information Behaviour Research, 3*, 143–159.

Thomas-Hunt, M. C., Ogden, T. Y., & Neale, M. A. (2003). Who's really sharing? Effects of social and expert status on knowledge exchange within groups. *Management Science, 49*(4), 464–477.

Tsai, W., & Ghoshal, S. (1998). Social capital and value creation: The role of intrafirm networks. *Academy of Management Journal, 42*(4), 464–476.

Tyler, T. R., & Blader, S. L. (2001). Identity and co-operative behaviour in groups. *Group Processes & Intergroup Relations, 4*(3), 207–226.

Tymon, W. G., & Stumpf, S. A. (2003). Social capital in the success of knowledge workers. *Career Development International, 8*(1), 12–20.

Upadhyayula, R. S., & Kumar, R. (2004). Social capital as an antecedent of absorptive capacity of firms. DRUID Summer Conference 2004: Industrial Dynamics, Innovation and Development, Elsinore, Denmark.

Van House, N. (2003). Digital libraries and collaborative knowledge construction. In: A. Bishop, B. Buttenfield & N. Van House (Eds), *Digital library use: Social practices in design and evaluation* (pp. 271–296). Cambridge, MA: MIT Press.

Widén-Wulff, G. (2001). *Informationskulturen som drivkraft i företagsorganisationen.* Åbo: Åbo Akademi University Press.

Widén-Wulff, G. (2003). Information as a resource in the insurance business: The impact of structures and processes on organisation information behaviour. *New Review of Information Behaviour Research, 4,* 79–94.

Widén-Wulff, G. (2005). Business information culture: A qualitative study of the information culture in the Finnish insurance industry. In: E. Maceviciute & T. D. Wilson (Eds), *Introducing information management: An information research reader* (pp. 31–42). London: Facet.

Widén-Wulff, G., Allen, D. K., Maceviciute, E., Moring, C., Papik, R., & Wilson, T. D. (2005). Knowledge Management and Information Management. In: L. Kajberg & L. Lörring (Eds), *LIS education in Europe: Joint curriculum development and bologna perspectives.*

Widén-Wulff, G., & Ginman, M. (2004). Explaining knowledge sharing in organizations through the dimensions of social capital. *Journal of Information Science, 30*(5), 448–458.

Wilson, T. D. (2000). Human information behaviour. *Informing Science, 3*(2), 49–55.

Wittenbaum, G. M., Hollingshead, A. B., & Botero, I. C. (2004). From cooperative to motivated information sharing in groups: Moving beyond the hidden profile paradigm. *Communication Monograph, 7*(3).

DISCIPLINARY SOCIALIZATION: LEARNING TO EVALUATE THE QUALITY OF SCHOLARLY LITERATURE

Vesa Kautto and Sanna Talja

ABSTRACT

There is an increasing interest in incorporating information literacy (IL) instruction into undergraduate curricula in higher education (HE) as a stand alone specialism, "a soft applied discipline" on its own. However, diverse and conflicting views exist about whether information use and evaluation can be taught as discrete activities in isolation from disciplinary content and context, and who, faculty or librarians, should be teaching information literacy. This article seeks to shed additional light on these issues by empirically exploring how literature evaluation and use is taught by faculty in four fields: physics, medicine, social politics and social work, and literature. Using Becher's (1989) characterizations of academic fields along the dimensions hard-soft and pure-applied, convergent and divergent, rural and urban, we explore the relationships between the nature of knowledge production within the fields studied and their practices of teaching literature use and evaluation. The findings indicate that IL is best conceived as something that can not be meaningfully approached or taught as separate from disciplinary contents and contexts.

Advances in Library Administration and Organization, Volume 25, 33–59
Copyright © 2007 by Elsevier Ltd.
All rights of reproduction in any form reserved
ISSN: 0732-0671/doi:10.1016/S0732-0671(07)25002-3

Information skills must be taught in ways that are wholly integrated with the ways literature is searched, used, and evaluated within disciplines.

INTRODUCTION

In the past 30 years, more than 5,000 publications dealing with information literacy (IL) and bibliographic instruction have appeared (Rader, 2002), and there has been an increasing international interest in incorporating information literacy into undergraduate curricula in higher education (HE) as a stand-alone specialism, "a soft-applied discipline" on its own (Johnston & Webber, 2003). Information literacy teaching and research have traditionally been advocated mainly by library and information professionals, having evolved from library skills and bibliographic instruction. The most important and widely cited publications on information literacy have come from library associations, for example, American Library Association (ALA, 1989), the Society of College, National and University Libraries (SCONUL, 1999), and the Association of College and Research Libraries (ACRL, 2000). The rationale behind the conception of information literacy as a soft-applied discipline and a stand-alone specialty is that "the ability to identify, locate, evaluate, organize, and effectively create, use, and communicate information is a prerequisite for participating effectively in the information society, and part of the basic human right of lifelong learning" (Information Literacy Meeting of Experts, 2003).

Information literacy is an umbrella concept joining together diverse skills and abilities such as information retrieval skills, Internet use skills, information technology use, and competencies needed to seek, evaluate, and use information, with a special emphasis on "higher order skills" such as critical thinking and wise and ethical use of information (Johnston & Webber, 2003). Information literacy has mostly been used as a prescriptive concept guiding IL instruction. IL instruction within HE is typically based on information literacy standards listing performance indicators and indicative outcomes. For instance, in the ACRL (2000) standard, an information literate student is able to

- determine the nature and extent of the information needed;
- access needed information effectively and efficiently;
- evaluate information and its sources critically and incorporate selected information into his or her knowledge base and value system;
- use information effectively to accomplish a specific purpose;
- understand many of the economic, legal, and social issues surrounding the use of information and access, and use information ethically and legally.

Johnston and Webber (2003) argue that IL standards are limited in their view of information literacy as an acquired personal attribute of individuals. They say that the prescriptive approach trivializes human information practices, and Halttunen (2004) notes that it is likely to lead to de-contextualized, artificial instruction. Information use and evaluation are seen as being comprised of *generic skills* that are independent from content and context – the subject matter, practices, and discourses of different disciplines. Cheuk (2002) similarly argues that information literacy needs a context and subject-specific content to be meaningfully discussed.

Studies on faculty and student responses to information literacy classes have discovered that while faculty–librarian relationships are vital components of successful information literacy teaching, students and faculty may see both the information literacy concept and library instruction as library-jargon-centered and tangential to class content (Julien & Given, 2003). At odds with the ACRL and SCONUL standards stressing higher order elements of information literacy, Julien's (2005) survey on information literacy instruction showed that 20% of librarians did not believe that librarians have a responsibility to teach critical thinking in general, and 15% did not believe that librarians have a responsibility for teaching the understanding of ethical, economic, or sociopolitical issues.[1] We may thus conclude that diverse and conflicting views exist about whether information use and evaluation can be taught as discrete activities in isolation from disciplinary content and context, and who, faculty or librarians, should be teaching information literacy.

This article seeks to shed additional light on these issues. It contributes to existing research by empirically exploring disciplinary differences in literature evaluation criteria.[2] We report on a study investigating teaching of literature evaluation across four disciplines. The study is underpinned by the observation shared with Webber and Johnston (2004) that while librarians' voices and views are well represented in IL literature, the conceptions of faculty and students have received comparatively little attention (for exceptions, see Leckie & Fullerton, 1999; Whitmire, 2002).

RESEARCH AIMS AND QUESTIONS

This article is part of the recent efforts to contextualize information practices within the cultures, modes of thought, and nature of knowledge production within disciplines. A growing body of research within LIS embeds the information literacy concept firmly into sociocultural theories of learning (Kapitzke & Bruce, 2005; Halttunen, 2004; Sundin, 2004, 2005;

Talja, 2005a; Tuominen, Savolainen, & Talja, 2005). These studies attempt to reach a better understanding of the elements of information literacy that go beyond library use and information retrieval skills, and to understand the contextual considerations that are often overlooked in IL initiatives and standards but fundamental to their success.

The study at hand deviates from previous IL inquiries in that it builds on studies showing that each academic discipline has its own distinctive set of epistemic and social considerations (Becher, 1989; Whitley, 1984). Within LIS, empirical studies using a systematically comparative domain analytic approach are relatively few in number (Kling & Covi, 1997; Talja, 2003; Talja & Maula, 2003; Fry & Talja, 2004; Talja, Savolainen, & Maula, 2004; Talja, 2005b). Studies typically focus on single disciplines, and little attempt has been made to lay a framework for comparisons across disciplines.

This article applies the description of academic cultures developed by Tony Becher (1989) in his book *Academic Tribes and Territories* to address the following questions:

1. What differences exist in approaches to the evaluation of the quality of literature across scholarly disciplines?
2. How are these disciplinary quality norms and practices transmitted to newcomers, if they are?
3. How well does Becher's theory enable the understanding and explanation of disciplinary differences in evaluation criteria?

The purpose of this work is to contribute to the efforts for developing more domain-specific ways of teaching information skills and to address the issue whether IL is best conceived as a stand-alone specialism, or something that cannot be meaningfully approached as separate from disciplinary contents and contexts.

The first chapter describes Becher's (1989) theoretical concepts and introduces the hypotheses that underpin the study. The empirical study is then described, and the empirical findings are presented in the fourth section. The summary compares the hypotheses to the results reached, and the chapter ends by discussing the implications of the findings for information literacy efforts.

ACADEMIC CULTURES

Based on interviews of scholars across 12 disciplines[3] and a scrutiny of existing literature, Becher's (1989) theory stresses the mutually shaping interplay between the epistemological character of a discipline and the culture of that discipline, that is, the recurrent practices of its members. The first dimension refers to the *intellectual territory* of a field: the nature of its research questions, nature of knowledge produced within the field, and the permeability of its boundaries. The second dimension refers to the character of its *tribal culture*: customs, routines and patterns of behavior that are taken-for-granted. Along the intellectual territory dimension, Becher (1989, pp. 35–36) argues that reasonably clear differences exist between knowledge domains in terms of the following:

- characteristics of the objects of enquiry;
- the nature of knowledge growth;
- the relationship between the researcher and knowledge;
- enquiry procedures;
- extent of truth claims and criteria for making them;
- the results of research.

Leaning on Kolb's (1981) and Biglan's (1973) categorizations of disciplines as soft/hard or pure/applied, Becher (1989) classifies disciplines into four groups – "hard-pure," "soft-pure," "hard-applied," and "soft-applied," – and describes the nature of knowledge in each group according to the criteria mentioned above. The characterizations of these four groups are presented in Table 1.

Becher (1989, pp. 77–102, 154–158) stresses that disciplines differ greatly in their degree of internal integration. Some disciplinary communities are *convergent*: tightly knit with shared judgments of quality and agreement about what counts as appropriate disciplinary content. Some disciplinary groups are *divergent* and loosely knit. Their members lack a clear sense of mutual cohesion and identity, and their borders with other subject fields are ill-defined. Soft disciplines with relatively permeable boundaries are in their nature more tolerant of divergence than those whose subject matter is hard and whose boundaries are closely defined. In the more loosely knit disciplines, it is commonplace for different specialty groups within the discipline to adopt different standards of academic rigor.

The grouping of disciplines into the four groups with related epistemic characteristics is followed by a distinction between *rural* and *urban* academic tribes. According to Becher (1989, pp. 79–80), "urban" researchers characteristically select a narrow area for study, with discrete and separable problems. Their "rural" counterparts cover a broader stretch of intellectual territory, in which the problems are not sharply demarcated or delineated. The urban tribe is clustered around a few salient topics, and competition can

Table 1. Disciplinary Groupings (Becher and Trowler, 2001, p. 36).

Disciplinary Groupings	Nature of Knowledge
"Hard-pure": Pure sciences (e.g., physics).	Cumulative; atomistic (crystalline/tree-like); concerned with universals, quantities, simplification; impersonal, value-free; clear criteria for knowledge verification and obsolescence; consensus over significant questions to address, results in discovery/explanation.
"Soft-pure": Humanities (e.g., history) and pure social sciences (e.g., anthropology).	Reiterative; holistic (organic/river-like); concerned with particulars, qualities, complication; personal, value-laden; dispute over criteria for knowledge verification and obsolescence; lack of consensus over significant questions to address; results in understanding/interpretation.
"Hard-applied": Technologies (e.g., clinical medicine, engineering).	Purposive; pragmatic (know-how via hard knowledge); concerned with mastery of physical environment; applies heuristic approaches; uses both qualitative and quantitative approaches; criteria for judgment are purposive, functional; results in products/techniques.
"Soft-applied": Applied social science (e.g., education, law, social administration).	Functional; utilitarian (know-how via soft knowledge); concerned with enhancement of [semi-]professional practice; uses case studies and case law to a large extent; results in protocols/procedures.

be intense, as against the rural tribe spread out thinly across a wide range of themes. "Urban" research is cumulative, based on close-knit collaborations, can command sizeable resources, and utilizes cutting-edge technology. In "rural" research, overlap in research topics is less likely. There is a great range of choice in style, taste, and subject matter. Since there is no established starting point for work, establishing a framework for discussion may in itself require several years and a book-length treatment.

The distinction between rural and urban tribes and their description closely resembles Whitley's (1984) theory of the social and intellectual organization of academic fields. Becher draws to some extent on Whitley's description of disciplines along the axes of "task uncertainty" and "mutual dependence." Space does not allow for detailed comparisons between Becher's and Whitley's (1984) theories; however, the resemblances lend support to both theories, as does their dependence on empirical case studies.

As noted by Becher (1989, pp. 16–17) himself, categorizations such as "hard-pure" cannot do justice to the complexity and variation of inquiry processes. As he notes, differences between specialties within a field can be bigger than differences between disciplines. Pure and applied, hard and soft, and urban and rural specialties may well coexist within single departments.

Nevertheless, Becher's concepts potentially bring into view some essential dimensions and differences that help in understanding and analyzing variation. Such essential differences are easily obscured in more localized studies of single disciplines.

The framework described above is best seen as a toolbox that provides a set of basic terminology to begin explorations into scholarly work and literature evaluation practices. For the purposes of the study at hand, Becher's ideas regarding "disciplinary socialization" are particularly relevant.

DISCIPLINARY SOCIALIZATION

The concept of disciplinary socialization is based on the family of sociocultural or situated theories of learning that were developed as alternatives to constructivist theories of learning that stress the individual's sense-making. The best known works on situated learning are by Lave (1988), and Lave and Wenger (1991). Lave and Wenger explain how newcomers learn the practice in which they are engaged through moving from "legitimate peripheral participation" to being full participants in a sociocultural practice. In this process, newcomers absorb a body of practice and procedures that have evolved historically and are shared and developed by a community of practitioners (Lave & Wenger, 1991; Talja & Hansen, 2005). As part of their socialization into an academic discipline, students will learn two kinds of knowledge. The first kind is knowledge that has grown out of long experience in the discipline. This is a practical knowledge or competence that the department elite fully masters. The most important ingredient of this is the ability to recognize what counts as a relevant contribution, what counts as answering a question, what counts as having a good argument, what counts as valid evidence for a result reached, and what counts as good scholarly criticism (Rorty, 1979). The second kind of knowledge relates to the practical application of the disciplinary tradition and discourses, including evaluative abilities, in particular situations and work tasks (Rorty, 1979; Becher, 1989, pp. 22–27). Based on the concept of disciplinary socialization, our basic hypothesis is that:

Hypothesis 1. Academics' understanding of their disciplinary subject matter influences the approach they take to teaching the evaluation of literature; there are distinct ways of thinking about, talking about, and acting on quality evaluation criteria; which vary according to discipline.

Becher and Kogan (1992) offer some assumptions regarding differences in the nature of education within the four disciplinary categories described in Table 1. We use these hypotheses as a point of comparison for the empirical results reached in the case studies in the summary section.

Hypothesis 2a. Within the hard-pure area, teaching is theoretically oriented. The teaching has clear common goals and the contents of the curriculum are stable and clearly delineated. Because knowledge is cumulatively built, students must absorb the body of basic knowledge in a predefined in order to be able to understand the issues.

Hypothesis 2b. Within hard-applied sciences, the goal of teaching is practically oriented. Primary importance is placed on the application of knowledge, and mastery of skills and techniques, not in the assimilation of concepts and theories. The aim is to ensure that students really learn the professional skills required in working life.

Hypothesis 2c. In the soft-applied area, teaching is oriented to practice and the aim is to develop professional skills for future working life. Practice is based on softer knowledge than that in the hard-applied category, related to development of activities within human relationship and service professions.

Hypothesis 2d. Within the soft-pure area, teaching and study are individualistic in nature. It is expected that students to a large extent build their own study programs and formulate individual interpretations and conceptions of the issues involved. The goals of studies are personally defined, and teaching leaves room for students' own inclinations.

THE STUDY

The interview data to explore disciplinary differences in literature evaluation practices were gathered through choosing one field to represent each of Becher's four categories. Physics represents a "hard-pure" field; medicine was chosen to represent the "hard-applied" category. Social work and social politics, located in a single department, were chosen to represent the "soft-applied" category, and literary studies represent the "soft-pure" category. The physics informants were located in the University of Helsinki, Finland, and the rest in the University of Tampere, Finland. The informants were selected on the basis of their departmental affiliations (Kautto, 2004).

From each field, four faculty members and four students were interviewed. Pilot interviews conducted earlier were added to the overall corpus consisting of 34 interviews. Eighteen informants were faculty members and 16 informants were students. The criterion for recruitment of faculty members was involvement in teaching involving use and evaluation of scholarly literature. The faculty members taught seminars in which students were required to use literature, or supervised master's theses. All faculty informants hold a PhD degree. The student informants, in turn, were identified by their teachers. All student informants were in the final stages of their studies.

The faculty interviews lasted about 80 minutes on average, and the student interviews lasted on average 60 minutes. All interviews were tape-recorded and transcribed in full for analysis. The interviews were analyzed thematically. Additional data were gathered in the form of study guides. The draft analyzes were sent to the faculty informants for comments, and six faculty informants offered their comments and additions to the texts.

TEACHING OF EVALUATION CRITERIA

Physics

In the Department of Physical Sciences at the University of Helsinki, education is given in physics, theoretical physics, geophysics, and meteorology. The education of physics teachers also belongs to the tasks of the department. Those studying physics choose between areas of specialization such as high energy or nuclear physics, material physics, and applied physics. Within physics, the basic studies are common for all specialties, involving basic theories of classical physics, thermodynamics, the structure of matter, modern physics, and electronics. Laboratory and mathematics exercises form a sizable part of basic studies.

Textbooks have a central role in studies of physics before the advanced phase. As one student put it, "the content of textbooks relates to basic laws, they cannot be approached critically, the only errors that you can detect are printing errors." Within applied physics, students did analyze research articles in groups in the *Laboratory Work 2* course. They were required to analyze the research methodology, the trustworthiness of methods, the measurements, the treatment of results, and the trustworthiness of conclusions drawn. However, within physics, the independent searching and use of literature mainly begin at the advanced studies phase, and especially during the writing of master's theses. The cumulative nature of knowledge within physics means that students cannot conduct independent studies without first having adopted the basics of physics and the mathematical methods for solving problems. As expressed by one faculty member:

> Physics is a discipline in which everything is built on the foundations learned in basic courses. These courses offer the basis for understanding physics, conducting experiments, counting equations, forming equations, and solving problems (P1).[4]

The master's thesis in physics involves laboratory work and a written thesis. The laboratory work can sometimes be performed within the research groups operating in the department. Graduate seminars provide orientation to the use of scientific literature. However, research groups provide a more efficient forum for disciplinary socialization and a forum where literature selection and evaluation criteria are absorbed as a normal part of the groups' work processes. One research group within material physics, for instance, consisted of two faculty members, three doctoral students, and six graduate students. The group regularly held research monitoring and planning meetings where students could introduce the literature they had found, and the group discussed the relevance of the articles. The literature used mainly consisted of articles written in English. The group tried to publish one international journal article on the basis of each completed thesis. Learning to search, select, evaluate, and produce scholarly journal articles was hence an integrated process. Within the research groups, students learned about international research groups studying similar problems as their own group. They learned that the searching, selection, and evaluation of literature to a large extent involve knowledge about these groups and monitoring their output.

Concerning the evaluation criteria taught to the students, one physics faculty member said that he guided his students to focus on results, methods, and arrangements of experiments: whether the results would provide a point of comparison for the students' own results and whether the method and experiments were similar to his own. He stated that:

> The introduction and discussion parts come later, the graduate student will not benefit from them. The student will show me the structure of the results, and I will say, these are good references, go through these, or that, you can forget this, this is not relevant for your work (P3).

Within physics, judging relevance hence requires detailed analysis of methods and results, something that according to faculty is fairly difficult and not something graduate students could necessarily conduct alone despite their education. Within theoretical physics, the guidance in the choice and evaluation of literature was an even more comprehensive process than help in the judgment of relevance. A student could be given the literature to be used in the thesis, and the independent task for the student was not a choice of topic or selection of literature. Rather, the task could be to make sense of the articles themselves and to form an understanding of the problems treated in them. Given the highly specialized knowledge structure within this field, the student could not be left alone in the tasks of topic choice, literature searching, relevance, or quality evaluation. In this light, it is not surprising that students were not actively offered or had taken courses to learn independent searching skills.

In the program designed to educate physics teachers, the independent searching, use, and analysis of research literature is a compulsory and central part of studies. These are mainly taught within proseminars where students are required to conduct a small-scale independent study and that typically contain exercises in searching literature in journal databases and practices in the evaluation of scholarly articles. Critical reading and thinking and creative writing are central subject matter in physics didactics courses. However, what is meant by "critical thinking" in the context of physics differs greatly from what it means in, say, social politics, because it is contextualized to physical experiments. As put by a physics education faculty member: "The scientific experiment is the question that is put to nature, and, through the experiment, nature provides an answer."

Medicine

In Finland, the Faculty of Medicine in the University of Tampere was the first to base its curriculum entirely on the principles of problem-based learning (PBL) in 1994. According to faculty, the first rationale underpinning the adoption of PBL methods was the rapid rate of change of the medical knowledge base. An attempt to transmit this knowledge base to students in a traditional teacher-led manner would have led to the unrealistic expansion of the study program. One faculty member stressed that:

> Each textbook is dated by the time it appears. In any case, it is wrong to hide the most recent knowledge from the students. All that knowledge cannot be offered to students because of its sheer amount, and that is why the ball must be thrown to them. They must search information and make their own conclusions. And they succeed very well (M1).

The second rationale for the shift to PBL was the observation that the theoretical basic knowledge previously taught within the first two years of study did not easily and unproblematically "travel" to the context of medical practice and study of clinical skills. The shift to PBL involved courses in clinical practice and patient encounters from the beginning of the student's academic career. The first principle of PBL is that a problem is encountered at the beginning of studies without prior preparation. Second, the problem is presented in the same way as it would appear in a real situation. Third, the problem is treated as requiring independent judgment and the application of knowledge. The fourth principle is that it is essential to recognize the areas that are necessary to master. The fifth principle is that, through study and independent information seeking, the acquired information is applied to the problem situation leading to problem solution. A central form of teaching in PBL is small group work led by a tutor (Holmberg-Marttila, Hakkarainen, Viljo, & Nikkari, 2005).

Medical students complete their degrees (licentiate in medicine) in approximately six years. The first four years consist of integrated periods involving the study of problem cases and exams measuring progress. The solving of the problem cases requires independent information gathering and knowledge acquisition. Students are also given lists of textbooks and central literature. The goal of PBL, however, is to have students search for information from various sources, evaluate its relevance for practice, and determine its applicability in real contexts and situations:

> The idea of problem-based learning is that a student should, in principle, be able to assess what type of knowledge is necessary, and to critically evaluate whether a scientific article is made in the way that it is credible, regardless of whether it is published in a highly esteemed journal. The case may be that the observation is important, but that does not mean that it is generally applicable to the treatment of any patient or the patient currently being treated (M1).

Courses in information skills are compulsory for medical students. Within the first three study years, students take three courses in the library. Courses basically offer instruction about searching in the library and searching in reference and journal databases. In addition to the courses given by the library, teachers personally give guidance and practical tips for literature searches. One faculty member explained that he advised students to begin their searches from Finnish article databases and review articles. He gave advice concerning various types of searches, choice of search terms, and the narrowing of searches, which are all considered to be vital skills within the curriculum. In some courses, students were required to conduct literature searches, which were then examined by the teacher. One seminar explicitly focuses on the conduct of systematic literature reviews and the evaluation of various dimensions of evidence within research articles.

As explained by one student, evaluation of the quality of research articles concerns evaluating the relevance of the topic and the rationality of the hypothesis, method, and data:

> The evaluation of evidence levels and trustworthiness of results relate to the research hypothesis, whether the hypothesis takes enough factors into account, the size of the sample, how many persons were tested, if it is a patient study, and whether it can be generalized into the Finnish environment if the research has been conducted elsewhere. And, if statistical methods were used, how reliable are the values reached (MS1).

In the evaluation of evidence levels, A-level is the highest and signifies experimental studies with randomized control trials (with concealed allocation). B-level signifies experimental studies without randomization or observational study with a control group. C-level refers to observational studies without control groups. D-level refers to case reports and means that a treatment recommendation is based on expert consensus and cumulated experience rather than clinical evidence (Khan, Kunz, Klijnen, & Antes, 2003, p. 17). Also, within other courses, students were required to evaluate articles and the credibility of the results reached. Some study periods involve the use of social scientific literature, as well as orientation to the use of questionnaires, and potential sources of error in them. Some medical students experienced something of a culture shock using social scientific literature. Accustomed to weigh evidence and look for verified results, some commented that:

> The type of knowledge is so different, a medical student will not easily accept the interpretations that are brought forward in such a wordy and lucid manner (MS1).

> It [social scientific literature] not does concern facts, it concerns theory developed by someone, and ponderings over the issue at hand, not based on scientific evidence (MS3).

Student informants stressed that articles obtained from "official" databases such as MEDLINE could not automatically be trusted, since articles could contain overly confident conclusions. One student who participated in the work of a research group narrated how he had conducted an experiment described in an article five times without reaching the same conclusion. Some informants mentioned one highly esteemed publication forum that sometimes published surprising and disputed results to raise discussion.

The problem-based learning methods adopted in medicine involve close communication between faculty members and students. The faculty offer background information about peer-review practices, the significance of various publication forums, how journal impact factors are counted, and other aspects related to the trustworthiness of evidence within research articles. Evaluation of the quality of literature within medicine is deeply ingrained with the evaluation of effectiveness of treatments-in-use. Given this, information searching and systematic evaluation skills emerge as vital "craft skills" to be mastered.

Social Politics and Social Work

Students at the Department of Social Politics at the University of Tampere can specialize in social politics, social work, or social pedagogics. The professions they typically enter are in public administration, teaching and research, and social work. Those studying social politics can choose to specialize in particular issues such as city planning, employment, housing, or work conditions. The curriculum aims at transmitting professional skills such as communication and professional interaction skills, theoretical understandings of the workings of society, social problems and their background, a readiness to do research, and critical thinking skills. Studies in social politics and social work hence have a distinct professional orientation, but with the aim of firmly grounding professional practice on theory and research.

The curricula mainly consist of lectures and literature exams. The teaching methods hence differ notably from those used within medicine. PBL methods are not used, although social work involves problem solving in interaction with clients. The independent use of literature starts early in basic courses, for instance, within seminars and courses on research issues within social politics. Within seminars, literature is in part given by the teacher, in part independently sought by the student.

Courses on library use and information searching skills were not a compulsory part of studies within social politics at the time when the interviews were conducted, but were recommended. The methods of searching for literature differed from those used in medicine, because students mainly identified relevant literature from the university library's OPAC and did not use journal databases. A frequently used search method was backward chaining from recent publications. One faculty member explained that:

> When students start tackling a research problem, a method that I recommend is that they search for a recent source on that area, and then go step by step backward from that source to find earlier sources (S2).

The literature used in master's theses incorporated international theoretical and methodological literature. Classical social theoretical works were also considered be valuable. Differences in social service systems across countries meant that the empirical literature used was mainly Finnish or Scandinavian.

Students were advised that professional articles in general were not to be used as sources, but as objects of analysis. Thus, students were explicitly guided to distinguish scholarly literature from professional literature.

There were no departmentally stated guidelines for the use or evaluation of literature. The research method studies guide, however, states that "through the use of literature the student manifests her knowledge of earlier results, reports the use of methods, and the relation of the results to others' interpretations." The analysis and evaluation of scholarly articles or doctoral dissertations was incorporated by some faculty into research project studies. The students were guided to analyze the heading, aims and central message of the study, concepts and theory used, how methods were used, the nature of data analyzed, the audience addressed, and the criteria given to justify the success of the study.

The use of and approach to literature within social politics and social work differ notably from those in both physics and medicine in that theories and hypotheses presented in earlier literature can be either accepted as points of departure for the student's own contribution or taken as objects of analysis and criticism. One faculty member explained that a major goal was to teach "critical reading" of scholarly and professional literature and develop a readiness to follow scientific conversations:

> We try to teach students critical reading, we tell what it is and use examples. Students who have spent long periods working in the field will tend to lean on professional literature and administrative texts and refer to them as if they simply contained facts. We take concrete examples and tell that these should also be analyzed and approach as texts (S4).

Some faculty encouraged students to approach textbooks, professional literature, and scholarly articles in the same way as texts: to analyze their structure, arguments, and style of argumentation. Some faculty members advised students to analyze speaker positions: who talks in the journal articles and to whom; what kind of target group is the article intended for, what kind of role does the researcher adopt, and what is the relationship of the study to earlier studies. Other evaluation criteria mentioned were the importance of the study's problem in the light of current social problems, clarity of answers and conclusions drawn, practical implications, the quality and level of theoretical framework, conceptual clarity, readability, reliability of the analysis, and quality of evidence.

Writing their master's theses, students in social politics and social work have to choose between diverse theoretical traditions. There are many ways to frame a problem and embed it in a conceptual and theoretical framework. This condition had sometimes been demonstrated by faculty in research

methods courses where students had analyzed the same research data from
diverse viewpoints using different analytical concepts, for instance, metaphor theories and identity theories. Hence, faculty wanted to teach students
to pay attention to the epistemic assumptions underlying research studies,
and to the contexts in which they were produced. One faculty member
stressed that learning to distinguish between approaches and theoretical
traditions is a process that takes many years of study to master and that it
could not be expected that students could reach the same level as experienced researchers. Students could reach a good level of analytical thinking,
but senior faculty could place a research report within a distinct school of
thought by a single glance at the references, concepts, and terminology used.

Within social politics and social work, the conception of critical reading is
very different from that used in medicine. Finding and searching for literature did not emerge as a significant or central area to master. Embracing
the analytic skills for critically approaching and unpacking various types of
texts emerged as more crucial. Students were not always sure about the
extent to which their work was expected to be based upon existing literature,
or how to combine various sources in a meaningful way. They experienced
problems in defining their own contribution and placing it within the corpus
of existing research, because some texts and ideas could be objects of criticism, and others major sources of inspiration and ideas. Outlining what is
important in each work, and how to synthesize ideas in a way that would be
helpful for future studies, was the task that was seen as most demanding by
both faculty and students. The core task was not searching but choosing and
making sense of the literature.

Literature

Those studying literature at the University of Tampere choose between
studies in Finnish literature or Comparative literature. The Department of
Arts also hosts studies in media culture, art history, and theatre and drama,
but we only look at literature studies. Those who complete their master's
degrees in literature, depending on their other coursework, end up working
as teachers, librarians, journalists, researchers, authors, or in the new media.
The studies in literature aim at transmitting skills for the analysis of
literature and cultural textual practices, and the teaching of literature. One
faculty member described studies in literature as a process consisting of
three stages. At the first stage, the role of textbooks is to transmit "the
dogma," a language for talking about literature. In the second phase,

scholarly literature should ideally be used to formulate research questions. Students should learn to navigate in the scholarly landscape and make a choice as to where they themselves fit. In the third phase, they should have an individual goal of contributing to existing knowledge, and provide that contribution in the form of master's theses.

One faculty member remarked that students often came to the department expecting to concentrate on literature, but would instead learn a different, theoretical way of thinking about and approaching literature. One student stated that literature studies meant studies in and about philosophy. In addition, skills of expression, reflexivity, and self-reflexivity, developing a crystallized self-understanding related to emotional, aesthetic, and ethical stances, were mentioned as the processes required for the successful completion of studies. Studies in literature usually take fairly long, between six and eight years, to complete.

The major teaching methods used are lectures, literature exams, and writing essays. Seminars are offered in some topics in addition to proseminars and graduate seminars. Literature students typically pursue individual interests and individually chosen topics. One faculty member said that the range of topics pursued by students was so wide that it was sometimes difficult for faculty members to give substantial guidance. Examples of topics he mentioned were "Analysis of advertisements" and "Identities in the Internet." Faculty members stressed that it was very important for teachers to help students get their independent work going by providing at least a couple of books on which students could base their work. Since the topics, theories, and methods used in work were self-selected, teachers saw a necessity to ensure students would not lean on outdated literature or literature of poor quality. In addition to their accumulated knowledge and experience, they based their recommendations on high-quality book publishers, authoritative researchers, and, to a lesser extent, the reputations of journals. There existed no consensus on the field's major journals among faculty members. Due to the fragmented nature of the field, there is a wide variety of different types of journals, whereas within astrophysics, for instance, relevant publications are concentrated in four major journals (Kling & McKim, 2000, pp. 1313–1314).

Library skills and information searching courses were sometimes incorporated into research skills courses and offered to students on a voluntary basis. Neither faculty nor students regularly used or searched in journal or reference databases, however. The seeking, use, and reading of scholarly literature was less bounded by the topic of study and guided even more by the choice of a theoretical and methodological framework than in social politics. One faculty member stressed that a very systematic approach to searching literature could even prove to be harmful. The first reason was that systematic searches would yield a large amount of literature, which, due to the non-cumulative nature of research within this field, would not be easily synthetizable. The literature found might not necessarily have a good fit with the student's chosen theory frame, and in the worst case could fragment the student's thinking and discourage her from pursuing the chosen line of questioning. The second reason mentioned was that the most fruitful sources would often be ones that were not "on the topic" – either on the subject studied or the theory used – but ones that provided a model for expressing a problem, or drawing conclusions. Such "model works" could be found practically anywhere; hence, faculty stressed the importance of browsing in the library, echoing a statement made by Eco (1990, p. 72) that

> The crucial idea for research may prove to be something that is mentioned almost in passing within the pages on an otherwise useless book (or one that most would consider irrelevant), and this page must be found on the basis of instinct (and with some good luck); it is nothing that is offered on a plate [translated from Finnish].

Literature scholars are often heavy consumers of different types of texts, as observed also by Kling and Covi (1997). They can read diverse types of texts with their research problems in mind, but, in their publications, they may end up using and citing only a fragment of what they have read.

In the same way as social politics faculty, literature faculty members stressed that students could not be expected to be readily able to distinguish between texts belonging to diverse theoretical traditions. According to the faculty members, providing a basic understanding and appreciation of theoretical plurality was a major goal:

> Within this field, we have a very pluralistic situation, where we have many competing theories and no one can say anything about their superiority. What we try to convey is tolerance of pluralism, and perhaps an ability to read pluralism so that in reading a text, the student would be able to see and understand the conversation it belongs to, the terms under which the knowledge has been produced, and most importantly, the kinds of concepts that are used within that specific theory or theoretical approach (L1).

In a field whose core mission is to teach critical reading skills, the criteria for the evaluation of scholarly literature are rarely made explicit, which is perhaps a paradox. One faculty informant formulated this paradox by saying that the criteria are to a large degree kept implicit rather than explained, partly because they are personal, partly because once clearly stated, they become subject of debate and criticism:

> If the evaluation criteria were openly stated, they could be questioned, but when they are learned through socialization, through doing and implicit knowledge, they never become questioned. This may be a form of power that the criteria are not explicated, but then again, it is part of critical thinking to set them under scrutiny (L3).

Hence, within literature, because there are no generally agreed upon positions from which to make quality judgments, teachers – often implicitly – convey their long personal experience and knowledge regarding evaluation. Some criteria that faculty offered for the evaluation of scholarly literature were novelty, level of intelligence, quality of perception, and imaginative use of methods. The development of theories was so rapid that older theoretical literature could be considered dated.

Within literature, the core skill in literature use was to stay within the boundaries of a particular theoretical conversation, and since it is not possible to search databases using theoretical concepts or approaches, help from faculty experts was seen to be vital for this core task.

ANALYSIS OF HYPOTHESES

The empirical analysis of interview data lends support to the basic hypothesis that academics' understanding of their disciplinary subject matter influences the approach they take to teaching the evaluation of the literature of that discipline. There are distinct ways of thinking about, talking about, and acting on quality evaluation criteria, which vary according to discipline. Next we compare the findings with the hypotheses drawn from Becher and Kogan (1992). We will also compare our findings concerning the features of the fields studied with Becher's (1989) grouping of disciplinary cultures (Table 1).

Hypothesis 2a. *Within the hard-pure area teaching is theoretically oriented. The teaching has clear common goals and the contents of the curriculum are stable and clearly delineated. Because knowledge is cumulatively built, students must absorb the body of basic knowledge in a predefined order to be able to understand the issues.*

Becher's description of the features of "hard-pure" fields and the hypothesis concerning the nature of education within this group have a close fit with findings from the physics case study. Faculty and students within physics saw knowledge within this field as cumulative, impersonal, value-free, quantitative, concerned with universals, and, therefore, requiring a step-by-step absorption. The independent use and searching of literature within physics only really starts at the doctoral level. In graduate studies, students were given the topics to study and at least part of the literature to be used in their work. Physics is an urban and convergent field, and the selection of literature was based on knowledge of research groups working on similar problems. Literature was chosen as relevant and evaluated on the basis of research results and the use of research methods. Relevant materials are concentrated in the publication archive at arXiv.org and in each sub-field's core journals, indexed in Physics Abstracts.

There emerged clear differences between the specialties of applied physics and theoretical physics, however. Studies within applied physics involved more laboratory work and more orientation toward the independent searching and evaluation of literature than those in theoretical physics. Studies within physics didactics differed even more from those in the parent discipline in the approach to independent literature use and searching. However, the "critical thinking skills" taught within physics didactics still had a distinct disciplinary sense and meaning.

Hypothesis 2b. *Within hard-applied sciences, the goal of teaching is practically oriented. Primary importance is placed on the application of knowledge, and mastery of skills and techniques, not in the assimilation of concepts and theories. The aim is to ensure that students really learn the professional skills required in working life.*

This hypothesis about the nature and aims of teaching in hard-applied fields fits particularly well with the medicine case study. The problem-based learning methods used within medicine were oriented toward knowledge application, and the aim was to ensure that studies would result in both the acquisition and absorption of a predefined body of knowledge and in sustainable practical and professional skills

Becher's description of the nature of knowledge in hard-pure fields captures some important elements of the epistemic features of medicine while missing others. The pragmatic orientation of medical knowledge clearly emerged from the case study; as well the purposive and functional (situation-related) criteria for evaluation. The description of hard-pure fields captures less well the fact that although a large part of research within medicine is experimental with an orientation toward causal explanations, such explanations are more concerned with degrees of likelihood than definitive certainty. The informants stressed that many different factors can intervene in experiments and that only some specific factors can be controlled in each experiment. Consequently it was stressed that even the well-defined literature evaluation criteria developed and taught within the field did not replace the ability to judge the situational relevance of research results for real-life circumstances. Medicine is an urban field in that textbooks are seen to outdate rapidly, and a convergent field. Informants stressed that research is partly non-cumulative in the sense that it will lean on and test variable hypotheses and theories. This resulted in an emphasis on the ability to critically analyze and evaluate scholarly literature.

Hypothesis 2c. *In the soft-applied area, teaching is oriented to practice, and the aim is to develop professional skills for future working life. Practice is based on softer knowledge than in the hard-applied category, related to development of activities within human relationship and service professions.*

The Department of Social Politics and Social Work placed equal emphasis on the acquisition of professional skills and theories and scholarly literature. Even textbooks concerned with professional skills such as those addressing client encounters could, according to student informants, be fairly theoretical in nature. The fact that social politics and social work as fields are related to the development of professional practice within human relationships and service professions emerged in the case study as important to the teaching orientation, but that teaching was also oriented toward developing skills for enhancing practice through research. This was manifested in the emphasis on the distinction between professional and scholarly literature and the definition of the former as an object of analysis. Another feature distinguishing the case study from the above hypothesis is the fact that the criteria for analysis and evaluation of scholarly literature incorporated aspects such as positions of knowledge production, and epistemic background assumptions, as much as practical value and the utility of research results. Social psychology and social work is clearly a divergent field in that there is no consensus on the importance of specific problems and topics, theoretical approaches, or best research methods. Social politics and social work represent a rural academic tribe in that there is a great range of choice in research priorities, approaches, and topics, and books are considered to be major sources.

Social psychology and social work did not fit totally with Becher's description of the nature of knowledge in soft-applied fields. Knowledge within this field is often concerned with the nature of social problems, social interaction, and social theories, and not purely functional or aiming at the development protocols and procedures. Social politics and social work, as it emerged within the case study, had perhaps more in common with sociology than other fields classified by Becher as soft-applied.

Hypothesis 2d. *Within the soft-pure area, teaching and study are individualistic in nature. It is expected that students will build their own study programs and formulate individual interpretations and conceptions of the issues involved. The goals of studies are personally defined, and teaching leaves room for students' own inclinations.*

The case study of literature corresponds well with the hypothesis presented above. Literature students were relatively free to pursue self-selected topics. Both faculty and student informants in literature stressed the holistic, personal, and value-laden nature of knowledge within the field, and the nature of research results as interpretations resulting in understanding. Informants stressed the existence of disputes over criteria for evaluating scholarly contributions and noted that there is no consensus on what are the most significant questions to study.

Correspondingly, literature evaluation was not systematically taught within literature, though the very essence of the field is to teach critical analytic reading skills. These skills were expected to be applied in the analysis of all texts, regardless of origin, and, in this sense, strict divisions between different kinds of literature were not made. Faculty sought to ensure that students would not be left entirely on their own by offering references to at least some basic authoritative texts (which then could become either objects of criticism or supportive sources). Literature is a rural and divergent academic field in that it takes a long time to develop an approach to a problem, and research efforts are thinly spread among a large number of diverse topics and interests.

SUMMARY OF FINDINGS

In summary, the social and cognitive aspects of disciplines were clearly reflected in the criteria used in evaluation of scholary literature and the teaching of information skills. Literature evaluation criteria were most clearly stated within medicine and physics, relatively clearly stated within social politics, and more implicitly transmitted within literature. In general, the results corresponded well with Becher's (1989) description of the nature of academic tribes and the hypotheses regarding "tribal differences" in approaches to education drawn from Becher and Kogan (1992). The differences between specialties within physics, and the deviance of social politics and social work from the description of the cultures of "soft-applied" fields, also show the limitations of Becher's (1989) coarse-grained grouping of disciplines along the axes of hard-soft and pure-applied, and the need for further empirical and theoretical work on the relation between the nature of knowledge production within academic fields and their literature use and searching practices.

IMPLICATIONS OF THE FINDINGS FOR INFORMATION LITERACY EFFORTS

Concerning the division of labor in information literacy education between libraries and disciplinary teaching, our findings show that what is currently understood as higher order information literacy, abilities going beyond database and web searching skills, namely, literature use and evaluation skills, are inherently domain specific in nature, and, as such, cannot be meaningfully taught as separate from disciplinary discourses, contents and contexts. Literature use and evaluation criteria are absorbed through an invisible process of disciplinary socialization, where students gradually learn, through reading and practicing the production of scholarly texts, the norms for what represents credible research output, what is considered as good research, and what counts as a contribution to the field. Moreover, searching skills are not something that could be meaningfully discussed as separate from academic tribes and territories. The way tribe members search for scientific literature is embedded in how they think about science and literature. "Literacy" essentially means being able to enact in practice the rules of argumentation and reasoning that an affinity group in a specific domain considers good and pertinent (Tuominen et al., 2005).

Information literacy standards such as those advocated by the ACRL (2000) promote and enhance a standardized approach to teaching information searching skills. Teaching information retrieval skills such as using controlled vocabularies in searching journal and reference databases is an integrated part of core learning within medicine. In literature, students undertaking systematic searches by topic risk getting sidetracked, having their minds fragmented by the many different approaches and viewpoints present in the texts retrieved, and losing perspective as they struggle to clarify and express their ideas coherently in textual form. Our findings indicate that an approach to teaching information skills that will be adequate and useful for one discipline can be confusing, and even harmful, within the context of another.

Our findings show that the teaching of information skills necessarily needs to be grounded within discipline-specific ways of using, searching, and evaluating literature. Otherwise, information literacy instruction in higher education will implicitly convey certain assumptions of "rational" behavior in approaching information systems and searching research literature, which can only be artificial and superficial when compared to the way that literature searching, use, and evaluation is *ingrained* in the intellectual territories of disciplines, that is, their epistemic objects and "tribal" practices.

It is reasonably clear that objective possibilities of searching such as using citation indexes that faculty and students are not necessarily aware of and that would help them exist. However, to adapt IL instruction to forms and contents that have a good match with the epistemic and tribal features of disciplines and specialties, it may be necessary to move away from the traditional library-centered approach to teaching IL. There has been a long tradition of offering library use skills and information searching courses in critical phases of studies (e.g., in research project courses). The responsible teachers often acted as intermediaries between domain practices and the library context. Offering courses in information searching and library research skills as independent study units offers fewer possibilities for collaboration between faculty and information experts situated in the library. Our findings would recommend a reverse kind of integration: of information systems and retrieval expertise aspects integrated within disciplinary curricula and courses.

More research is clearly needed for exploring fruitful ways of teaching information searching skills in ways that are wholly integrated with the ways literature is searched, used, and evaluated within disciplines. There is also a clear need to revise the generalized learning criteria and objectives of information literacy standards to incorporate the findings of this study. Continued efforts are required to develop in-depth understandings of the life worlds of academic tribes.

NOTES

1. Julien's survey in Canadian academic libraries showed that librarians' preferred instructional objectives were:

- to teach general research strategies
- to teach how to find information in various sources
- to teach how to critically evaluate the quality and usefulness of information

- to teach how to locate materials in the library
- to teach how databases in general are structured
- to teach awareness of technological innovations (Julien, 2005).

2. "Literature use" and "literature evaluation" are preferred here to "information use" and "information evaluation." As observed by Davenport and Cronin (1998), use of the term "information" seems to alienate professionals from the texts they use at work and that to a large extent also constitute their work. Scholars do not literally search for "information" but for scholarly literature, books, and journal articles that are read, disassembled, and reassembled, as a part of the scholar's own contribution to knowledge (Bishop, 1999).

3. Becher's (1989) original intention was to conduct case studies within individual disciplines, but during the course of interviews, it was the differences between disciplines that emerged as more interesting and important.

4. Faculty informants are identified by interview number and letter referring to discipline (P = Physics). Students are discerned from faculty by the letter "S." "PS" refers to a physics student.

REFERENCES

American Library Association Presidential Committee on Information Literacy (January 1989). Available at http://www.infolit.org/documents/89Report.htm (accessed May 18, 2004).

Association of College and Research Libraries (2000). *Information competency standards for higher education.* Available at http://www.ala.org/acrl/ilcomstan.html (accessed May 18, 2004).

Becher, T. (1989). *Academic tribes and territories: Intellectual enquiry and the cultures of disciplines.* Milton Keynes: The Society for Research into Higher Education & Open University.

Becher, T., & Kogan, M. (1992). *Process and structure in higher education.* London: Routledge.

Becher, T., & Trowler, P. R. (2001). *Academic tribes and territories* (2nd ed.). London: The Society for Research into Higher Education & Open University Press.

Biglan, A. (1973). The characteristics of subject matter in scientific areas. *Journal of Applied Psychology, 57,* 195–203.

Bishop, A. P. (1999). Document structure and digital libraries: How researchers mobilize information in journal articles. *Information Processing and Management, 35,* 255–279.

Cheuk, B. W. (2002). *Information literacy in the workplace context: Issues, best practices and challenges.* White Paper prepared for UNESCO, the U.S. National Commission on Libraries and Information Science, and the National Forum on Information Literacy, for use at the Information Literacy Meeting of Experts, Prague, The Czech Republic (July 2002). Available at http://www.nclis.gov/libinter/infolitconfandmeet/papers/cheuk-fullpaper.pdf (accessed May 18, 2004).

Davenport, E., & Cronin, B. (1998). Texts at work: Some thoughts on "just for you" service in the context of domain expertise. *Journal of Education for Library and Information Science, 39,* 264–274.

Eco, U. (1990). *Oppineisuuden osoittaminen eli miten tutkielma tehdään* (2nd ed.). [Translated from *Come si fa una tesi di laurea*.]. Tampere: Vastapaino.

Fry, J., & Talja, S. (2004). The cultural shaping of scholarly communication: Explaining e-journal use within and across academic fields. In: *ASIST 2004: Proceedings of the 67th ASIST Annual Meeting*, Medford, NJ: Information Today (Vol. 41, pp. 120–130).

Halttunen, K. (2004). *Two information retrieval environments: Their design and evaluation*. Doctoral dissertation, Tampere, University of Tampere. Available at http://acta.uta.fi/pdf/951-44-6009-X.pdf

Holmberg-Marttila, D., Hakkarainen, K., Viljo, I., & Nikkari, S. (2005). A tutorial script in medical education – the PBL-model designed for local needs. In: E. Poikela & S. Poikela (Eds), *PBL in context – Bridging work and education* (pp. 135–144). Tampere: Tampere University Press.

Information Literacy Meeting of Experts (2003). *The Prague declaration: Towards an information literate society*. National Commission on Library and Information Science; National Forum on Information Literacy & UNESCO. Available at: http://www.nclis.gov/libinter/infolitconf&meet/post-infolitconf&meet/post-infolitconf&meet.html

Johnston, B., & Webber, S. (2003). Information literacy in higher education: A review and case study. *Studies in Higher Education, 28*, 335–352.

Julien, H. (2005). A longitudinal analysis of information literacy instruction in Canadian academic libraries. In: L. Vaughan (Ed.), *Data, information, and knowledge in a networked world. Annual Conference of the Canadian Association for Information Science*, London, Ontario, June 2–4, 2005.

Julien, H., & Given, L. (2003). Faculty-librarian relationships in the information literacy context: Faculty attitudes and pedagogical practices. *Canadian Journal of Information and Library Science, 27*, 65–87.

Kapitzke, C., & Bruce, B. C. (2005). *Libr@ries: Changing information space and practice*. Hillsdale, NJ: Lawrence Erlbaum.

Kautto, V. (2004). *Tieteellisen kirjallisuuden arvioinnin ohjaus yliopisto-opetuksessa. Neljän tieteenalan tarkastelu.* [Teaching research literature evaluation in higher education: An analysis of four disciplines.] Doctoral dissertation, University of Oulu, Oulu. Available at: http://herkules.oulu.fi/isbn9514274725/

Khan, K. S., Kunz, R., Klijnen, J., & Antes, G. (2003). *Systematic reviews to support evidence-based medicine*. London: Royal Society of Medicine Press.

Kling, R., & Covi, L. (1997). *Digital libraries and the practices of scholarly communication: Report of a project*. Available at: http://www.slis.indiana.edu/kling/SCIT/SCIT97.htm (accessed September 13, 2000).

Kling, R., & McKim, G. (2000). Not just a matter of time: Field differences and the shaping of electronic media in supporting scientific communication. *Journal of the American Society for Information Science, 51*, 1306–1320.

Kolb, D. A. (1981). Learning styles and disciplinary differences. In: A. Chickering (Ed.), *The modern American college* (pp. 232–255). San Francisco, CA: Jossey-Bass.

Lave, J. (1988). *Cognition in practice: Mind, mathematics and culture in everyday life*. Cambridge: Cambridge University Press.

Lave, J., & Wenger, E. (1991). *Situated learning: Legitimate peripheral participation*. Cambridge: Cambridge University Press.

Leckie, G., & Fullerton, A. (1999). Information literacy in science and engineering undergraduate education: Faculty attitudes and pedagogical practices. *College and Research Libraries, 60*, 9–29.

Rader, H. (2002). Information literacy 1973–2002: A selected literature review. *Library Trends*, *51*, 242–259.

Rorty, R. (1979). *Philosophy and the mirror of nature*. Princeton, NJ: Princeton University Press.

Society of College, National and University Libraries (1999). *Information skills in higher education: A SCONUL position paper*. Available at: http://www.sconul.ac.uk/pubs_stats/pubs/99104Rev1.doc (accessed May 18, 2004).

Sundin, O. (2004). Användarundervisning inför informationssökning i yrkeslivet: en kunskapsöversikt [User information seeking education in professional life: A review]. *Human IT*, *7*, 265–321.

Sundin, O. (2005). Conflicting approaches to user information seeking education in Scandinavian web-based tutorials. In: *ASIST 2005: Proceedings of the 68th ASIST Annual Meeting*. Medford, NJ: Information Today (Vol. 42).

Talja, S. (2003). Information sharing in academic communities: Types and levels of collaboration in information seeking and use. *New Review of Information Behavior Research*, *3*, 143–159.

Talja, S. (2005a). The social and discursive construction of computing skills. *Journal of the American Society for Information Science and Technology*, *56*, 13–22.

Talja, S. (2005b). The domain analytic approach to scholars' information practices. In: K. Fisher, S. Erdelez & L. McKechnie (Eds), *Theories of information behavior: A researcher's guide* (pp. 123–127). Medford, NJ: Information Today.

Talja, S., & Hansen, P. (2005). Information sharing. In: A. Spink & C. Cole (Eds), *New directions in human information behavior*. Dordrecht: Springer.

Talja, S., & Maula, H. (2003). Reasons for the use and non-use of electronic journals and databases: A domain analytic study in four scholarly disciplines. *Journal of Documentation*, *59*, 673–691.

Talja, S., Savolainen, R., & Maula, H. (2004). Field differences in the use and perceived usefulness of scholarly mailing lists. *Information Research*, 10. http://informationr.net/ir/10-1/paper200.html

Tuominen, K., Savolainen, R., & Talja, S. (2005). Information literacy as a socio-technical practice. *Library Quarterly*, *73*, 329–345.

Webber, S., & Johnston, B. (2004). Information literacy in the curriculum: Selected findings from a phenomenographic study of UK conceptions of, and pedagogy for, information literacy. In: C. Rust (Ed.), *Improving student learning: Diversity and inclusivity. Proceedings of the 11th ISL symposium*, Birmingham, 6–8 September 2004. Oxford: Oxford Brookes University.

Whitley, R. (1984). *The intellectual and social organization of the sciences*. Oxford: Clarendon Press.

Whitmire, E. (2002). Disciplinary differences and undergraduates' information seeking behavior. *Journal of the American Society for Information Science and Technology*, *53*, 631–638.

NEW PREMISES OF PUBLIC LIBRARY STRATEGIES IN THE AGE OF GLOBALIZATION

Ari-Veikko Anttiroiko and Reijo Savolainen

ABSTRACT

Drawing mainly on the ideas of Manuel Castells, this article discusses how globalization and informatization condition the development of public libraries. To explore this issue, recent public library strategies developed in Britain and Finland are analyzed. The analysis demonstrates how public libraries stand for structures that support and consolidate life forms in local communities that need to adjust to contextual changes. In this way, public libraries serve as mediating and filtering mechanisms in local-global interaction. To do this they may utilize the tools derived from the following four strategic options: institutional resource strategy; networking strategy; commercialization strategy; and civil society strategy. Whatever is the strategic choice or their mix at the national or local level, it seems essential that libraries utilize the potential of a hybrid library, which as a new library paradigm combines traditional local dimension with networked and ubiquitous library services.

Advances in Library Administration and Organization, Volume 25, 61–81
© 2007 Published by Elsevier Ltd.
ISSN: 0732-0671/doi:10.1016/S0732-0671(07)25003-5

INTRODUCTION

The present article focuses on the changing role of public libraries with specific regard to the requirements posed by globalization and information society development. These two megatrends have already transformed our world, but in the next 10 to 15 years their impact on the role of institutions such as public libraries will certainly be dramatic. These are not, however, changes that are only imposed outside our societies, local communities, and institutions, but the kind of transformation that is shaped by a dialectic of external and internal changes. Thus, these contextual changes set new kinds of constraints, and present new kinds of challenges and opportunities to public libraries. These changes are visible in such areas as computer literacy, inclusiveness of local communities, equal access to information, and practices of deliberative democracy. Most of these are "local" matters, but they, nevertheless, have a global dimension.

The question of the changing role of libraries is not a new one as such. It has been on the agenda since the 1960s as a minor theme of the modernization of public service delivery systems. Yet, within the framework of information society discussion intensified since the 1980s, when the impact of information technology on society became a highly popular topic. For example, in their book *Managing Libraries in Transition*, Cargill and Webb (1988) identified a number of factors contributing to the new development phase of libraries. In their view, the most important factors challenging the traditional ways of organizing library services are the development of information technology in general, the growing utilization of networks and projects, and the growing needs of various groups using library services. According to them, the above factors will bring out a fundamental change that lead libraries to rethink their objectives and functions, and, in fact, their ultimate rationale in society. In the mid-1990s, the breakthrough of the Internet magnified the libraries' challenges to survive in the information society and to find strategies that would be effective in the "digital future" (see, e.g., McClure & Bertot, 1997).

Discussion about the changing role of public libraries tends to reflect the social and economic changes occurring at local, national, and global levels. Let us take Britain as an example. There, the changing role of public libraries had already been noted in the 1960s. At that time, however, the change was seen as a result of a series of structural innovations by which the activities of local authorities were reorganized in the purpose of moving toward efficient and customer-oriented service culture (Kinnell Evans, 1991,

p. 3). In fact, the breakthrough of the public library in most of the industrialized countries followed the increased division of labor and democratization of society, which took place between 1950s and 1970s. The next turn of events that was most striking in Britain was a neo-liberalist policy under Thatcher's premiership in the 1980s, which resulted in considerable cuts in public funding for libraries. Since the late 1990s, the values of the so-called "third way" propagated by Tony Blair have been reflected in the government's public library strategy. Blair's Government has been keen to develop public libraries as a "people's network", putting computers and Internet connections in every public library. This development has been shadowed by tight economic constraints and the continuously increasing demands of innovations, efficiency, and value for money. In strategy papers, public libraries are depicted as social places that are welcoming all. Public libraries are also conceived as networked gateways to knowledge, enabling forces for learning and social inclusion and catalysts for change (Library and Information Commission, 1998; Department for Culture, Media and Sport, 2003; see also Muir & Douglas, 2001).

In this article, we review how the major social and economic contexts of public library action are going to change with the current information society development spurred by globalization. We will seek answer to the question of what kinds of challenges these changes pose to library services. In particular, we will review the role of the public library from the viewpoint of changes taking place with regard to its social function. We hypothetize that institutions such as public libraries stand for structures that support and consolidate life forms in local communities that need to adjust to contextual changes. In this way, these public libraries can and do serve as mediating and filtering mechanisms in local–global interaction.

Another question closely related to this issue concerns the strategic management of public libraries. In this respect, our main attention will be devoted to the analysis of the current environment of library organization and the basic ways of adjusting libraries to their requirements. When discussing extensive contextual factors, in particular globalization, we draw substantially on Manuel Castells' (1996, 1997, 1998) theory of the development of an informational network society. In order to find links between the general level conceptualization of globalization and the specific issues of library developments, we make use of national public library strategy documents. We focus on strategy papers recently produced in two European countries, Britain and Finland, in which the role of public libraries has traditionally been important.

GLOBALIZATION AS A FACTOR OF CHANGE

The Basic Tension of Globalization

In the beginning of 21st century, the trends of change and central factors affecting the development of society can be characterized as follows:

• The structural change and globalization of the economy (informational economy, free mobility of capital, intensifying global competition, and flexible use of labor force).
• The development and adaptation of new information and communication technologies (ICTs).
• The transformation of institutions and networking as the basic logic of organization (e.g., changes in family institution, the role of women, church, education, state and local governments, and political parties).
• The post-modern characteristics of culture and mentalities (e.g., increased individualism, cognitive globalization, disintegration of communities, and new forms of citizen activism).
• Environmentalism and the demand for sustainable development.

In order to ground the above-mentioned issues theoretically, we draw on Manuel Castells' (1989, 1996, 1997, 1998) conceptions of the inherent tension that directs the development of the "informational" network society. Castells' theory is particularly helpful in that it clarifies the nature of the dynamics of change. It provides a well-founded framework for under-standing the contextual changes that affect the role of public libraries in contemporary societies.

Castells paints a picture of the emerging network society that brings var-ious new social tensions with it. At a metalevel, the most prominent tension is the one between the Net and the Self. According to Castells, economy is directed by globalized networks that are engaged in instrumental exchanges. This refers to dynamic networks of capital, information, and governance; which determine the underlying logic of informational economy. In the configurations of economic power, individuals, groups, communities, and even states are switched on and off, depending on how relevant they happen to be to the attainment of the goals posited by the key actors in the Net. A true meaning of this tension is expressed by Castells by saying that "[o]ur societies are increasingly structured around a bipolar opposition between the Net and the Self" (Castells, 1996, p. 3).

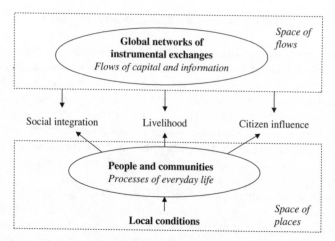

Fig. 1. Aspects of the Fundamental Tension between the Net and the Self.

The logic of the networks of instrumental exchanges is very different from the logic of people's everyday life and experiences. Yet, it seems that the life worlds of ordinary people are increasingly bound to such instrumental networks. Daily living, interaction with other people, self-development, and participation are more and more connected with the ways in which global networks position people according to their use value. These developments are indicators of the fundamental tension between the Net and the Self (Fig. 1).

The tensions between global networks of instrumental exchange and the place-specific, historically determined life forms at local and individual levels have been reacted and mediated in various ways. Some of these strategies of action are based on spontaneous reactions of citizens, while others draw on societal and institutionalized forms of mediation. This repertoire ranges from individual alienation and citizen activism to the activities of non-governmental organizations and state interventions. For example, the exploitation of developing countries by multinational companies has given rise to social movements and consumer boycotts. Similarly, this kind of mediation – particularly its institutional form – is manifested in the ways in which nation states, regions, and cities make attempts to increase their attractiveness on a global level by creating innovative milieus, regional innovation systems, and favorable conditions for business (see, e.g., Anttiroiko, 2004b). In a similar sense, we may assume that libraries have a role as cultural mediators in the global–local dialectic.

Globalization as a Conditioning Framework

What do the changes associated with globalization mean for public libraries and the conditions of their action? In general, globalization refers to the intensification of worldwide social relations, linking localities to each other and making local transformations as inherent part of the logic of globalization (Giddens, 1990; Hirst & Thompson, 1999; Scholte, 2000). As the processes of globalization include economic, cultural, social, and political aspects, it is likely to affect public libraries in various ways. The impacts of globalization are rarely direct, which means that they must be analyzed as a kind of conditioning framework rather than as a single factor with direct causal impact on libraries. Thus, globalization may be seen as a complex setting of contextual factors that are not causally determining the strategies and measures of individual public libraries. However, since public libraries function as an integral part of local communities subject to the same structural and contextual changes as the community at large, libraries can hardly avoid being responsive to such changes, not least because most of them have their manifestations at local community level.

Another important factor of change that has a close connection to globalization is information society development. In essence, it revolves around the informational logic of development, which increasingly determines the ways in which material, social, and human resources are allocated and used in society. Public libraries as cultural and informational institutions have a role to play in this transformation. For example, they may provide services and support in the fields of communication, life-long learning, and the use of networked services. In fact, during their history, libraries have contributed to fields related to "information society"; nowadays these contributions have just received new forms. In addition, public libraries have a significant role as mediators and arenas of culture. In a general sense, they may relieve orientation and identity problems, increase the openness and transparency of society, activate discussion and information transfer, and dampen the externalizing and instrumentalizing effects of globalization.

From the perspective of the critical factors of change outlined above, public libraries seem to have two possible directions. A conservative route is to adhere to traditional models of action such as, for example, borrowing books from the local library. Given the severe pressure from and changes in worklife, civic education, and library and leisure services consumption patterns, it is unlikely that conservative or reactionary strategies such as these would garner political support for a library. Thus, it is more likely that libraries will be required to apply more responsive and adaptable strategies in order to guarantee that they will maintain their productive and reproductive mediating functions in changing conditions of globalization and informatization. The starting point of this alternative is that the library can function as a democratic node and public arena at local level in order to provide access to knowledge and enhance interaction in the community and in local–global exchange relations. In this way, the role of the public library may be profiled as a mediator at two levels and in two realms, i.e. connecting the local and the global, and creating new links between the space of flows and the space of places. At a very fundamental level this implies that the library may provide a value-based element supporting the formation of identity in a network society that is permeated by instrumental relationships of exchange. It may contribute to more inclusive globalization as well as the democratization of the space of flows. In our view, this is perhaps the major message that Castells provides to the discussion concerning the changing social role of institutions, including public libraries.

NEW ROLE FOR PUBLIC LIBRARIES: FINNISH AND BRITISH EXPERIENCES

Evolution of Public Libraries

Since the 19th century, public libraries have leaned toward the conceptions of freedom originating from the liberal democratic ideology. From this perspective, public libraries are assigned both social and educational missions. Along with the ideas emphasizing the values of enlightenment and democracy, the libraries were given the task to encourage people to learn and seek for information they need freely and without external pressure (Kinnel Evans, 1991, pp. 53–54). For example, in Finland, discussion about the public libraries gained momentum in the 1840s. The idea was simply that if individuals could not afford to purchase books for themselves, their acquisition and mechanism for making the materials available should be organized by collective arrangements. As a consequence, by the end of the 19th century, there were almost 2,000 libraries available for use by the common people (Hietala, 2001, p. 12).

In general, the breakthrough of the idea of the public library in the late 1800s and the beginning of 1900s drew on the division of labor and the pursuits of democratization in the context of industrialization. In Finland, a considerable growth of public libraries and the use of their services took place in the 1960s and the following decade. In Finland, as in other Nordic countries, the development of public libraries epitomized the welfare state ideology, which meant that a wide range of public services – including public libraries – were provided by public authorities and financed by tax revenue. Looked from the historical perspective, this equalization policy in the public library field was an integral part of the welfare society development. Some part of this development has become almost universal, for not only in Nordic countries but also in most of the other developed countries all core library services, such as borrowing books and other printed material and their use within the library premises, are provided free of charge to citizens (cf. Egholm & Jochumsen, 2000, p. 299).

In addition to welfare state ideology, the ideas of the "service society" and the "post-industrial society" affected the ways in which public services have been developed since the 1970s. The development of institutionalization originating from industrialization concerned also public libraries in that they were incorporated in the hierarchical machinery of public administration. As an "informational bureaucracy", public library was bound to contribute to the reproduction and service functions of the welfare state. Later, hierarchically organized public library became an object of re-evaluation in the wake of new approaches to public management since the 1980s.

The functions of public libraries were discussed in a new light in the 1990s, when discussions about globalization and information society development intensified. In particular, along with the renaissance of liberalism and right-wing conceptions of new public management (NPM), the entire landscape of public service started to change, bringing new principles to the forefront of public service management: value for money (cost-effectiveness), new managerialism, utilization of market-mechanism (incl. compulsory competitive tendering), consumer choice, and public–private partnerships. In Europe, it was Great Britain that led this turn, showing the way that has gradually become legitimized by international organizations (e.g., the World Trade Organization), the European Union, and also national governments. On the other hand, libraries have so far been among the last local public institutions to be subordinated to this new policy line, due to its special cultural role. This is also why there are some weak counter-balancing trends, such as the rehabilitation of public libraries as institutions that support the values of communality, inclusiveness, and democracy.

Public Library Services and IT Revolution

The role of technology in libraries was mostly seen as an internal matter that revolved around library catalogues (see, e.g., Lamb, 1973). The first IT-based visions for libraries were presented as early as the early 1960s, but the picture of the "computerized library" started to broaden in the 1980s. By the mid-1980s it had become clear that the library of the future will offer a wide range of services beyond the provision of a computerized catalogue and the availability of printed material (Arbib, 1984, p. 331). Arbib's (1984, p. 334) conclusions show illuminatingly how the future directions were seen in the early 1980s:

> In short, it seems that the library will remain as a repository of books, but it will be enriched by the increasing availability of audiovisual materials. Access to these materials will be aided by a computerized catalog ... it is likely that the library will remain a place to which people actually go. The new technologies, however, will give individuals the opportunity to obtain an overview of a wide range of information without leaving their homes.

Another good example of the views of the 1980s is the report on the future of the use of IT in libraries in which Finnish experts in the field of information and media forecasted how the major tasks of libraries will change until 2010 (Huhtanen, 1988, p. 3). The following developments were expected to take place:

- Self-service in libraries will become more common.
- Distance use of library services will become more popular.
- Library opening hours will be extended.
- Libraries will provide telephone answering services.
- Libraries will provide multiple services (e.g., so-called telecottages will be established in the premises of public libraries).
- Individual (isolated) library units will be replaced by an extensive network of libraries.
- Services not yielding added value will be replaced by information services of new kinds.

Even though all of the above trends did not materialize as expected, this list shows that the effects of technological developments could be identified quite well in the late 1980s. It should be remembered that the economic recession in the early 1990s slowed down the actual creation and adoption of innovative practices in almost all areas of public services, including libraries, so it can be assumed that, while predictions may change, it is likely that some of the predictions may still be fulfilled in the near term.

From the point of view of the understanding of the role of ICTs in libraries, the most profound turn has come as a result of the Internet revolution of the 1990s. It started to remold libraries both internally and from the outside. What happened was a totally new vision for the public library, which started to look something like an easily accessible multimedia department store capable of offering everything from books to audiovisual and multimedia products, and from material to be borrowed to a wide range of services. One of the main factors of this change was the new horizon of interactivity opened up by the Internet. Consequently, more attention was devoted to information networks, Internet-based service systems, and new information services. In some cases, electronic library services became among the most popular Web services of local government (see, e.g., Drüke, 2005).

It is almost a cliché to remind people that the technological development of library services does not mean that the role and societal function of the library should be ignored. On the contrary, the very basic questions of civic education, access, and the finance of library services remain important in the future. For example, Webster and Dempsey (1999) have a strong conviction that libraries should provide information and recreative material without charge also in the future. This viewpoint is highly relevant when considered against the growing use of increasingly technologically mediated and market-oriented provision of public services.

A Paradigm Shift: Toward a Hybrid Library

Along with the breakthrough of electronic information services, particularly the Internet, the conceptions of digital, electronic, and virtual libraries have developed since the early 1990s (see, e.g., Borgman, 2000, pp. 40–51; cf. Rowlands & Bawden, 1999). In the early years, digital libraries were often sharply contrasted with traditional libraries in order to emphasize the revolutionary features of the former. Later, however, the contrasting viewpoints have been largely abandoned and a new concept of "hybrid library" has gained popularity particularly in library strategy papers (see, e.g., European Communities, 1997; Ministry of Education, 2001, 2003).

Hybrid library may be defined as a "networking library of mixed types, offering access to global information via various kinds of media, material and networks" (European Communities, 1997). Thus, hybrid library means extended service and collections available both in the physical library and as remote, virtual, and mobile services (Ministry of Education, 2003, pp. 14–16). In addition to printed material, hybrid libraries provide CD-ROMs, DVDs, and e-books. Further, they provide access to licensed Web material, such as electronic journals and databases. In the hybrid library strategies, the social aspect of library space is of utmost importance. They also bring new dimensions to the access to information (Henderson & King, 1995). On a concrete level, this means that every citizen should have access to vital information, an opportunity to communicate with public administrators, and an opportunity to use public services electronically. Hybrid libraries may also offer information about local events and provide feedback channels, remote information service, and chat-rooms. Finally, there are a number of interactive, personalized, and sectored services available, for example, mastering one's own loan data, searching information from the Web, and novelty follow-up and booking services aimed at diverse groups of users.

The hybrid library approach is central, for example, in the public library strategy adopted in Finland (Ministry of Education, 2001). The strategy assumes that the library's traditional cultural and enlightening mission will not disappear but will merge with the modern information and support services. From this perspective, the public library becomes a local cultural center, a "quality portal", which makes its accumulated cultural and intellectual resources available to people who can then use it according to their needs, either in the library or on the net. As information, recreative and entertainment materials are increasingly digitized and transferred to the net, libraries may become the nodes of diverse networks and portals giving access to information and cultural services, thus supplementing their role as real arenas for interaction and culture (Gorman, 2000, p. 40).

As the service provision is renewed, the cooperation of libraries and networking of libraries can and should be strengthened. In this way, for example, the services of inter-library lending may be made more effective, theoretically even at the level of the global library network, and connections with the institutions of education can be intensified. Moreover, libraries may sharpen their profile as mediators of information produced in the local community. This viewpoint has emphasized, for example, in the report on *Public Libraries in the Information Society* published by the European Union (see European Communities, 1997) and in some more recent national and state level strategy documents (e.g., Department for Culture, Media and Sport, 2003; Ministry of Community, 2004). By utilizing networked services, public libraries may provide more diversified services to various groups of users, including diverse professional groups, ethnic minorities, and disabled people.

A transformation toward hybrid library goes through the extension of the public library mission. The trends in Finnish libraries can be used here as an illuminating example. By now practically all public libraries are computerized. They provide services online, as well as free public access to their catalogues through the Internet.

Another new dimension emphasized by the Finnish Government has been the promotion of inter-library networking. (Kekki, 2001). One concrete local example is the Tampere City Library, one of the leading Finnish libraries, which also serves as a major regional library. It offers such online services as online lending/return, information service (each department has its own service providing information from the library's own collections as well as national registers), and material from other libraries and inter-library lending. Since 2002, the so-called PIKI (Pirkanmaan kirjastot) NetLibrary system has been in operation, which, as a joint library system for 23 public libraries in the Tampere Region, provides a database of the collections available in all of the libraries involved in the system. An additional service known as OmaPIKI, available free of charge, is a special service that provides reminder of the due dates, a collection note of a reservation to the customer's e-mail or mobile phone (SMS), information on new items purchased by the library that match search criteria specified by the customer, the capacity to make reservations for items on the shelf in the library (normally reservations can be made only when all the copies of an item are on loan), and other similar services.

A new dimension in library services has emerged in the early 2000s when such leading "mobile cities" as Tampere and Oulu started to provide the option to reloan books, make inquiries on the availability of books, and receiving messages about newly arrived books by mobile phones, thus strengthening the aspect of ubiquity of hybrid libraries.

As important as this development is, it is only one side of the development of a hybrid library. The other side of the coin is the adoption of new roles for the "physical library" and extensions of this aspect with branch libraries, networks, and mobile libraries. This community dimension is briefly discussed next.

Integrating Public Libraries with Local Communities

John Dolan (1999) has aptly pointed out that the starting point of the active and innovative role of libraries is their integration with the local, national, and global environment. By drawing on discussions that occurred in Britain in the late 1990s, Dolan specified three areas that libraries should approach more actively:

- *The modernization of administration.* One of the basic requirements of democratic governance is sufficient communication and openness, opportunities to obtain information, and access to information. To support this aspect of governance:
  - Libraries provide access to local networks.
  - Libraries provide resources for learning.
  - Libraries provide a communication forum that can be shared by the public and the local authority.
- *The library strengthening participation and community.* Integration with society and participation are important social questions. To support social integration:
  - Libraries may strengthen social inclusion and pluralism.
  - Libraries can provide networked connections based on the needs of the local community.
  - Libraries must be considered shared public places that are valuable in itself from the viewpoint of the community.
- *The library as the promoter of wealth and creation of economic value.* In the knowledge-based economy, one of the basic requirements to enhance wealth and standard of living is the ability to use information and learning resources. To support economic development:
  - Libraries provide a lot of opportunities to help people in their everyday life.
  - Libraries are centers of skills, access to information, learning and interaction, thus creating fruitful soil for knowledge-based economy and social, human, and cultural capital.

One of the main challenges to the attainment of goals such as these presents itself in the way in which information resources of various kinds available in local and regional communities can be made available more effectively. People looking for information often face the problem of separate information "islands"; information that is scattered into diverse sources such as libraries, health service providers, and voluntary agencies (Atherton, 2002). Digitization provides a significant way to bridge these information islands. *SeamlessUK* recently launched in Britain exemplifies ambitious projects of these kinds in that it aims at providing a single point of search and retrieval for selected local, regional, and national information sources. Emphasis will be laid on improving access to community information, but it will also support lifelong learning, active citizenship, and digital literacy. *SeamlessUK* enables cross-searching of existing community information databases, library catalogues, and harvested websites. Naturally, also various Web search engines are available for the users of the information system (Atherton, 2002, p. 470).

Public libraries may significantly contribute to individual, organizational, and collective knowledge processes not only by providing networked library catalogues but also by offering assistance in the organization of information and improving the search capabilities of the electronic community information systems (Rowley & Farrow, 2000). Interest in projects leading to integrated information gateways is growing also in the sense that public library units will be developed as entry points to electronic information by implementing *"One Card"* library systems. For example, in British Columbia in Canada, there are plans to introduce *One Card* access to library collections, giving all British Columbians free, equitable, and seamless access to library holdings 24 h a day, 7 days a week from any computer in the world connected to the Internet (see Ministry of Community, 2004, p. 12).

Strategic plans such as these indicate that, in the reflective modernization of administration, the role of libraries as the site of learning, creativity, and entertainment, has so far not been paid sufficient attention. Libraries contribute to learning in local community, to harnessing the creative potential of people, and to the development of inclusive local governance. This relates to the fact that the capacities and potential of public libraries have not been sufficiently utilized to strengthen the cultural competence of citizens. This is important since cultural competence is obviously one of the critical success factors in the competition between creative and knowledge-based territorial communities.

DESIGNING ADJUSTMENT STRATEGIES FOR LIBRARIES

Creating Vertical and Horizontal Connections

As the discussion above implies, public libraries need to take care of their governance relations with various stakeholders in different sectors. They need to focus on three activity levels: to mobilize their own potential as an institution, to grassroot their activities to local community, and to connect citizens and customers upwards and outwards (cf. FITLOG, 1999, p. 10). This is illustrated in Fig. 2.

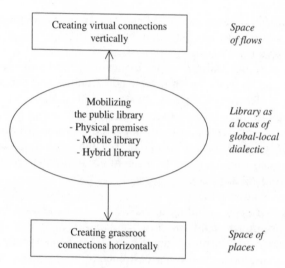

Fig. 2. Mediating Role of Public Library.

What Fig. 2 pictures is the basic setting of the public library as a mediator in the global–local dialectic. To take the strategic governance challenge to a more concrete level, we may identify four major stakeholder relations of libraries and their characteristic forms of governance: higher level public authorities (hierarchies), inter-sectoral multi-actor fields (networks), market-based exchange relations (markets), and local associations, voluntary groups, and individual citizens (communities) (cf. Anttiroiko, 2004a). These will be discussed briefly in the next chapter.

Four Directions for the Public Library Strategy

As the territorial communities outline strategies in the times of globalization, technological development, and new governance, they have to take into account several viewpoints that affect the acquisition of resources for libraries and their action. On the basis of fourfold governance model, we may identify at least four complementary strategic lines:

a) Institutional resource strategy
   – Attempt to utilize all existing institutional resources to maintain and develop library services available at local, regional, national, macroregional (the European Union), and international levels.

- This strategy is based mainly on governance by hierarchies, multi-level public governance, and public–public networking.

b) Networking strategy
  - The networking of libraries with the institutes and units functioning in library field as well as with diverse communities and expert organizations (e.g., Rowley & Farrow, 2000, pp. 378–381).
  - Leveling out differences between regions and levels of knowledge, and differences between libraries through the creation of centralized and regional target services, available via the Web for common use, and through support given to regional library services (cf. Ministry of Education, 2003, p. 26).

c) Commercialization strategy
  - Selective strategy including a wide spectrum of actions from privatization to outsourcing of core or support services. This strategy also includes the introduction of user fees and chargeable services for business enterprises and other customers.
  - Acquiring additional resources and saving costs by means of partnership projects, sponsoring and outsourcing individual services whenever cost-effective.

d) Civil society strategy
  - Strengthening the legitimacy of the public library and acquiring the support of civil society for the library by means of a responsive, customer-centered, and community-oriented service culture.
  - Contributing to the achievement of e-government and providing access to electronic services in order to facilitate the development of digital citizenship (cf. Department for Culture, Media and Sport, 2003, pp. 34–37). This strategy builds upon strengthening public libraries' role as one of the anchoring institutions in local communities and as one of the major membership institutions in civil society (cf. Department for Culture, Media and Sport, 2003, p. 42). One of the core tasks is to promote information literacy and narrow digital divide (cf. Tuominen, Savolainen & Talja, 2005).

These strategies suggest that, in addition to tax revenues and public funding gained within a hierarchical system of public governance, resources can be acquired by relying on partnerships, markets, and communities. It is equally important that libraries are able to utilize the logic of the "space of flows" by means of networking and participating in policy and innovation networks. Fig. 3 summarizes the basic trends of social change and public

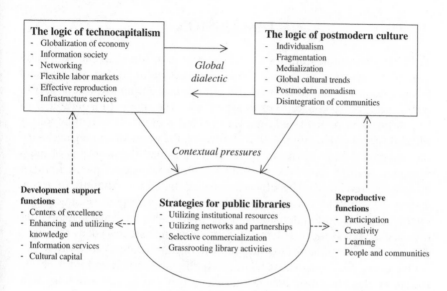

Fig. 3. Strategies for Public Libraries in Context.

library strategies discussed above from the point of view of development and reproductive functions of institutions, suggesting that libraries may well serve both and meet the requirements of the age of globalization when designed properly.

The main message of the above setting is connected with the social tension between the Net and the Self, and related mediation task of public libraries. Libraries should be developed by taking heed of the economic megatrends, but it is equally important to fend off – or at least to relieve – the side effects brought about by these trends, side effects that cause for example, social polarization, growing inequality, and a digital divide. This mediation task emphasizes the importance of the relationships between global networks of instrumental exchanges (the Net) and local actors in their historically determined local contexts (the Self) with regard to information and knowledge processes. In this role, public library may function as a support system of civil society, which dampens the problematic effects of globalization at the local level (cf. Johansson, 2004, p. 48). Lastly, public libraries may also strengthen participation in society and foster the values of democracy by increasing inclusion and transparency and serving as a locus of public hearings and other events and a place for innovative democratic experiments.

DISCUSSION

Traditionally, public libraries were primarily understood as public institutions and memory organizations providing access to organized collections of printed books to guarantee that the information resources were available openly and free of charge to ordinary people. The Internet revolution challenged this development and significantly contributed to a rethinking of the societal role of public library. In recent years, the issues of supporting users' information seeking by means of the new ICTs and the problems of managing information have become central when the services of public libraries have been developed. The other megatrend that gave stimulus to recent discussion of public library is globalization, that is, the increasing global interdependence and interactions that poses new challenges for public libraries serving as local centers of information and as knowledge exchanges. This is also how globalization and informatization relate to each other.

One of the basic issues that relates to both globalization and information society is the democratic dimension of the formation of the emerging new form of society. From this perspective, public libraries can be seen as a key institution of our time. This is reflected, for example, in the so-called *Glasgow Declaration* issued by the International Federation of Library Associations and Institutions (IFLA) in 2002. According to this document, libraries are "gateways to knowledge, thought and culture", and they "contribute to the development and maintenance of intellectual freedom and help to safeguard democratic values and universal civil rights" (see Byrne, 2004, p. 12). Naturally, these issues are connected with the ways in which libraries adjust themselves in the new demands of the global knowledge-based economy. One of the challenges is to guarantee access to the basic networked services and to make the organization of electronic resources more effective in order to facilitate information seeking and other value-adding information and knowledge processes.

Despite the revolutionary changes that have emerged since the early 1990s, printed and electronic information resources should not be seen as competitors. Rather, they complement each other. This is, in fact, a development that has already happened in most of the advanced countries in which the role of library is important. Finland is a good example of this. The extension of the role of libraries has recently become crystallized as a goal to develop high-quality hybrid libraries. This goal or the respective transformation that is emerging as a result is reflected in such projects as *SeamlessUK, Idea Stores,* or *Discovery Centers* that reinterpret the role of libraries in a new setting (Atherton, 2002; Department for Culture, Media and Sport, 2003). These projects and organizations not only provide hybrid library services but also combine libraries with museums, health facilities, leisure activities, and e-government services. The idea is that, through visiting libraries, people should discover a large collection of resources that can be utilized to draw them into new activities, including health, education, sports, and business development support (Department for Culture, Media and Sport, 2003, p. 22).

Public libraries have found an important role in the area of culture, and this is likely to remain as one of their characteristic features. Public libraries have a potential to build upon their distinctive and long-standing role in promoting reading and informal learning (Department for Culture, Media and Sport, 2003, p. 23). This distinctiveness should be remembered when profiling library strategies in order to avoid duplicating the efforts of other public and private sector providers. However, the distinctive strategies should not be seen as a barrier for cooperation but as a fruitful basis of partnerships with various organizations and service providers. For example, in the Finnish public library strategy the cultural role of libraries is emphasized from this viewpoint (Ministry of Education, 2001). One of the major visions of this program is that public libraries should function as the mediator of cultural heritage and supporter of multi-cultural developments by providing access to information relevant to other cultures. In the cultural mission of public libraries, the issues of information literacy and self-realization are central. In the above-mentioned Finnish program, references are made to important civic educational and holistic tasks: a true challenge to public libraries is to provide "the sense of wholeness" that goes beyond the fragments of information by building connections between diverse issues and materials. This is ultimately how they contribute to meeting the challenge of globalization.

CONCLUSION

Viewed from the angle of the globalization, the connections between production and culture seem to become closer than before (cf. Castells, 1989). Apparently, a significant growth potential may be found in the field of content production, culture, and artistic creativity. The whole cultural competence on which high-quality content production is based can be one of the central success factors in the globalizing information society. In this picture, public libraries may provide new opportunities, for they have a capacity to strengthen civic competence and to serve communities by utilizing the potentials of a hybrid library. As exemplified by recent public library strategies developed in Britain and Finland, libraries have identified this opportunity. New library strategies signal clearly that public libraries are significant not only in connecting institutions of public governance and civil society but also in functioning as catalysts for cultural innovations.

REFERENCES

Anttiroiko, A.-V. (2004a). Introduction to democratic e-Governance. In: M. Malkia, A.-V. Anttiroiko & R. Savolainen (Eds), *eTransformation in Governance: New directions in government and politics* (pp. 22–49). Hershey, Philadelphia: Idea Group Publishing.

Anttiroiko, A.-V. (2004b). Editorial: Global competition of high-tech centres. *International Journal of Technology Management, 28*, 289–323.

Arbib, M. A. (1984). *Computers and the cybernetic society* (2nd ed.). Orlando, FL: Academic Press.

Atherton, L. (2002). SeamlessUK – building bridges between information islands. *New Library World, 103*, 467–473.

Borgman, C. L. (2000). *From Gutenberg to the global information infrastructure. Access to information in the networked world.* Cambridge, MA: The MIT Press.

Byrne, A. (2004). Libraries and democracy – management implications. *Library Management, 25*, 11–16.

Cargill, J., & Webb, G. M. (1988). *Managing libraries in transition.* Phoenix: Oryx Press.

Castells, M. (1989). *The informational city. Information technology, economic restructuring, and the urban-regional process.* Oxford: Basil Blackwell.

Castells, M. (1996). *The information age. Economy, society and culture: The rise of the network society* (Vol. I). Oxford: Blackwell.

Castells, M. (1997). *The information age. Economy, society and culture: The power of identity* (Vol. II). Oxford: Blackwell.

Castells, M. (1998). *The Information age. Economy, society and culture: End of millennium* (Vol. III). Oxford: Blackwell.

Department for Culture, Media and Sport. (2003). Framework for the future. Libraries, learning and information in the next decade. http://www.culture.gov.uk (accessed 4 January 2005).

Dolan, J. (1999). Inside out. The shape of new library. In: S. Pantry (Ed.), *Building community information networks: Strategies and experiences* (pp. 84–91). London: Library Association.

Drüke, H. (Ed.) (2005). *Local electronic government. A comparative study.* London: Routledge.

Egholm, C., & Jochumsen, H. (2000). Perspectives concerning user fees in public libraries. *Library Management, 21*, 298–306.

European Communities (1997). *Public libraries and the information society.* Luxembourg: Office for Official Publications of the European Communities (EUR 17648 EN).

FITLOG (1999). *The Connected Council. Leading the community in the information age.* Bristol, UK: Foundation for Information Technology in Local Government (FITLOG).

Giddens, A. (1990). *The consequences of modernity.* Stanford, CA: Stanford University Press.

Gorman, M. (2000). *Our enduring values. Librarianship in the 21st century.* Chicago: American Library Association.

Henderson, C. C., & King, F. D. (1995). The role of public libraries in providing public access to the Internet. In: B. Kahin & J. Keller (Eds), *Public access to the Internet. A publication of the Harvard Information Infrastructure Project* (pp. 154–171). Cambridge, MA: The MIT Press.

Hietala, M. (2001). Foundation of libraries in the historical context. In: I. Mäkinen (Ed.), *Finnish public libraries in the 20th century* (pp. 7–22). Tampere, Finland: Tampere University Press.

Hirst, P., & Thompson, G. (1999). *Globalization in question. The international economy and the possibilities of governance* (2nd ed.). Cambridge, UK: Polity Press.

Huhtanen, A. (1988). *Tietohuollon tuleva tekniikka. Tietotekniikka kirjastossa ja tietopalvelussa 2010 [The future technology of information provision. Information technology in libraries and information services in 2010].* Helsinki, Finland: Valtion painatuskeskus.

Johansson, V. (2004). Public libraries as democratic intermediaries. Some examples from Sweden. *New Library World, 105,* 47–59.

Kekki, K. (2001). Public libraries in Finland – gateways to knowledge and culture. Ministry of Education. Culture and Media Division, July 2001, http://www.minedu.fi/minedu/culture/libraries_gateways.html (accessed 3 March 2005).

Kinnell Evans, M. (1991). *All change? Public library management strategies for the 1990s.* London: Taylor Graham.

Lamb, G. M. (1973). *Computers in the public service.* London: George Allen & Unwin.

Library and Information Commission. (1998). New library: the people's network. http://www.ukoln.ac.uk/services/lic/newlibrary/full.html (accessed 4 January 2005).

McClure, C. R., & Bertot, J. C. (1997). Creating a future for public libraries: Diverse strategies for a diverse nation. *Library Trends, 46,* 36–51.

Ministry of Community, Aboriginal and Women Services. Public Library Branch (2004). Libraries without walls: the world within your reach. A vision for public libraries in British Columbia. http://www.mcaws.gov.bc.ca/lgd/public_libraries/plplan/library_strategic_plan.pdf (accessed 4 January 2005).

Ministry of Education. (2001). A wide range of culture and quality information retrieval in the library. The salient points in the Finnish library policy programme 2001–2004. Committee's report. http://www.minedu.fi/minedu/publications/librarypolicyprogramme.pdf (accessed 4 January 2005).

Ministry of Education. (2003). Library strategy 2010. Policy for acces to knowledge and culture. http://www.minedu.fi/minedu/publications/2003/kseng.pdf (accessed 4 January 2005).

Muir, L., & Douglas, A. (2001). Where now the UK public library service. *Library Management, 22,* 266–271.

Rowlands, I., & Bawden, D. (1999). Digital libraries: A conceptual framework. *Libri, 49,* 192–202.

Rowley, J., & Farrow, J. (2000). *Organizing knowledge. An introduction to managing access to information* (3rd ed.). Aldershot, UK: Gower.

Scholte, J. A. (2000). *Globalization: A critical introduction.* Basingstoke: Macmillan Press.

Tuominen, K., Savolainen, R., & Talja, S. (2005). Information literacy as a socio-technical practice. *Library Quarterly, 75,* 329–345.

Webster, F., & Dempsey, L. (1999). Virtual library – false dawn? http://www.ukoln.ac.uk/services/papers/ukoln/dempsey-1999-01/index.htm (accessed 4 January 2005).

THE UNIVERSITY LIBRARY'S INTELLECTUAL CAPITAL

Mirja Iivonen and Maija-Leena Huotari

ABSTRACT

The article is concerned with the university library's intellectual capital (IC) as a part of the university's IC. The concept of IC is analyzed as consisting of the three main components: human capital, structural capital, and relational capital. These components are described in the context of the university library. It is suggested that certain kind of professional understanding and knowledge could be used to integrate the library's IC with the university's IC. It is claimed that this integration could enhance the library's contribution to the overall performance on the university. It is seen as a very important issue to demonstrate the role the university library can play in the growth of the university's intellectual capital, performance, and outcomes at a time when public funding for the universities is diminishing.

INTRODUCTION

Some focal changes are taking place globally in universities. As performance and impact have become the main interests of funding bodies of educational institutions, universities are pressured to achieve better outcomes in teaching, learning and research, and also in administration. They face

Advances in Library Administration and Organization, Volume 25, 83–96
Copyright © 2007 by Elsevier Ltd.
ISSN: 0732-0671/doi:10.1016/S0732-0671(07)25004-7

requirements to improve their rankings in the quality assessments of research and teaching which are their primary tasks. Among the wider audience, universities are more and more often imaged as brands indicating high-quality education, research and services to society.

Along with this development, many universities compete for funding and human resources more than ever before. They pay increased attention to staff competence and recruitment and student selection. High-quality faculty and students who meet high standards are critical to provide high-quality products and services. Moreover, these requirements challenge universities' management and leadership practices.

Universities' performance is usually assessed by applying certain, almost universal, criteria. Thus far, at least, the yearly student intake and the number of bachelor's, master's and doctoral degrees' students have been used. Moreover, research activities and tasks of expertise are used as performance indicators. These include, for example, publishing, research funding and projects carried out and other service provided for society (e.g. contract research, vocational training, etc.). Sometimes citations by peers within the field and in other fields are also used as indicators for research quality in particular. However, the emphasis might soon shift to increased assessment of outcomes based on research due to the need to improve research quality and develop the national innovation systems in general.

We believe that university performance depends on its intellectual capital (IC) that is a more crucial factor than physical assets, and even more important than financial resources. Therefore, it is to the university's benefit to aim at adding to its IC. For improving the overall performance, we have to understand how the library's IC is integrated with the university's IC.

In a recent article, we (see Huotari & Iivonen, 2005) introduced a framework of knowledge processes as the strategic foundation for the partnership between the university and its library. In this article, our foci are on the university library's IC in enhancing the university's IC. We will consider the components of the library's IC and suggest that certain kind of professional understanding and knowledge could be used to integrate the library's IC with the university's IC. By this we will try to indicate how the library contributes to the overall performance on the university.

INTELLECTUAL CAPITAL

The concept of IC has raised interest since the beginning of the 1990s when Stewart introduced it though there is no universal definition of the concept

Table 1. A Description of the Human Capital.

Component of Intellectual Capital	Edvinsson and Malone (1997)	Magic Project (see Seetharaman et al., 2002)	Castellanos et al. (2004)	Johannessen, Olsen, and Olaisen (2005)
Human capital	All individual capabilities, the knowledge, skill and experiences of the company's employees and managers	The basic potentials of an organization	The set of explicit and tacit knowledge of the people in the organization, shared or not amongst them, that has value to the organization	The sum of internal and external knowledge bases in a system

(see Seetharaman, Sooria, & Saravanan, 2002). Stewart has defined IC as the sum of everything people know which can give them a competitive advantage in the market. His concept of IC consists of three components: human, structural and customer capital (Stewart, 1997). Castellanos, Rodriquez, and Ranguelov (2004) in turn described IC as the set of knowledge that creates, or can create in the future, value for the organization. The common feature in these rather extensive definitions is that IC adds to existing outcomes by producing something more, a competitive advantage or additional value.

Still at the end of last millennium, at the 3rd International Conference on the Management of Intellectual Capital, it was argued that too much of the nature of IC is unknown and hard to capture in explicit terms (see Seetharaman et al., 2002). In spite of these doubts, many researchers have aimed at describing IC in more detail by analysing its components. The major components of IC are summarized in Tables 1–3 below.

We claim that the university library's IC, including its major components, might enhance the university's IC. Thus we assumed that the whole university's performance will improve when the library's IC is integrated with the whole university's IC. One way to increase understanding of how the library's IC and its major components impact on the university's IC is to consider what kind of professional understanding and knowledge is needed for integrating them. By applying the idea presented by Castellanos et al. (2004), we identify these areas of professional knowledge as knowledge drivers.

Table 2. A Description of the Structural Capital.

Component of Intellectual Capital	Edvinsson and Malone (1997)	Magic Project (see Seetharaman et al., 2002)	Castellanos et al. (2004)	Johannessen et al. (2005)
Structural capital	The embodiment, empowerment and supportive infrastructure of human capital		The explicit knowledge related to the internal processes: organizational and technological	Organizational learning and innovation
Organizational capital	The company's investment in systems, tools and operating philosophy that speeds the flow of knowledge through the organization, as well as out to supply and distribution channels	The ability to transfer human potentials to products and services		
Innovation capital	The renewal capability and the results of innovation in the form of protected commercial rights, intellectual property and other intangible assets and talents	The capability to improve and develop continuously all potentials and environmental variables		
Systemic capital				The ability to adjust to changes in the environment demonstrated by the social system, in addition to the ability to create one's own future
Process capital	Work processes, techniques and employees, programs that augment and enhance of manufacturing or the delivery of services			

Table 3. A Description of the Relational Capital.

Component of Intellectual Capital	Edvinsson and Malone (1997)	Magic project (see Seetharaman et al., 2002)	Castellanos et al. (2004)	Johannessen et al. (2005)
Relational capital			The set of explicit and tacit knowledge concerning the way in which the organization deals with the external agents	
Customer capital	Relationship of the company to its customers			
Market capital		The competence to manage and integrate the external interfaces with the organization's stakeholders		
Network capital				Social relations internally in organizations and between organizations and the external world

LIBRARY'S HUMAN CAPITAL IN ENHANCING THE UNIVERSITY'S INTELLECTUAL CAPITAL

Human capital (HC) seems to be widely accepted as one major component of IC. The content of HC has clearly been connected to the employees' competence, though descriptions of IC vary to some extent (see Table 1).

For defining the university library's HC, we can apply Edvinsson and Malone's (1997) definition and notice that the university library's HC is the collective capability, the knowledge, skill and experiences of the library's staff. The library's HC is linked to its capability to perform its activities and to produce services to the university community. The members of the library staff hold wide competence (i.e. a set of knowledge and skills that enable employees to orient and solve problems in their work-related setting) and various capabilities. Traditionally, the basic competencies of the library staff have included such elements as knowledge of information resources and the content of various subject areas, knowledge of various techniques used in the library work (cataloguing, subject description, etc.), knowledge of foreign languages and knowledge of customer service. Today the basic competencies of library work cover a wider area, and basic competencies include the technical skills required to utilize information and communication technology, knowledge of legislation, pedagogical skills, communication skills and the ability to share knowledge, the ability to perform in international markets, cognitive capability to react to changes, interest in the latest developments in the field, among others (see e.g. Abell, 1998; New Information Technologies, 1998).

However, competence is a resource that is not easily divided into smaller units, converted or exchanged because it is linked to individuals (see e.g. Johannessen, Olsen, & Olaisen, 2005). Therefore, knowledge of leadership and staff recruitment is a critical part of the library's HC, as well as continuous staff development and training. Such knowledge and skills could be outlined, for example, as follows:

- Management skills (analytic thinking and problem solving, ability to innovate), leadership skills, knowledge of marketing strategies and cost–benefit analysis, understanding of customer needs, knowledge of markets, strategic planning and goal orientation.
- Organizing skills (ability to build, coordinate and manage teams, flexibility with alternative arrangements related to projects and collaboration, ability to create and organize public services).
- Creativity (innovative, long-term planning related to product and service

development, visionary thinking) (see e.g. Abell, 1998; New Information Technologies, 1998).

The university library's HC includes both explicit and tacit knowledge of the employees and is strongly related to the cultural aspects of organizational knowing. Tacit knowledge has a vital role in the library's HC because by deriving advantage from the implicit knowledge of employees, it promotes learning and innovations (see e.g. Choo, 1998). However, when deeply rooted in organizational practices and culture, it may also have a negative impact by causing resistance to change among staff members (Stewart, 1997). If this happens, embedded tacit knowledge may even reduce the university library's ability to enhance the university's performance.

We claim that the ability to change is crucial for libraries to increase their HC, because it is based on continuous development and renewal of expertise (see Iivonen, 2003). Therefore, it is necessary to take a new viewpoint towards the libraries' competencies and their development. As libraries develop their own key competencies to be utilized by their partners, they will be nourished by the partners' key competencies.

Castellanos et al. (2004) provide an interesting viewpoint to the development of the university's IC. They consider what kind of knowledge is needed in the creation of scientific and technical knowledge and its transfer to the social environment (Castellanos et al., 2004). By applying their ideas, we can assume that special areas of professional understanding and knowledge are also crucial at the university library as drivers to integrate the library's HC with the whole university's IC. We can recognize at least the following knowledge drivers of the library's HC:

1. Updated professional and technical knowledge of library work.
2. Understanding and knowledge of the needs of the customers (students, researchers, teachers, administration and management).
3. Understanding and knowledge of the processes at the university and the library's role in these processes.
4. Understanding and knowledge of the need to collaborate with other actors (e.g. students, teachers, researchers, administration and management) at the university, and also inside the library.
5. Knowledge of people management in managing knowledge workers.

The competence, capabilities and brainpower of the library staff are an essential part of the HC of the whole university. Many changes which have taken place in the external information environment, such as electronic publishing and the fast development of information technology, have affected library work and requirements substantially. However, it is not enough that the library staff hold new key competencies, new knowledge of information environment and information resources. They have to under- stand what the value of this knowledge is to the whole university. Further, they have to be able to integrate their own knowledge to the HC of the university. In this process, a shared understanding of the importance of collaboration plays a crucial role.

LIBRARY'S STRUCTURAL CAPITAL IN ENHANCING THE UNIVERSITY'S INTELLECTUAL CAPITAL

In addition to HC, an organization also needs the second component of IC which includes internal processes and is often called structural capital (SC). Structural capital can be both organizational (e.g. organizational learning, management and business processes and organizational culture) and tech- nological (e.g. databases, licenses and information systems). The organiza- tion's capability to improve and develop continuously all potentials and environmental variables (innovation capital) and its ability to adjust to changes and to create its own future (systemic capital) are an essential part of SC (see Table 2).

The university library's structural capital can be described as the explicit knowledge related to the internal processes in the library. It includes organizational capital, such as the library's ability to produce and offer services to its customers, to innovate and develop its services and processes and the library's ability to learn. It can also include technological capital like information systems and information resources available in the library.

The library's SC also relates to its organizational structure. We claim that a networked mode of activity is more appropriate in adapting changes in an environment that is not adequately facilitated by the traditional hierarchical structure. Concerted efforts have been made to restructure library organ- izations to increase their responsiveness and effectiveness, for example, by creating flattened hierarchies and work teams. Lateral communication between the departments and teams has been enhanced by providing staff a wider perspective on the entire organization. However, it has been noted that university libraries still are rather large units with cumbersome organ- izational structures that do not currently support fast transformation, though they aspire and are striving to become learning organizations (Moran, 2001). It has also been suggested that they have to become more client-centred, to redesign work processes in light of organizational goals, and to restructure their operations in order to support front-line perform-ance (Wilson, 1998, p. 17).

University libraries have traditionally played an important role as a part of the university's information system and information resources. They are responsible for acquiring, selecting and providing access to the external knowledge for the whole academic community. Digital technology provides new opportunities and challenges ways users approach library resources, as well as the way libraries store and preserve them (see e.g. Lynch, 2000). It is clear that the provision and use of electronic materials will increase substan-tially in the future. This requires that libraries improve access to and instruc-tion in using both printed and electronic materials. For scientific work, it is extremely important to acquire new external information, above all, to select and assess it on the basis of its potential usefulness in supporting research.

Complex and integrated library systems are the essential tools of the library work. Simultaneously, one part of the structural capital of the whole university, namely, content description, metadata and database work, have an impact on the creation of new knowledge by providing an access to information resources.

Although a huge amount of external information is available via various channels and networks, research findings show that university researchers appear to be reading more than ever and that they rely on the library's collection (both electronic and print) more than before. The evidence shows that the information obtained from scholarly articles improves scientists' quality of work and productivity (see e.g. King & Tenopir, 2001; King, Tenopir, Montogomery, & Aerni, 2003).

Castellanos et al. (2004) recognized that the knowledge drivers of uni-versity's SC refer to organizational and technological factors. We suggest that their ideas can be applied to identify the following types of professional knowledge, which can be understood as the drivers of the library's SC to the university's IC and to the overall performance of the university:

1. Knowledge of the management of the library.
2. Understanding and knowledge of the development of library work and its meaning as a part of value system.
3. Understanding and knowledge of the assessment and performance meas-urement of the library's service quality.
4. Knowledge related to information systems (catalogues, portals, etc.) that offers an access to information resources, such as printed collections, electronic journals and other resources.
5. Knowledge related to information resources.

Libraries provide for universities both modern and sophisticated information systems and diverse information resources. Certainly, they constitute an essential proportion of the SC of the whole university. It is even possible that the staff and students of the university assume that having access to these types of information resources is axiomatic without thinking about the library behind them. This suggests that the library itself can be understood as one part of the SC of the whole university. However, the library cannot have a crucial role in SC of the university without taking care of the quality of its own processes and their quality. Therefore, the continuous development of quality is needed at libraries to assure the library's SC.

LIBRARY'S RELATIONAL CAPITAL IN ENHANCING THE UNIVERSITY'S INTELLECTUAL CAPITAL

The third major component of IC is related to the organization's relationships and ability to deal with its stakeholders. This component of IC might be called relational capital (RC), customer capital, market capital or network capital (Table 3). In spite of the variety of terms used to describe it, RC is seen as a crucial component of IC in organizations.

The university library's RC can be described as the library's relations and ability to deal with customers, suppliers and other stakeholders either within the university or with other actors outside the university. The university library's relational capital also includes the library's internal relations.

The library's stakeholders can be viewed as partners. This provides a new perspective that helps to make the nature of customer relations that are based on loyalty and continuity more understandable. Because partners have a joint interest in value creation and in each other's success, they must learn to trust in a joint future despite occasional mistakes and shortcomings without looking for new service providers when dissatisfied (see e.g. Siess, 2003; Huotari & Iivonen, 2004). The partnership may add to the library's visibility within the university and an understanding among all of its constituencies of its strategic impact on the university's IC.

Teaching information literacy might represent an area of the library's RC and its relations and ability to deal with university teachers, researchers and students. Although the academic faculty is mainly responsible for teaching, the library has a crucial role as a partner in teaching information literacy and supporting network-based teaching. This partnership may improve the overall performance of the university (for example, by increasing the efficiency of the system, it may decrease the time spent studying prior to graduation). However, this requires internal networking and crossing organizational boundaries. Success in collaboration is determined by the university library's and the university's strategic linking capability, and this may vary from unit to unit within the university,

Publishing is also the major area of research activity at the university which demands that the library is able to deal with other internal actors. It is an essential part of scholarly communication which is impossible without the academic community. Researchers make their expert knowledge available for use and further development through scholarly communication. The libraries could contribute to publishing in at least the following ways:

- Participating in teaching scientific communication for degree students and researchers.
- Publishing doctoral dissertations, journals and monographs in print and in digital forms. Electronic publishing in general is a field of activity in which libraries can collaborate effectively within their universities and as the partners produce joint value with other internal stakeholders. For example, the delivery of the latest research findings in the form of electronic articles and reports could have an impact on the growth of the discipline. However, this requires close collaboration with the customers because the impact of such publication depends on the nature of the discipline.
- Promoting the benefits of open access (OA) publishing as an alternative, faster channel for the publication of the latest findings. During the last years, open access publishing has gained quite a deal of visibility and this trend is likely to continue (see Björk, 2004).
- Training researchers and administrative staff to understand citation processes in general and reading of citation indexes in particular.

Castellanos et al. (2004) considered which type of knowledge is needed as the drivers of university's RC to its social environment. Similarly these drivers are needed in libraries to assure the transfer of the libraries' RC to the academic community. Such drivers could be:

1. Knowledge of the information needs at the university level in general.
2. Knowledge about information-seeking behaviour of partners/customers.
3. Knowledge of collaboration and partnership building.
4. Knowledge of ways to develop the image and reputation of the library as a producer of valuable benefit to the university community.

In spite of the understanding that we all are already living in the era of the knowledge economy and that knowledge is a success factor in the whole society, universities still differ from many other organizations. Their main task is to add IC of the whole society, by producing and creating new knowledge through research and giving academic education at the highest level. The library can contribute to the university's main task in a very profitable way, but its success in this area demands that information needs and information-seeking behaviour at the universities are understood by those who work in the library. However, knowing information needs and behaviour is not enough. Libraries have to collaborate with researchers, teachers and students and aim to improve their abilities to find relevant information to meet their needs. The library's RC is manifested in its ability to build these kinds of partnerships.

CONCLUSION

In this article, our aim was to increase understanding of how the university library's intellectual capital constitutes a part of the university's intellectual capital. We described the human, structural and relational capital of the library. Furthermore, we discussed which kind of professional understanding and knowledge are needed at libraries as drivers to help integrate the library's intellectual capital with that of the university.

We believe that the competence, capabilities and brainpower of the library staff are an essential part of the human capital of the whole university. However, libraries have to be able to integrate their own knowledge with the human capital of the university. We described the many features of the library's structural capital and suggested that the library itself can be understood as one part of the structural capital of the whole university. We considered the library's relational capital as the library's relations and its ability to deal with customers, suppliers and other stakeholders.

Further research should focus on a more detailed examination of how to measure the university's performance and outcomes, on indicating in detail how the library's work impacts these critical issues, and how this impact could be measured. This type of examination will be important at a time when public funding for the universities is diminishing and the portion of external money required is increasing. The infrastructure of the universities, including libraries, has in many cases been funded from public sources, so declining public funding could lead to harmful limitation of the libraries' operations with a simultaneous enlargement of research activities supported by external funding. Because universities are forced to achieve better outcomes in teaching, learning and research, it is very important to demonstrate the role that the library plays in the growth of the university's intellectual capital, performance and outcomes.

REFERENCES

Abell, A. (1998). Skills for the 21st century. *Journal of Academic Librarianship & Information Science, 30*(4), 211–214.

Björk, B.-C. (2004). Open access to scientific publications—an analysis of the barriers to change. *Information Research, 9*(2) Available at http://www.InformationR.net/ir/9-2/paper170.html. Read in August 2005.

Castellanos, A. R., Rodriquez, J. L., & Ranguelov, S. Y. (2004). University R&D&T capital: What types of knowledge drive it? *Journal of Intellectual Capital, 5*(3), 478–499.

Choo, C. W. (1998). *The knowing organization: How organizations use information to construct meaning, create knowledge and make decisions.* New York: Oxford University Press.

Edvinsson, L., & Malone, M. S. (1997). *Intellectual capital: Realizing your company's true value by finding its hidden roots.* New York: HarperBusiness.

Huotari, M.-L., & Iivonen, M. (2004). Managing knowledge-based organizations through trust. In: M.-L. Huotari & M. Iivonen (Eds), *Trust in knowledge management and systems in organizations* (pp. 1–29). Hershey, PA: Idea Group Publishing.

Huotari, M.-L., & Iivonen, M. (2005). Knowledge processes: A strategic foundation for the partnership between the university and its library. *Library Management, 25*(6/7), 324–335.

Iivonen, M. (2003). Future scenarios for libraries – Finnish perspective. *Signum, 36*(4), 96–98.

Johannessen, J.-A., Olsen, B., & Olaisen, J. (2005). Intellectual capital as a holistic management philosophy: A theoretical perspective. *International Journal of Information Management, 25*, 151–171.

King, D. W., & Tenopir, C. (2001). Using and reading scholarly literature. In: M. E. Williams (Ed.), *Annual Review of Information Science and Technology* (Vol. 34, pp. 423–477). Medford, NJ: Information Today.

King, D. W., Tenopir, C., Montogomery, C. H., & Aerni, S. E. (2003). Patterns of journal use by faculty at three diverse universities. *D-Lib Magazine, 9*(10) Available at http://www.dlib.org/dlib/october03/king/10king.html. Read in August 2005.

Lynch, C. (2000). From automation to transformation. Forty years of libraries and information technology in higher education. *Educause Review, 35*(January/February), 60–68.

Moran, B. B. (2001). Restructuring the university library: A North American perspective. *Journal of Documentation, 57*(1), 100–114.

New Information Technologies. (1998). Draft Recommendation No. R(98): On cultural work within the information society. New professional profiles and competencies for information professionals and knowledge workers operating in cultural industries and institutions. Council of Europe. Council for Cultural Co-operation, Cultural Committee 17th meeting 14–16 October 1998.

Seetharaman, A., Sooria, H. H. B. Z., & Saravanan, A. S. (2002). Intellectual capital accounting and reporting in the knowledge economy. *Journal of Intellectual Capital, 3*(2), 128–148.

Siess, J. A. (2003). *The visible librarian: Asserting your value with marketing and advocacy.* Chicago, IL: American Library Association.

Stewart, T. A. (1997). *Intellectual capital. The new wealth of organizations.* New York: Currency Doubleday.

Wilson, T. D. (1998). Redesigning the university library in the digital age. *Journal of Documentation, 54*(1), 15–27.

FROM THE RHETORIC OF QUALITY MANAGEMENT TO MANAGING SELF-ORGANIZING PROCESSES: A CASE STUDY ON AN EXPERT ORGANIZATION

Jarmo Saarti and Arja Juntunen

ABSTRACT

Quality management was introduced to the European higher education with the decision made by European Union Ministers of Education in Bologna, year 1999. This paper describes its effect on the Kuopio University Library, Finland. Quality management has been used in the library as a tool for reorganizing the management, as well as, a tool for marketing and improving customer oriented library and information services.

INTRODUCTION

Quality management ideology began to have an impact on the public sector in Finland during the 1990s (see Poll & Boekhorst, 1996, which is a good summary of the development in academic libraries). Some of its principles,

Advances in Library Administration and Organization, Volume 25, 97–112
© 2007 Published by Elsevier Ltd.
ISSN: 0732-0671/doi:10.1016/S0732-0671(07)25005-9

such as changes in management and evaluating and setting goals for results, were adapted from the private sector. A clear example of this was the so-called "New Public Management" – movement, which started using private sector instruments within the public sector:

> ... instruments of such policy interventions are institutional rules and organizational routines affecting expenditure planning and financial management, civil service and labor relations, procurement, organization and methods, and audit and evaluation. (Barzelay, 2001, p. 156)

These instruments can also be found in the descriptions of quality management in the Finnish public sector published by the Ministry of Finance (Sorri-Teir, Pallas, & Westerlund, 1998, p. 8). They list the pressures for the public sector actors as:

- Economic situation and continuing demands for savings
- Results management; the need for development and goals set by the Ministries
- Ministries have demanded quality improvement from civil service departments
- Budgeting has changed from sub-item specified to framework budgets
- Clients require quality services and are eager to provide feedback
- Civil service departments have become more independent and thus they have become more able to improve quality
- There has been a strong emphasis on the total quality management (TQM) during the 1990s

Publicly funded higher education institutions, like all the universities in Finland, are under the umbrella of the Ministry of Education, and these policy definitions have a great effect on how universities may, should and actually do act. The Finnish universities must adhere to the statutes of the Act, which determine the distribution of educational responsibilities between universities by means of decrees issued separately for each field of study. The university performance is monitored in annual budget negotiations with the Ministry of Education. Thus, the Ministry has the responsibility for the quantitative evaluation of higher education institutions. At the beginning of this millennium, quality evaluation began to be used actively and now auditing is being introduced as a public management tool into Finnish higher education institutions.

In addition to the developments triggered by the policy makers, there has also been a major change in how scientific information is disseminated that has affected university libraries and changed their ways of "doing business".

The traditional, reactive way of building and owning collections has, at least partly, changed to a more reactive way of intermediating printed and electronic resources as part of the university's learning and knowledge creating processes (see, e.g., Huotari & Iivonen, 2005). On the other hand, libraries can be seen to be moving to become the knowledge management centers of their parent organizations (Parker, Nitse, & Flowers, 2005).

Libraries face vast challenges as they move into the digital environment. There is a huge number of publications available, especially within bio- and health sciences, and they seem to be among the most expensive scientific journals. Increasingly, publishing of hard science is seen more and more as a business, and it has been claimed that commercial pricing bears little relation to production costs and is relatively immune to competitive pressures (see, e.g., Morgan Stanley Equity Research, 2002; La Manna, 2003). For a medium-sized university, such as the University of Kuopio, this means that we have to struggle to balance the needs of our researchers and students against the commercial interest of international publishing houses.

In the digital world the library also faces competition from other providers of information, all competing for the same clientele. Clients have become more quality conscious, and they want to participate in the development of the information services within the campus. Information technology not only enables the interaction between clients and libraries but also provides opportunities to engage the active client in developing innovations (see, e.g., Prahalad & Ramaswamy, 2000).

But there are also challenges for management in this modern result- and profit-oriented culture. It has been quite difficult to define what a result is when one evaluates a university library. Results should be quantifiable, but this is clearly problematic when one considers learning and the creation of new knowledge (see, e.g., Poll & Boekhorst, 1996; Quinn, 1997).

On the other hand, the consumer culture ideology can create inequality among users. Libraries have always defended the idea that all individuals should be able to utilize the library's resources and services but they are now confronted by the fact that more and more digital resources are drifting away from open to restricted access. Goodman and Cohen (2004, p. 76) define two types of inequality: stigmatizing inequality that exists in a direct, less ambiguous and more transparent manner, and anonymous inequality, the kind that is indirect and not resulting from any deliberate intention. The digital revolution has clearly increased this anonymous inequality.

Unequal access poses major challenges for the leadership and management of university libraries. Fig. 1 depicts the different pressures faced by a

Culture	Management
-Market oriented culture	-Quality system management
-Digitalization	-Evaluation
-Individualism	-Need for evidence based librarianship
-Networked resources	
-Internationality	
Policy	**Employees**
-Politics/policy making	-Expertise
-Higher education policies in Finland	-Self-direction
and parent organization	-Teamwork
-Information society policies	
-Resource allocation	

Fig. 1. Challenges in Managing the Customer-Oriented Organization within Public
Sector in Finland.

library in the modern world. On the one hand, we live in a culturally more open and international environment that needs sophisticated and varied services, but on the other hand, public sector decision makers seem to want to decrease this sector as a participant in the economy and open almost all services to competition. Thus, in order to compete for resources, libraries need to create competitive services and base their evaluations on hard facts, which means that the work-force must be flexible, committed to lifelong learning and highly trained. To sum up: more and better services have to be achieved while financial support is being reduced.

In this paper, we present a case study on how we have tried to confront and combat these challenges in our university's library and its management.

FINNISH HIGHER EDUCATION POLICIES AND HOW THEY IMPACT ON THE UNIVERSITY OF KUOPIO

The University of Kuopio, Kuopio, Finland (for further information see http://www.uku.fi/english/) has an international reputation in the fields of health, environmental science and well being, with particular strengths in biotechnology, life sciences and biomedicine. It is one of the 20 universities in Finland and has about 6,200 students, 1,500 staff members, and the annual budget is about m€ 95.

Kuopio University Library is an academic library, open to everyone, not simply students and staff. The library was established in 1972. Its collections and expertise are focused on health sciences, pharmacy, biosciences, environmental sciences, information technology, business and social sciences. The annual budget of the library is about m€ 2.5. There are 37 staff members in the library, and the collections consist of approx. 160,000 monographs, 900 printed journals (subscriptions), 8,000 electronic journals, 16,000 electronic books and 5,500 audiovisual sources and other material. Information literacy teaching is provided and accounts for 580 h/840 student credits each year.

The provision of higher education is being debated in Finland because international competition is becoming more intense in education and because almost all European countries are faced with declining birthrates. One solution to make education more cost-effective is to implement quality control. During the past couple of decades, different types of quality management and evaluation systems have become integrated into higher education institutes. One impetus for these systems, especially for the evaluation process, was the decision of the member states of the European Union to create a European Higher Education Area, a process that started in Bologna in the summer of 1999. This led to the establishment of European policies and decisions on how this should be implemented in member states. The Finnish Ministry of Education has listed aims for quality control in Finland (Korkeakoulujen laadunvarmistus, 2004, also see, e.g., Standards and Guidelines, 2005) as follows:

1. Universities and polytechnics will establish quality systems that will cover all of the processes undertaken within the institution.
2. To meet the goals set in the Communiqué of the Conference of Ministers responsible for Higher Education in Berlin on 19 September 2003 (2003) in Finland, evaluations or auditing of the universities and polytechnics will be implemented.

Thus the higher education institutions have responsibility for quality control on their campuses. The auditing is carried out by the Finnish Higher Education Evaluation Council (FINHEEC) (see http://www.kka.fi/). The timetable for these evaluations is such that the piloting phase will take place during 2004–2005, and all the higher education units will be evaluated at least once by the year 2010.

As stated, this can all be viewed as a response to the new perspective of what a university education should mean. As Vartiainen (2004, p. 49) stated:

> Today's societies, on the other hand, have changed their concepts and attitudes toward university education. The requirements for today's universities can simply be stated in eight words: more value and more results of high quality.

Universities are currently redefining their roles taking into account both the market ideology (the concept of university that turns out a product) and the academic ideology (the seat of learning and the preserver of cultural values) (*ibid.*, p. 51). One outcome is that the universities as well as their libraries will be under a stricter control: measuring and evaluation is now and will be a continuous process. It should also be remembered that the evaluation can be viewed from different points of view. The following approaches have been used (Vartiainen, 2004):

- Evaluation with outcomes and goals
- Evaluation of costs
- Evaluation of implementation processes
- Client-oriented evaluation
- Stakeholder evaluation
- Consumer needs evaluation

In Finland, all these approaches have been used. At the present, one can see that the auditing policies are nudging the system in the direction of stakeholder evaluation and consumer need evaluation – both clearly adopted from the private sector. The pressure from the growing global education market could well lead to the creation of some kind of certification in the near future leading to accreditation, without which education institutes will not be able to attract students and faculty.

The University of Kuopio has been active in quality management for the past 20 years, but the pace has accelerated during the past few years because of the developments described above. To be able to compete for national and international funding and status, one must be able to demonstrate one's quality. One also must be critical of the evaluation rhetoric. As stated earlier, there are a great many instruments, concepts and values in use, many taken from the private sector, even from manufacturing industries with their techniques for optimizing the production of goods. Furthermore, according to Koenig's (2005) bibliometric analysis there is a tendency for business management fads to become popular for a time and then to fade into obscurity being replaced by some new model – e.g., articles about TQM peaked at the beginning of the 1990s and have decreased radically in number since that time. Thus, the crucial question that must be asked is are these instruments suitable, per se, for the university environment and how can they effectively be implemented in the daily work being done on campus and in the library?

MANAGING LIBRARY'S PROCESSES AND CREATING TEAMS TO IMPLEMENT THE POLICY

Teamwork and the process-oriented approach to management have been highlighted as tools for better leadership (see, e.g., Sheard & Kakabadse, 2004). Higgs (1999) defined the following criteria about teams, saying that they worked best when they had:

1. Common purpose
2. Interdependence
3. Clarity of roles and contribution
4. Satisfaction from mutual working
5. Mutual and individual accountability
6. Realization of synergies
7. Empowerment

Thus when creating a team-based organization, one must set goals for the teams, give them independence and establish avenues for exchanging information between teams, leadership and clients. It is important for the management to realize that teams need time to come together as a group and that each individual needs time to learn how to become a member of a team. Teams cannot be made to perform well – leaders can only create conditions that increase the likelihood that teams can facilitate their work. One can say that the leader's responsibility here is to be able to clearly delegate authority to the team and help it to function as a self-governing unit (see Hackman, 2002, p. 52).

Modern information technology provides us with tools for aiding teamwork by building a supportive context for the teams (Hackman, 2002, p. 147). In the Kuopio University Library, we started this by strategically working to define our role in the Finnish and international library network (Saarti, 2005). An individual university's library can build its own services in Finland from two sources: consortiums that acquire and maintain the services and collections needed in the digital environment (e.g., library systems, digital object management systems and acquiring e-material licenses, in Finland the FinELib); and the National Repository Library that ensures the availability of less extensively used and older printed material (at the present time an increasing proportion of the new printed materials are also found in its collections).

The next step was to define the core processes of our library. We started this part of the review by undertaking user surveys in order to identify the

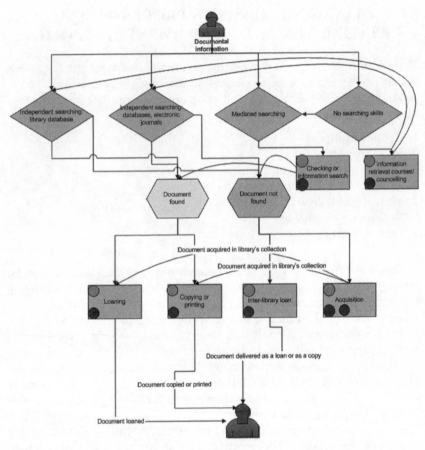

Fig. 2.   The Main Quality Scheme of Kuopio University Library (see also Juntunen,
Ovaska, Saarti, & Salmi, 2005).

needs of our users. These surveys revealed that a clear shift toward the
e-library had occurred on our campus (Ovaska & Saarti, 2004). Thus we
concluded that fulfilling our clients' need for documented (scientific)
information had to be our main mission. Subsequently, we started to model
ways in which we could help our clients. We devised one diagram that shows
these processes and shows how they are interrelated (see Fig. 2 and http://
www.uku.fi/kirjasto/english/palvelut/toimintokaavio.shtml). Then we rede-
signed our web- and intranet-pages so that they would provide support for

our clients (web pages and light dot link in figure) and staff (intranet and dark dot link in figure).

Thus we have tried to answer the need to define and support the intangible assets essential for implementing the strategy as defined by Kaplan and Norton (2004, p. 203):

Human capital

Strategic competencies: The availability of skills, talent and know-how to perform activities required by the strategy.

Information capital

Strategic information: The availability of information systems and knowledge applications and infrastructure required to support the strategy.

Organizational capital

Culture: Awareness and internationalization of the shared mission, vision and values needed to execute the strategy.

Leadership: The availability of qualified leaders at all levels to mobilize the organization toward their strategies.

Alignment: Alignment of goals and incentives with the strategy at all organization levels.

Teamwork: The sharing of knowledge and staff assets with strategic potential.

THE CASE OF THE KUOPIO UNIVERSITY LIBRARY

In the University of Kuopio, information service provision is done by the Centre for Information and Learning Resource Services. It consists of three separate departments: the Information Technology Centre, the Learning Centre and the library (see Fig. 3).

The idea of providing these services jointly by these departments gradually evolved from the beginning of the 1990s. The greatest influence and need for co-operation is attributable to the fact that a growing number of information services are implemented via information technology and software. Thus, in order to use resources efficiently, we in the library need to access and utilize the expertise found in other departments. If one examines Fig. 4, it can be seen that most of our services consist of maintaining information systems and teaching, supporting and developing these services, as well as making them available to help our customers on the campus.

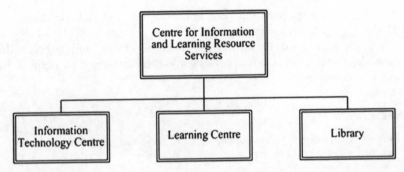

Fig. 3. University of Kuopio Centre for Information and Learning Resource Services.

Co-operation has also been crucial due to the fact that the actual resources have not expanded at anything like the increase in the number of researchers and students working in the University. For example, it is now impossible to maintain the library's core functions without expert level knowledge on databases, their creation and maintenance.

The aim for the library's quality work has been to improve the quality of the services provided. In this discussion, the term services include functions that impact on the collection and information literacy education provided by the library. Also improving the know-how of the staff has been focused in implementing the concept of organizational learning. Quality work also provides tools for the management, strategy work and objective definition for the library. On the other hand, the requirement for measurability provides evidence-based facts and practices and helps in negotiations with the university's management about the library's resources.

The clientele of the Kuopio University library consist of students, teachers and researchers. The library is also open to the general public, so in theory, anyone can access its services. The Finnish library network also creates one special circle of customers – other libraries and information services (e.g., inter-library loans). In addition to acquiring, organizing and supplying documents, the library also delivers curriculum-based information literacy courses for graduate students.

The quality work started in the beginning of the year 2003, beginning with the renovation of the library's web pages. A project was established for this, the aim of which was to help our client find the information they need as efficiently as possible using the website and to make the pages clear, concise and logical. A project team was created to undertake this task, and the pages were tested by our university's web experts.

SERVICES	CUSTOMERS
	Researchers Teachers and students Other University's management
Acquisition, organization and support of the ICT-environment	E-library, library and digital object management systems Data communication: data network, e-mail, web-services etc. Technical infrastructure: Workstations including peripherals and software, servers, videoconferencing equipment etc. Computer classrooms and hardware for short-term loan
Information management	Data security, data administration, data and system architecture
Acquisition, organization and mediation of knowledge resources	Library material (printed and e-material) Web-based teaching resources Graphics and other digital material
Support of the teaching and studies	Web-based teaching course management systems and tools Student information systems, e.g. academic records database Information literacy teaching, aiding in the acquisition of information Pedagogic education and helpdesk services for computer aided teaching and resource creation
Support of the publication process	Information management software, e.g. citation management University's publication database Image processing, graphic design, photography Publishing, e.g. series and dissertations
Support of the research process	University's research database Statistical methodology support Information retrieval support IT-based communication support for research teams
Other support	University administration information systems support
Research and product development	R&D and product development

Fig. 4. Services Provided by the University of Kuopio Centre for Information and Learning Resource Services.

At the same time, we started to renew the library's organization. Our intention was to convert the library's office-based structures into service process-based teams. As part of this effort, the teams and staff members were empowered to make decisions. The aim here was to help all the members of the staff to appreciate that they carry part of the responsibility for improving the library's quality of service (Carter, 2004, p. 9).

There are currently three standing teams: the lending services team, the information and teaching services team and the administration team. It is also possible to establish ad hoc teams to undertake specific projects. Teams are instructed to function in an orderly manner. They prepare an annual plan of action; they establish meeting practices and schedules, and they report their work to the library's management team. This helps management in its strategic planning and in communication between management and the staff. This more formal management was implemented in the fall of 2005, though the teams have functioned on an informal basis for years. This new policy also confers a more official status on the teams.

The quality team was in charge of the quality work done in the library during its first phase from the year 2002 to 2005. It was responsible for the establishment of the quality work and started the documentation underpinning the quality system. The team consisted of 14 members of the staff from all the departments of the library and its wide representation ensured that it was effective in its role of motivating and assimilating other personnel into quality work. The library's head of services was chair of the team and acted also as the quality manager who was in charge of the quality system development within the library. Quality manager also acts as a contact person with the university's quality manager. The quality team held its last meeting in the beginning of the year 2006. Today, quality considerations are integrated into the work of standing teams, which bear responsibility for ensuring improvements that the quality of service is improved in the future.

The actual quality work has been target oriented from the onset. One goal was that it should be subjected to internal auditing – a policy established by the university – and that this should be undertaken for two services, local lending and inter-library lending. The auditors were from different departments of the university who had been clients of the library but were not familiar with the actual library work. The library has also been active in auditing other departments library director acting as a one of the university's internal auditors. The aim in this process has been twofold: to improve the library's own processes and to show that the library is a vital part of the university's core processes, teaching and conducting research (see also Juntunen et al., 2005).

An intensive documenting process preceded the auditing with the intention of creating documented terms of reference for the clients within the intranet, implemented together with the library services provided via the web. The desk staff involved in routine work can also use these services.

Intranet pages were established for the staff including minutes and other communication of the teams, terms of reference for internal use such as *Lending practices, On call routines, The Library system reference manual and Discretion rules*. Each of these has a named person who is responsible for the maintenance of the reference materials. The library's quality manual consists of the library's internet and its intranet pages. The Centre for Information and Learning Resource Services also has a paper version of its quality manual, which includes more ISO standard-like documentation.

This documentation formed the foundation for the internal auditing that took place in 2004. The auditors evaluated in detail the management system and loaning and also visited two of the library's lending premises and the inter-library lending office. What was the evaluation like? To begin with, the auditors were highly motivated and had examined our documentation thoroughly. They had been granted access and passwords to the library's intranet in order to peruse the documentation. The library's management system was under transition as described earlier, and the auditing process encouraged us to ensure that the documentation should be at the same level as the Centre for Information and Learning Resource Services in order to achieve conformity. Another fact that we appreciated was that the auditors provided feedback about the amount of "librarian-slang" used in the documentations. As Quinn (1997) (see also Phipps, 2001) states, libraries have a tendency to devise their policies from library service standards, not from the customers' needs, and this was very clear in our documentation, including guidelines and forms intended for library users.

The actual work of librarianship and its substance were omitted from this type of auditing. Evaluating this part of what we do can be best achieved by peer reviewing and benchmarking from other libraries and librarians from both our home country and foreign libraries. This is an on-going process, and we have already found good partners and had benchmarking sessions.

It was also important that all of the staff be involved in this process. Thus, we have been able to concentrate on the creation of quality documentation from the bottom up and in committing our staff to the success of this process. Auditing has been a learning process for our library; a lot of issues were raised, which now need to be debated, assessed and documented. Auditing and the discussions that followed have provided new perspectives for us and an impetus to hold joint discussions on our library's future development.

The proposals given in the audit report have been discussed in the quality team and the modifications needed have been implemented. The rapidly changing technological environment is very challenging in this respect.

Documentation needs to be updated monthly. Also customer feedback –
face-to-face and survey-based – affects our ways of carrying out our
services. Group discussions with the staff about the feedback are the most
efficient way of improving one's services.

CONCLUSIONS

What have we learned during this process in our library? First of all, it is
important to define, separate and address the two aspect of quality
management. The most important from our point of view is the library's
core processes and their documentation. This helps our staff in fulfilling the
library's goals and our clients' needs. This also helps in integrating both the
university's and library's strategies into our everyday work. Modern
information technologies are a great help in this documentation process
and should be exploited as extensively as possible.

Another aspect of quality management that is indirectly as important to
the library is the political and rhetorical quality work. Which facets do
policy makers wish to see addressed: in Finland there are many levels to be
addressed, civil servants, especially those in the Ministry of Education;
within the University, especially the University's management. These
individuals set the political agenda and goals for higher education.
Crucially, they also hold the strings to the purse, deciding who will be
funded and who will be allowed to wither. Libraries must also be active in
this political debate because it is the only way that their voice can be heard.

Both arguments, service provision and policy influencing, need to be
backed up by facts. The requirements for evidence-based librarianship and
measuring the cost-effects, as well as, assessing the impact and effectiveness
of library services are becoming increasingly important (see, e.g., Poll, 2005).
Decision makers need facts and they prefer simple, mathematical numbers.
Thus, libraries must be active in making these measurements by themselves
and must be creative in ensuring that they are unambiguous and
comprehensible. This is our next goal – to create a set of key figures to
describe the library's effectiveness on the University's core processes.

It is also important to benchmark against other types of libraries and
information services. On the one hand, it is important to keep pace with the
competition, and on the other hand, it helps us identify niches for
specialization and in that way improve the flexibility of our library services.
The ideal that libraries are a part of global network that has the mission of
enabling everyone to access scientific knowledge must be enshrined as a goal

in spite of the economical and political pressures bearing down on the libraries.

This sets a new goal for library management. Libraries and their leaders must become more and more open to the society and to ongoing cultural changes. We must adopt a more proactive attitude and be ready to influence the decision makers and legislation that places restrictions on our activities. Ultimately, information must be free and not be subjected to any borders.

ACKNOWLEDGMENT

The authors are grateful to Dr. Ewen MacDonald for revising their English.

REFERENCES

Barzelay, M. (2001). *The new public management: Improving research and policy. Dialogue* (Wildavsky Forum Series, 3). Berkeley: University of California Press.

Carter, N. (2004). *Auditointi ja ISO 19011* [Finnish translation of the Auditing the ISO 19011 Way]. Helsinki: SFS.

Communiqué of the Conference of Ministers responsible for Higher Education in Berlin on 19 September 2003 (2003). *Realising the European Higher Education Area.* Berlin: European Union Available from: http://europass.cedefop.eu.int/img/dynamic/c1400/ type.FileContent.file/Berlin_en_US.PDF (Last visited 4.11.2005).

Goodman, D. J., & Cohen, M. (2004). *Consumer culture: A reference handbook.* Santa Barbara, CA: ABC-CLIO.

Hackman, J. R. (2002). *Leading teams: Setting the stage for great performances.* Boston, MA: Harvard Business School Press.

Higgs, M. (1999). *Teams and team working: What do we know?* Henley Management College Report, No. HWP 9911.

Huotari, M.-L., & Iivonen, M. (2005). Knowledge processes: A strategic foundation for the partnership between the university and its library. *Library Management, 26*(6–7), 324–335.

Juntunen, A., Ovaska, T., Saarti, J., & Salmi, L. (2005). Managing library processes: Collecting data and providing tailored services to end-users. *Library Management, 26*(8–9), 487–493.

Kaplan, R. S., & Norton, D. P. (2004). *Strategy maps: Converting intangible assets into tangible outcomes.* Boston: Harvard Business School Press.

Koenig, M. E. D. (2005). KM moves beyond the organization: The opportunity for librarians. *Paper presented at the World Library and Information Congress: 71th IFLA General Conference and Council.* 2nd Version: June 17, 2005. Hague, IFLA. Available from: http://www.ifla.org/IV/ifla71/papers/123e-Koenig.pdf (Last visited 3.11.2005).

Korkeakoulujen laadunvarmistus *[Quality assurance of higher education]* (2004). (Opetusministeriön työryhmämuistioita ja selvityksiä 2004:6). Helsinki: Ministry of Education. Available from: http://www.minedu.fi/julkaisut/koulutus/2004/tr06/tr06.pdf (Last visited 3.11.2005).

La Manna, M. (2003). The economics of publishing and the publishing of economics. *Library Review*, *52*(1), 18–28.

Morgan Stanley Equity Research (2002). Scientific publishing: Knowledge is power. Available from http://www.econ.ucsb.edu/~tedb/Journals/morganstanley.pdf (Last visited 3.20.2005).

Ovaska, T., & Saarti, J. (2004). Availability of library materials and access to information resources. *EAHIL Newsletter* (69), 2004. Can be accessed from http://www.eahil.org/newsletter/69/69%20.pdf

Parker, K. R., Nitse, P. S., & Flowers, K. A. (2005). Libraries as knowledge management centers. *Library Management*, *26*(4), 176–189.

Phipps, S. (2001). Beyond measuring service quality: Learning from the voices of the customers, the staff, the processes, and the organization. *Library Trends*, *49*(4), 635–661.

Poll, R. (2005). Measuring the Impact of New Library Services. Paper presented at the World Library and Information Congress: 71th IFLA General Conference and Council. Version: June 9, 2005. Hague, IFLA. Available from: http://www.ifla.org/IV/ifla71/papers/081e-Poll.pdf (Last visited 3.11.2005).

Poll, R., & Boekhorst, P. (1996). *Measuring quality: International guidelines for performance measurement in academic libraries* (IFLA publications, 76). München: Saur.

Prahalad, C. K., & Ramaswamy, V. (2000). Co-opting the customer competence. *Harvard Business Review*, *78*(1), 79–87.

Quinn, B. (1997). Adapting service quality concepts to academic libraries. *Journal of Academic Librarianship*, *23*(5), 359–369.

Saarti, J. (2005). From printed world to a digital environment: The role of repository libraries in a changing environment. *Library Management*, *26*(1–2), 26–31.

Sheard, A. G., & Kakabadse, A. P. (2004). *A Process Perspective on Leadership and Team Development*. Bradford, Emerald Group Publishing Limited, 2004. (Journal of Management Development, 23(1): 7–106.) Accessed via http://site.ebrary.com/lib/uku/Doc?id = 10058619 (Last visited 8.11.2005).

Sorri-Teir, E., Pallas, K., & Westerlund, A. (1998). *Julkisen sektorin laatulinjauksia*. [*Definitions of the public sector's quality policies*.] Julkaisija: Valtiovarainministeriön hallinnon kehittämisosasto. (Tutkimukset ja selvitykset, 5/98). Helsinki, Valtionvaraiministeriö [Ministry of Finance].

Standards and Guidelines for Quality Assurance in the European Higher Education Area. (2005). European Association for Quality Assurance in Higher Education, 2005, Helsinki. http://www.enqa.net/files/BergenReport210205.pdf (Last visited 10.10.2005).

Vartiainen, P. (2004). *The legitimacy of evaluation: A comparison of Finnish and English institutional evaluations of higher education*. Frankfurt am Main: P. Lang.

OPEN ACCESS PUBLISHING AS A DISCIPLINE-SPECIFIC WAY OF SCIENTIFIC COMMUNICATION: THE CASE OF BIOMEDICAL RESEARCH IN FINLAND

Turid Hedlund and Annikki Roos

ABSTRACT

Open access to scientific publications is in this study looked at from the perspective of Finnish biomedical research. In the study we outline the development of open access in Finland and the different channels for open access publishing as well as the recommendations from officials. We argue that the discipline-specific patterns of communicating research should be taken into account when studying open access adoption, and when planning for initiatives and recommendations. We have in the case study on the prevalence of open access articles on the Internet, in the field of biomedical research, found that incentives to publish in open access channels could be developed and that the impact of open access in research publishing is growing and therefore future research is needed.

Advances in Library Administration and Organization, Volume 25, 113–131
© 2007 Published by Elsevier Ltd.
ISSN: 0732-0671/doi:10.1016/S0732-0671(07)25006-0

INTRODUCTION

Open Access means that a reader of a scientific publication is granted free access to the text and can print it out and distribute it for non-commercial purposes, the only constraint being that the authors retain the right to control the integrity of their work and the right to be properly cited and acknowledged. In scientific publishing, this is a world-wide phenomenon made possible by the development of the Internet. When we talk about open access, we generally mean free access to original research results in the form of journal articles, doctoral theses, research reports and other forms of publishing. However, open access publishing can even include material that normally is not published such as research data and appendices.

Open access can be seen as a movement where the initiative comes from researchers and librarians in universities and resembles the open source movement in computer software programming (see, for example, Szczepanska, Bergquist, & Ljungberg, 2003). Pioneers in this effort have focused on two strategies on the road to open access, both defined at a meeting in Budapest in December 2001 by the Information Program of the Open Society Institute.[1] The first strategy defined was to create new journals or to convert existing ones to open access formats. The second strategy was to urge authors and institutions like universities to start "self-publishing" copies of their articles in subscription-based journals on the Internet. The idea was and is to create openly accessible searchable archives where the articles can be accessed free of charge.

Open access has a history that goes beyond the introduction of the World Wide Web. The best-known example is the subject-specific repository for high-energy physics[2] (Ginsparg, 1996) that was founded in 1991. Subject-specific repositories have emerged in research areas where traditions for the exchange of preprints have existed prior to the Internet and where the speed of publication is an essential factor (Kling & McKim, 2000). For example, in economics the circulation of working papers has a long tradition and since 1998 also resulting in the digital library RePEc.[3] The guiding principle behind such electronic archives is that researchers themselves or their institutions upload article manuscripts, conference papers, etc. into the repositories. As a result, papers in a repository are available globally much earlier than final published versions of the manuscripts in traditional journals with publishing schedules that include a certain number of issues per volume.

As an alternative to traditional subscription-based journals, open access scientific journals have emerged since the beginning of the 1990s. These journals are defined as journals that distribute their content free of charge to the user. There are several business models for open access journals and so-called hybrid journals that give delayed open access to content as described in Hedlund, Gustafsson, and Björk (2004). According to the directory of open access journals (DOAJ),[4] there were 1,900 peer-reviewed journals listed in the directory in November 2005, and that number is growing.

Self-archiving also provides an important source for open access information. From the earliest days of the web, individual researchers have distributed copies of their own publications on their personal homepages or on the homepage of the research group. We do not know the extent of this kind of self-publishing or self-archiving, but it is still the most common open access channel available today.

Besides open access journals, subject-specific repositories and self-archiving, publication archives are also maintained by universities and their libraries. The increasing interest in recent years in institutional archives brings a more systematic and long-term commitment to this activity. It is in the interest of universities and their libraries to collect and distribute the university's production of research papers and theses in electronic form instead of exchanging copies in paper format, and, today, most universities concentrate on publishing doctoral theses and the university's own publication series in electronic format. But the core research in the form of scientific articles is still lacking for the most part from the institutional archives. Stevan Harnad wrote on the posting list of the American Scientist open access forum on December 13, 2004[5] that only 15% of the scientific articles produced in the world can be found in institutional archives.

It is generally recognized that filling and coordinating institutional archives is a problem. Jean-Claude Guedon (2001), one of the well known proponents of open access scientific journals, admits that experiences from the last decade show that system change in scholarly communications has been slow and tedious. Several open access journals have emerged during that period, and the percentage of new open access journals among all new journals starting up has been rising (Hedlund et al., 2004). The problem with the open access journals is that they publish, on the average, relatively few articles per year, and that several journals have ceased publication after their first year before getting enough submissions or developing a good reputation. Björk (2004) characterizes the barriers to open access into six types: legal frameworks concerning copyright; IT-infrastructure; business models; indexing services and standards; academic reward system; and marketing and critical mass. The IT-infrastructure barrier is mostly solved and most of the work has been completed on standardizing metadata. But the problem is still to find sustainable business models, to influence the academic reward system and to get a critical mass of open access articles.

In this paper, we start by outlining the pre-requisites for Finnish open access publishing regarding scientific articles. We will look at the present systems (institutional archives, subject-based archives and open access journals) and recent recommendations from officials. Next, we will focus on e-publishing, particularly the open access publishing of scientific articles either in open access journals or as secondary publishing on the web. The author's incentives to publish are to disseminate the research results to a large audience and to gain a reputation among his/her colleagues by publishing in high-class journals, journals that normally carry high subscription fees. Open access publishing on the web provides visibility (Lawrence, 2001). Kling and McKim (1999) and Kling, Spector, and McKim (2002) discuss the importance of the scholarly discipline in shaping legitimate communication forms. They also point to the link between the academic social contexts and its reward and meriting system to publishing patterns. Whitley's (1984) theory of social organization of scholarly fields is used to position the characteristics of differences in scientific fields.

The objective of this empirical study is to find out how much open access publishing is going on and what types of publishing channels are being used in the biomedical sciences in Finland. We also wanted to know whether researchers used open access journals like BioMed Central (BMC), society publishers with delayed open access in PubMed Central (PMC), or self-archiving in institutional archives or own home pages. Also, the location and format of the articles found on the Internet were of interest.

In the discussion part of the article, we try to identify the incentives for publishing open access among medical researchers.

OPEN ACCESS IN FINLAND

The open access initiative started in Finland on the basis of the activities of a set of stakeholders that formed an informal group called FinnOA. The members were scientists engaged in an EU-project on open access, university librarians, representatives of the scientific societies, and the Academy of Finland. In January 2004, the group organized a successful conference on open access that increased the general awareness on open access issues. During 2004–2005, this group has been actively participating in conferences and network building both nationally and internationally. In September 2004, the Finnish minister of education appointed a committee to develop a policy on open access. Policies defined on the governmental or ministry level are still quite rare and would seem to have a strong impact. The recommendations were sent out in March 2005, signed by the minister of education, to all institutes of higher education as well as to other stakeholders (e.g. funding institutions). The central part of the report contains a list of about 30 recommendations directed to the major stakeholders in the Finnish research community,[6] such as higher education institutions, research institutes, funding agencies, journal publishers, learned societies and libraries. The main recommendation was to encourage researchers to publish using open access channels.

The committee first recognized that most scientific research would be published in traditional subscription journals and fee-charging conference proceedings in the coming years. In order to improve the circulation and availability of such publications, the committee gave recommendations. The primary recommendation was for researchers to mount copies in institutional or subject-based repositories. To provide the infrastructure for this, higher education institutions working in concert with one another or together with their libraries were asked to facilitate the building of repositories. Funding agencies were asked to underwrite author or page charges for submissions as research project expenditures. It was also recommended that Finnish scientific journals (which currently total about 70) and the learned societies offer open access to their articles and journals as soon as possible after publication and to allow their authors to deposit articles in open access archives. In this case, delayed access is also considered proper since many societies that publish scientific journals provide them as member service and are dependent on member fees.

The kind of institutional archives that are recommended are not specified in the recommendations, but it is likely that an OAI-compliant archive is preferred. Today (November 2005) only a few universities and one research institute have OAI-compliant archives. Open access institutional publication archives exist in the university sector mainly for doctoral theses and other research reports and series, but these publication archives vary widely, ranging from HTML pages to databases. Most universities today publish their doctoral theses in electronic form as open access publications on the Internet, and the pilot testing of open source software for use in supporting institutional archives has begun on many campuses.

FIELD DIFFERENCES IN SCIENTIFIC
COMMUNICATION AND PUBLISHING PATTERNS

Open access publishing is in the official declarations and in statements mostly directed to one single academic community of researchers, institutions and libraries. However, research reports and scientific articles give a more differentiated view of the scientific fields regarding scientific communication. Kling and McKim (2000) state that there is a high likelihood that differences in communication patterns in various academic fields and the use and meaning given to different media and forums will persist in the electronic age. Fry and Talja (2004) point out the importance of the overall context of domain differences in studies of the use of scientific journal articles. Domain differences are seldom probed in depth, and this can be seen as a common shortcoming in research on user habits, for example, in questions like "When do researchers prefer electronic to paper formats?" Fry and Talja also suggest that Whitley's theory of the social organization of scholarly fields is useful as an exploratory model of e-journal use in different disciplines. The model can probably also be used to describe publishing patterns in scientific fields even though e-journal use and publishing patterns do not coincide in all aspects. Björk and Turk (2000) carried out a survey on e-journals use and publishing patterns within the community of construction engineers. Their results show that researchers like to retrieve publications directly from the web via open access but that the main criteria they use in choosing where to publish are the academic status of the journal and the relevant readership.

Whitley (1984) argues that scientific disciplines can be understood in similar ways as work organizations. The differences in scientific fields can be characterized in terms of two dimensions: *degree of mutual dependence* and *degree of task uncertainty*. The concept of mutual dependence is associated with the degree of dependence that exists among scientists or groups of colleagues that is required to make a proper contribution to collective goals to increase the researcher's reputation among his/her fellow scientists. Two analytically distinct aspects to mutual dependence are considered: the degree of functional dependence and the degree of strategic dependence. The first aspect refers to the extent to which researchers have to use specific results, ideas and procedures as scientists in the field to establish the legitimacy of their claims to be making competent contributions to their field of study. The second refers to the extent to which researchers have to convince the scientific field of the significance and importance of the research problems addressed and the research approaches taken (*ibid.*, p. 88). The concept of the degree of task uncertainty is associated with differences in patterns of work organization and control and varies in relation to changing contextual factors. Whitley finds that this includes two major facets: technical task uncertainty and strategic task uncertainty. The first refers to the "visibility, uniformity and stability of task outcomes," while the second refers to the "uniformity, stability and integration" of research strategies and goals (*ibid.*, p. 148). A high level of task uncertainty leads to greater direct personal control of research and is associated with theoretical diversity. Especially, high levels of technical task uncertainty limit the technical control of empirical phenomena, make the results more difficult to interpret and give way to alternative views and difficulties in coordination (*ibid.*, p. 148). Whitley's example of a scientific field with high degree of technical task uncertainty and low degree of strategic task uncertainty is Economics as it has developed since 1870.

Whitley's taxonomy of scientific field differences can be concretized to the fact that when the degree of mutual dependence increases, the methods used for scientific communication become more controlled and the competition increases. Citation patterns become very important in a field with high mutual dependence. This fact may affect publishing patterns, making them more restrictive and standardized. Publishing in highly respected journals with high impact factors and high rank becomes increasingly important.

In fields with high degree of task uncertainty, publishing patterns might be less controlled, but in the case of economics where the problems and goals are restricted and tightly structured, the visibility and communication of scientific results at an early stage are important. The distribution of working papers might be an indication of this fact.

From the Finnish study by Ursin (2004, p. 28) on characteristics of medical research groups, we find that the increased demands from society and officials on productivity and accountability are probably a factor affecting the publishing of research. Also, the visibility and reputation of the researcher are important personal factors. When reviewing studies of collaborative research among scientists, Ursin (2004, p. 28) picks up factors that have been found in earlier studies to motivate researchers to cooperate. Among these, the increased demands from society and officials on productivity and accountability are probably factors that also affect the publication of research.

Regarding open access publishing, the CUL Open Access Publishing Task Force Report (2004) stresses that there is no single academic community but multiple communities with various cultures and that an appreciation of this point is crucial when trying to organize and analyze academic interest in open access publishing.

Open access author behavior has been studied probably most extensively by the CIBER research group in the United Kingdom during 2004–2005 (Nicholas & Rowlands, 2005). Attitudes towards open access publishing were gathered in a world-wide survey directed to authors publishing in peer-review journals indexed in Thomson Scientific's Citation databases (ISI). One of the findings was that open access is not a well understood concept among researchers in general. Only 5% knew a lot about open access, while an additional 48% said they knew a little about it. However, there were several interesting points to be noted. Younger authors and authors already publishing in open access journals are more positive about it than were senior authors. There are also differences in geographical location; researchers in Western Europe and North America were least likely to have published in open access journals, while researchers from South America and Asia have the most experience in publishing there. Also, differences in attitudes between scientific disciplines could be seen. Respondents from immunology, material sciences and medicine thought that authors would publish more in open access journals in the future. Authors from chemistry and economics were of the opinion that open access gives less choice to the author and the reader. The opposite opinion was prevailing in neuroscience, immunology and biochemistry.

Studies on authors' attitudes towards open access publishing have also been carried out by Swan and Brown (2004) and Schroter, Tite, and Smith (2005). The results from the first study indicate that open access is no longer an unfamiliar concept among researchers and that self-archiving is also increasing, although the awareness of the archiving possibilities is still low. The latter study explores authors' attitudes towards journals using author charges and was conducted among *British Medical Journal* authors. The results from the study were that the perceived journal quality is more important than open access.

From the literature study on previous research, we were able to characterize and identify incentives for publishing open access into factors depending mostly on the social environment and factors mostly depending on personal factors of the researcher.

Environmental or external factors:

• Policymaking, governmental policy in science and technology, policy of other funding bodies, interest groups and officials
• Increased demands for productivity and accountability
• Internationalization and strong competition in the scientific field
• Geographic location

- Availability of subject-based and institutional archives and open access journals
- Institutional policies that promote open access publishing
- Communication patterns of the scientific field and the field's willingness to early adoption of new techniques

Personal factors:

- The importance of reputation and meriting to the researcher
- Speed of publication and visibility of research results
- Personal communication patterns and willingness to adopt new techniques
- Personal values

OPEN ACCESS INITIATIVES FOR MEDICINE

One of the main actors in the open access movement in biomedicine has been the National Institutes of Health (NIH) in the U.S. The mission of NIH is to disseminate new knowledge that will lead to better health for everyone. The primary mechanism for accomplishing this mission is the sharing of ideas, data and research findings.[7] This mechanism perfectly fits the principle of open access. The main advocate for open access at NIH has been the former director, Dr. Harold Varmus, who proposed in 1999 that an electronic repository for all biomedical research (called E-biomed, later PMC) should be established at the National Library of Medicine (NLM) (Homan & Watson, 2004, p. 83). The establishing process of the repository, the public discussion surrounding its founding and the role of other main actors besides Dr. Varmus, namely, the scientific societies, are described in an article by Kling et al. (2004).

NIH supports the availability of research results in several ways. It has an official policy statement concerning public access of NIH-funded research results, and beginning in May 2005, NIH has requested and strongly encouraged all researchers funded by NIH to make final manuscripts available to other researchers and to the public through NIH and through the National Library of Medicine's (NLM) PubMedCentral (PMC).[8] According to an estimate provided by Elias Zerhouni, the current director of NIH, NIH funds at least 10% of annual biomedical literature. This should mean a yearly addition of about 65,000 articles to PMC (Zerhouni, 2004a).

In biomedicine there are two current, successful open access publishing models that provide immediate access to research articles. The first one is

BMC, a commercial publisher. The second is Public Library of Science (PLoS), a non-profit organization that consists of an independent group of researchers who have committed to providing free access to biomedical literature.[9] Both of these publishers allow free access, but in each case, authors are charged for publishing their articles. BMC and PLoS also submit all articles to PMC (Zerhouni, 2004b). These publishers have similar fee structures. In each case, there is an article fee and a membership fee. Institutions can pay a certain amount of money in advance and discount the article fees. BMC allows new customers to join at quite a low institutional price, but after a certain amount of time the charge will be based on the amount of articles actually published in BMC. In most cases, this means quite a big increase in the price. Finland has had a national license with BMC since the year 2004. However, this license ended by the end of 2005. The license was negotiated by FinElib, the National Electronic Library of Finland. Since that date (1.4.2004–30.9.2005), 58 open access articles have been published by Finnish researchers.

THE CASE STUDY ON FINNISH BIOMEDICAL OPEN ACCESS PUBLISHING – NATIONAL PUBLIC HEALTH INSTITUTE AND UNIVERSITY OF OULU

National Public Health Institute (KTL)[10] is a research institute and an expert body under the Ministry of Social Affairs and Health. The aim of KTL is to promote the possibilities to a healthy life for the Finnish people. The functions of the institute are research, expert functions, health monitoring, public health services, education and training, international collaboration, laboratory research and participation in the dissemination of health information and health education. KTL addresses the public health field on a broad spectrum and creates synergy between research and public health functions. KTL has a staff of over 900 people, of whom 360 are researchers. About 500 original scientific articles are published every year.

The University of Oulu[11] is a multidisciplinary university in Northern Finland with a staff of 3,100 and a student body of over 15,800. There are nine educational areas in the university organized in six faculties. The focus areas are biotechnology, information technology and northern and environmental issues. The Faculty of Medicine is divided into 27 departments. The research in the faculty is concentrated in seven main areas: cancer biology and cancer diseases, cardiovascular diseases, connective tissue research, cartilage and bone diseases, environment and health, life span and gerontological research and neuroscience.

Methodology to Identify Publications

This study was conducted between April and May 2005. The reference data used in this article for the empirical study of published articles relating to medicine were collected from research information registers for the years 2003–2004 from the National Public Health Institute (KTL) and from the Faculty of Medicine at the University of Oulu: a sample from KTL of 340 articles (170 from 2003 and 170 from 2004) and another sample from the faculty of Medicine at the University of Oulu of 47 published articles in 2003 and 77 in 2004. In the case of Oulu, the articles represent the single department of Biochemistry and Molecular Biology.

Google and Google Scholar were used as search tools to find out about available publications in open access format. The general search engine Google was chosen because of its popularity among the general public, and the Google Scholar version was chosen because of its focus on scientific material. Google Scholar is popular among researchers who want to collect information about a researcher through his/her web page and to look up references directly from the web using a general search engine. The search criterion used in the study was the full article title. In this case study, only two search engines and one criterion were used, and we are aware that the results might differ if other search engines or other search criteria, such as author name or affiliation, were introduced. However, this study is not intended to show every possible way in which one might find an article online, but rather to study the publishing patterns of a scientific field as it relates to open access. The subject-based database PubMed was used to identify bibliographical data about the publication. Information about the journals was collected from the journal page or the web page where the article is found or in some cases from Ulrich's Periodical Directory. ISI Journal Citation Report was used to study the impact factor of the journals and the rank of the journal (sorted by impact factor) in the respective subject category.

RESULTS

The publishing of Finnish scientific articles either as open access copies or in open access journals is still rather low as can be seen from Table 1, which presents data on the percentage of articles found to be openly accessible on

Table 1. Number of Articles Found on the Internet Using Standard Search Engines Google and Google Scholar.

	Number of Articles	Found on the Internet	Percentage
KTL			
Original articles 2003	178	59	34.14
Original articles 2004	178	34	19.10
University of Oulu			
Original articles 2003	47	17	36.17
Original articles 2004	77	21	27.27

Table 2. Open Access Articles Found With a Specific Search Engine.

Article Information	KTL, 2003	KTL, 2004	Oulu, 2003	Oulu, 2004
Search engine				
Google	12	13	4	6
Google Scholar	3	3		
Both	44	18	13	15
Total	59	34	17	21

the Internet. As could be expected, the percentage varies a lot between the years. The percentage is 34 for KTL and 36 for Oulu in 2003. In 2004, the percentage dropped to 20 for KTL and 28 for Oulu. The reason for the decrease in the percentage in 2004 could relate to the delayed access that is provided for some journals. In comparison, we might add that in 2003 the researchers at the Swedish School of Economics and Business Administration published 70 articles in refereed journals, but only 6 (8.5%) were available through open access.

In the case of KTL, a total of 461 articles were produced in 2003 and 540 were published in 2004. The set of articles in Table 1 formed a sample of the total. There are 63 different journal titles in the sample for both years, meaning that on average 5.6 articles are published per journal.

In Table 2, the specific numbers of articles found using each search engine are displayed. As can be seen from the table, most articles were found through both search engines.

We have also looked in detail in Table 3 at types of publishers. The most common type is the society publishers who tend to publish their articles online and make them available free of charge to the user either immediately or after a delay of six months to a year. The commercial publishers follow the

Table 3. Open Access Articles According to Type of Journal Publisher.

Type of Publisher	KTL, 2003	KTL, 2004	Oulu, 2003	Oulu, 2004
Society publishers	43	15	14	18
Commercial	10	12	3	1
BioMed Central	1	6		
Other OA-journals	5	1		2
Total	59	34	17	21

same pattern of delayed access. In some cases, it has been hard to distinguish between society publishers and commercial publishers, and in the study, the criterion for designating a house as a society publisher has been that the publication was noted somewhere on the journal page of a society. We are aware that some scientific societies use a commercial publisher for the publishing process of their journal and that this is a fact that we might not be able to recognize from the web page of a journal. In view of the sample, the researchers at KTL had published in one BMC journal in 2003, and that number rose to six for the year 2004. It should be noted that a license agreement for Finnish universities and research institutes covering the costs for the article processing or the author charge fee has been signed for the years 2004–2005 and at the same time, it should be noted that KTL was a member of BMC before the license was signed, and the publishing cost has been carried by the institute almost from the beginning. However, after the end of the national license in 2005, the situation has been open in Finland. The main reason for KTL researchers to use BMC might have been that BMC has been a quick publishing channel and researchers have become familiar with it during the years. The impact factors of at least some BMC titles have been rising. The category, other open access journals, contains only a few articles for both years and for both institutions.

The format of the journal articles available through open access is displayed in Table 4. PDF is the most common format, but HTML is also available as an alternative in a majority of cases. The available version was in all cases the exact copy of the journal article. This might be due to the fact that we studied publishing patterns for the years 2003 and 2004 in the spring of 2005. The initial data about the articles were taken from research databases where only published articles are registered and where articles accepted for publication or submitted publications are not included.

The full text of the articles could be located using several types of web services (see Table 5). The majority of articles were found on the

Table 4. Open Access Articles According to Format.

Format	KTL, 2003	KTL, 2004	Oulu, 2003	Oulu, 2004
HTML	2			
PDF	15	15	11	8
Both	42	19	6	13
Total	59	34	17	21
Exact copy	59	34	17	21

Table 5. Article Information According to Location.

Article Information	KTL, 2003	KTL, 2004	Oulu, 2003	Oulu, 2004
Location				
Journal page	43	27	17	20
PubMed Central	4	1		
IngentaConnect	1	3		
Institutional archive	11	3		1
Total	59	34	17	21

journal's web site, and fewer were found on web sites like that of PMC. Surprisingly few articles were found on personal web pages, although some of the articles were found on institutional web sites even though many (including KTL) did not have an institutional archive at the time of the research.

The impact factor in Table 6 is taken from the ISI Journal Citation Report. Most of the articles examined (51) were published in journals with an impact factor of less than 5.0, but nearly an equal number are published in journals with an impact factor between 5.0 and 10.0. Only a few open access articles are published in journals that would be classified as a very high impact journal with an impact factor of over 10.0. The rank of the journals was studied comparing the impact factor to the impact factors of journals in the same-subject category. Since the subject categories in ISI differ a lot in terms of the number of journals published, one has to be cautious when drawing conclusions based on the rank of a journal. As shown in Table 6, 42 articles were published in journals with a rank in the interval rank 1–9, 26 in journals with a rank in the interval rank 10–19, 31 in journals with a rank in the interval rank 20–49 and 10 in journals with a rank in the interval rank over 50.

Table 6.   Open Access Articles According to ISI Impact Factor and Rank.

ISI Ranking	KTL, 2003	KTL, 2004	Oulu, 2003	Oulu, 2004
Impact factor				
Less than 5.0	25	18	7	1
5.0–10.0	23	7	9	10
Over 10.0	4	1	1	3
Total	52	26	17	14
Rank				
1–9	23	10	4	5
10–19	16	8	1	1
20–49	7	5	11	8
Over 50	6	3	1	
Total	52	26	17	14

DISCUSSION

On a general level, we can say that biomedicine is a scientific field where publishing of research results in the form of scientific articles is the prevailing standard procedure accepted by the community. Different business models, even page charges, are tolerated in biomedical sciences because of the researcher's desire to publish in the most prestigious journals. It is probably not a coincidence that a business model that collected author/article charges and provided open access is used by the publisher BMC and was applied first in the medical sciences. The large number of journals that are produced by society publishers is also a specific characteristic of the academic field. However, the dual role that society publishers sometimes play in the e-publishing debate was described above in the study conducted by Kling et al. (2004).

The recommendation from NIH to open up the content at least on a delayed basis was probably the main reason that the large proportion of society publishers put up their content in PMC. The role of NIH and PMC was important and influenced other agencies to follow suit. KTL made 35% of its open access publications available via PMC in 2003 and increased that to 45% in 2004.

We can also see a growing rate of publishing in BMC journals from both KTL and Oulu. The National Public Health Institute (KTL), like some universities in Finland, joined BMC a few years prior to the signing of the national license, and KTL's researchers have published 29 research articles during the years 2002–2005 (Nov.) in BMC. The University of Oulu published 12 research articles in BMC during the same period, the University of Kuopio 23 articles, the University of Tampere 24 articles and the University of Helsinki 59 articles. The number of published articles has risen substantially in 2005. It seems that, at least in this respect, some of the OA-titles have gained a stable or even a growing position in the market.

We argue that the most important factors in the social environments promoting open access publishing have been the political and practical initiatives made by the NIH and the NLM. The importance of the subject-based open archive PMC cannot be overlooked. The successful new business model developed by BMC and support provided to encourage use of that channel on national and institutional level have also had an impact on publishing patterns. The impact of the Finnish open access recommendations in the future is not yet clear, but the recommendations concerning the building of institutional archives in universities and research institutes seem to interest at least the libraries. Whether the policy of the organizations will be that uploading of articles by researchers to the archives is mandatory is yet to be determined. In this respect, the attitude and policy of each university and research institute as well as the research funding bodies, especially the Academy of Finland, are important. The future copyright policy of journals and the opportunities that are provided for researchers to retain the right to put up a copy of the article in an institutional archive will be crucial as we fill these archives.

The status or ranking that researchers have within the research community will continue to be based on their capacity to publish in "the right" journals, and this will continue to benefit the researchers' organizations by enhancing their reputation for quality. Therefore, it will be interesting to see if open access journals can gain the kind of reputation that will place them among the ranks of "the right" journals.

One important actor in medical research is the industry. According to Richard Smith, the former editor-in-chief of the *British Medical Journal*, approximately 70% of all published drug studies are financed by the drug industry (Järvi, 2005, p. 13). However, in this study, we will not take a stand as to whether open access is profitable to the medical industry.

Regarding the personal factors affecting publishing patterns of the researcher, we cannot draw any conclusions on the basis of the limited cases. However, we can argue that the trend in medical science that impact factors are important also prevails in open access publishing. At least in biomedical research institutes like KTL, the researchers want to publish original articles in journals that have as high an impact factor as possible. It seems that it is the main criterion for the choice of journal. This is mainly because impact factor of journals and the number of times their articles are cited are the main indicators used in the evaluation of the quality of research by those who fund research. The other reason for an author's choice might be the speed of the publishing process. In certain circumstances, speed of publishing can be even more important than the impact factor. This speaks for online only and OA-publishing. The high degree of internationalization in the field is indicated by the high number of coauthorships and the use of English as the publishing language.

Thomson ISI (Institute for Scientific Information) counts the impact factor of a few open access titles. The impact factors of BMC titles varied between 1 and 5.4 in 2004, and many of the BMC titles are competing very well with traditional journals, e.g. BMC Bioinformatics, which ranked sixth (IF 5.4) in its category (total number of titles is 51, median IF 2.1) and Arthritis Research and Therapy (IF 4.5) ranked second (total number of titles 22, median IF 1.6). Public Library of Science Biology is doing even better. Its IF is 13.8, and it is ranked eighth in the large competing category of biochemistry and molecular biology, which has a total of 261 journals and a median IF 2.3. (The impact factors were collected from ISI's Journal Citation Reports dated November 13, 2005). These examples show that in the near future, it can be expected that traditional publishers might face more challenges in getting the best articles for their journals. Researchers regard factors like visibility and speed of publishing as important to their choice of journal, and this might increase publishing in open access journals as their ranking improve, thus further enhancing these journals' standing in the academic community.

In this study, we have looked at publishing patterns regarding open access for a specific scientific field in a specific place, namely, biomedical research in Finland. We have identified incentives to publish via open access channels as they relate to environmental or external factors and in relation to personal factors. Even though the study was limited in scope, it indicated that the publishing patterns and scientific field differences are important when implementing open access initiatives and recommendations. The study also indicated that the impact of open access is important and growing and therefore deserves future research attention. As a continuation of this study, we will study more in depth the publishing patterns regarding open access in the field of medicine and other scientific fields as, for example, economics.

NOTES

1. For more information see http://www.soros.org/openaccess/index.shtml
2. The archive for physics mathematics and computer science can be found at http://arxiv.org/
3. The digital library of research papers in economics can be found at http://repec.org/
4. http://www.doaj.org/
5. http://www.ecs.soton.ac.uk/~harnad/Hypermail/Amsci/4247.html
6. The full memorandum text in English is available from http://www.minedu.fi/julkaisut/tiede/2005/tr16/tr16.pdf
7. For more information on the National Health Institute, see http://www.nih.gov/about/ and http://publicaccess.nih.gov/publicaccess_background.htm
8. http://www.pubmedcentral.gov/
9. http://www.biomedcentral.com/ and http://www.plos.org/
10. http://www.ktl.fi/portal/english/osiot/ktl/organization/aim_and_function/
11. http://www.oulu.fi/english/index.html

REFERENCES

Björk, B.-C. (2004). Open access to scientific publications – An analysis of the barriers to change? *Information Research, 9*(2).

Björk, B.-C., & Turk, Z. (2000). How scientists retrieve publications: An empirical study of how the internet is overtaking paper media. *Journal of Electronic Publishing, 6*(2).

Fry, J., & Talja, S. (2004). The cultural shaping of scholarly communication: Explaining e-journal use within and across academic fields. In: *ASIST 2004: Proceedings of the 67th ASIST Annual Meeting* (Vol. 41, pp. 20–30). Medford NJ: Information Today.

Ginsparg, P. (1996). Electronic publishing in science. Paper presented at a conference held at UNESCO HQ, Paris, 19–23 February, 1996, during session *Scientist's View of Electronic Publishing and Issues Raised*, Wednesday, 21 February, 1996. http://arXiv.org/blurb/pg96unesco.html

Guedon, J. C. (2001). In Oldenburg's long shadow: Librarians, research scientists, publishers and the control of scientific publishing. In: *ARL (American Research Libraries) Proceedings*, 138. May 2001. Membership meeting. http://www.arl.org/arl/proceedings/138/guedon.html

Hedlund, T., Gustafsson, T., & Björk, B.-C. (2004). The open access scientific journal: An empirical study. *Learned Publishing, 17*(3), 199–209.

Homan, J. M., & Watson, L. A. (2004). STM publishing meets NIH Digital Archive: Librarian service on the PubMedCentral National Advisory Committee. *Reference Services Review, 32*(1), 83–88.

Järvi, U. (2005). BMJ:n ex-päätoimittaja Richard Smith: Tieto ja tiede ovat vapaita – mutta kustannustoiminta on bisnestä [The former editor in chief of BMJ, Richard Smith: Information and science are free – But publishing is business]. *Suomen Lääkärilehti, 60*(1), 13–15.

Kling, R., & McKim, G. (1999). Scholarly communication and the continuum of electronic publishing. *Journal of the American Society for Information Science, 50*(10), 890–906.

Kling, R., & McKim, G. (2000). Not just a matter of time: Field differences and the shaping of electronic media in supporting scientific communication. *Journal of the American Society for Information Science, 51*, 1306–1320.

Kling, R., Spector, L., & McKim, G. (2002). The guild model. *Journal of Electronic Publishing, 8*(1) http://www.press.umich.edu/jep/08-01/kling.html, Retrieved 20 November 2005.

Kling, R., Spector, L. B., & Fortuna, J. (2004). The real stakes of virtual publishing: the transformation of E-Biomed into PubMed Central. *Journal of the American Society for Information Science and Technology, 55*(2), 127–148.

Lawrence, S. (2001). Free online availability substantially increases a paper's impact. *Nature*, 31 May 2001. http://www.nature.com/nature/debates/e-access/Articles/lawrence.html

Nicholas, D., & Rowlands, I. (2005). Open access publishing: The evidence from the authors. *The Journal of Academic Librarianship, 31*(3), 179–181.

Report of the CUL Task Force on Open Access Publishing: Presented to the Cornell University Library Management Team August 9, 2004 http://techreports.library.cornell.edu:8081/Dienst/UI/1.0/Display/cul.lib/2004-3

Schroter, S., Tite, L., & Smith, R. (2005). Perceptions of open access publishing: Interviews with journal authors. *British Medical Journal, 330*(7494), 756–758.

Swan, A., & Brown, S. (2004). Authors and open access publishing. *Learned publishing, 13*(3), 219–224.

Szczepanska, A. M., Bergquist, M., & Ljungberg, J. (2003). High Noon at OS Corrall – Duels and shoot outs in open source discourse. In: J. Feller, B. Fitzgerald, S. Hissam & K. Lakhani (Eds), *Perspectives on Open Source and Free Software* (pp. 431–446). Cambridge: The MIT Press.

Ursin, J. (2004). Characteristics of Finnish Medical and Engineering Research Group Work. *Jyväskylä Studies in Education, Psychology and Social Research 244.*

Whitley, R. (1984). *The intellectual and social organization of the sciences.* London: Clarendon Press.

Zerhouni, E. A. (2004a). Access to Biomedical Research Information, National Institutes of Health. Department of Health and Human Service. *National Library of Medicine, 14,* 12p. http://www.taxpayeraccess.org/docs/NIH_access_report.pdf

Zerhouni, E. A. (2004b). Information access: NIH Public Access Policy. *Science, 306*(5703), 1895.

USE OF SOCIAL SCIENTIFIC INFORMATION IN PARLIAMENTARY DISCUSSION

Kimmo Tuominen and Timo Turja

ABSTRACT

The article examines how social scientific information is discursively utilized as an argumentative and rhetorical resource at debates held during
plenary sessions at the Finnish parliament. The authors analyze the
speeches given by members of parliament by using the methodological
perspective of constructionist discourse analysis. It is found out that the
objectivity and authority of social scientific information in parliamentary
discussion can be undermined by using at least four types of arguments
stressing (1) contradictions, (2) politicization of information, (3) uncertainty of information and (4) the inability of scientific knowledge to solve
value conflicts. The speakers utilize social scientific information instrumentally to solve a certain social problem defined in advance, to provide
statistical evidence, to show a causal relationship, or to justify an individual argument. However, social scientific information can also be used
conceptually to bring larger perspectives to conversation or to reveal
unnoticed aspects of the problem under discussion. Social scientific information often penetrates the symbolic definition struggles under way, and in
this respect it alters social reality. In conclusions, the serious difficulties
built into the professional position of librarians as providers of neutral
facts are considered.

Advances in Library Administration and Organization, Volume 25, 133–154
Copyright © 2007 by Elsevier Ltd.
All rights of reproduction in any form reserved
ISSN: 0732-0671/doi:10.1016/S0732-0671(07)25007-2

133

INTRODUCTION

Within library and information science (LIS), information use is often considered a difficult topic to study (Tuominen & Savolainen, 1997). Traditionally, information use has been seen as the end point of the chain of actions proceeding from information need to information seeking and – after relevant information sources or channels have been found – to information use. According to this traditional *constructivist* viewpoint, information use is seen as a mental process in which the user builds his or her meanings and interpretations on the basis of found or received information (see, for example, Todd, 1999). This kind of approach opens up fruitful perspectives into the study of cognitive and physical information retrieval processes. However, it is not very enlightening when the objective is to understand the roles and uses of information in various and often complicated social practices (Talja, Tuominen, & Savolainen, 2005).

Tuominen and Savolainen (1997) have suggested that LIS should adopt a *social constructionist* (in short, constructionist) approach for studying information use. The constructionist approach is interested in various explicit or implicit interpretative disputes and conflicts (i.e., in situations where the meanings attached to states of things and events are not predetermined but – at least in principle – objects of constant negotiation) (Tuominen, Talja, & Savolainen, 2002). Because politics consists, above all, of disputation and negotiation about various interpretations and ways of seeing the world, debates held during plenary sessions at the Finnish parliament are a useful field of study for applying this constructionist approach. Politics involves a struggle for symbolic power, and its objective is to legitimize a certain conception of social reality (Bourdieu, 1991). Members of parliament (MPs) representing different parties compete over whose version of reality gains hegemony. In this competition, MPs use various means of argumentation and rhetoric in order to reinforce their own interpretation – and to undermine the credibility of their political opponents' interpretations. One such means is to rely on various authoritative information sources in situations where, for instance, evidence is needed to support one's own views and arguments.

In the following, we concentrate on debates held during plenary sessions at the Finnish parliament. We approach these debates and discussions from the perspective of discursive information use, applying the constructionist approach. In our view, the constructionist approach provides a novel and useful way to explore the character of parliamentary debates. The information use of MPs is a new topic of study in LIS; but the constructionist approach has been applied earlier empirically in studies of everyday life information seeking (ELIS), mainly in the context of information seeking on health issues (McKenzie, 2003; Tuominen, 2001, 2004). Our goal is to give an overall description of discursive information use during parliamentary debates and to focus on some illustrative cases in more detail.

The debates held during the plenary sessions of the Finnish parliament, and the minutes of debates during the past 100 years would be an enormous topic of study. Therefore, we have limited the scope of material used, paying attention primarily to the use of social scientific information in parliamentary discussion. As we shall show, the role of social scientific information in society and in political debate is different from the role of, say, bioscientific or medical information. Owing to the wealth of material available, our findings will – despite the rather narrow area we have addressed – remain general and preliminary.

The article is structured as follows: The next section characterizes the constructionist approach as it is applied in the present study. In the third section, we briefly discuss the features that must be taken into account when studying discursive information use. In the fourth, we describe the general nature of plenary session debates and take a closer look at discursive information use taking place in parliamentary discussion. The fifth section focuses on the use of social scientific information in parliamentary discussion, and the sixth analyzes the instrumental and conceptual uses of social scientific information. The seventh and last section presents conclusions and suggests some ways to deepen the study of discursive information use in parliamentary contexts. In this section, we also discuss how the discursive and political uses of information might endanger the neutral professional position generally adopted by librarians.

THE CONSTRUCTIONIST RESEARCH APPROACH

We justify the choice of our research approach by the fact that plenary session debates have tacit links not only to politics, but also to culture and to the modern media reality: the audiences or interlocutors of an individual speaker may for the most part exist outside the Session Hall. Thus, for instance, the methodologically disciplined perspective offered by conversation analysis for the close reading of face-to-face interaction cannot be applied as such as a tool for understanding the cultural and rhetorical nature of plenary session debates. In terms of our research problems and material, a constructionist approach with discourse analytic orientation provides a consistent and sufficiently open methodological perspective for examining the construction of social reality in the context of parliamentary discussion.

The constructionist approach examines power and the use of power from the perspective of *discursive struggles over meanings and definitions* (Potter, 1996). When one version of reality has gained an established position, proposed political actions and decisions based on this generally accepted version also begin to seem obvious and natural. Thus, political groups compete for the most credible way to make sense of an issue under discussion.

In constructionism, the object of study is not the world per se. Instead, constructionist researchers concentrate on 'worlding', because from their angle, social reality should not be understood as a completed, given fact (Pollner, 1987). Therefore, the constructionist researcher focuses on the social practices and resources used to uphold the conception of the world's stability and permanence. He or she examines the methods and tools that members of a community use for constructing an inter-subjectively shared (natural, believable and self-evident) feeling of credibility in their mutual interaction. An integrated, credible and stable interpretation of the states of things and events is not a given feature of a speech or text; instead, it is an *achievement* that is reached by constructing descriptions, reports and stories (Potter, 1996).

In order to be taken seriously, members of our culture have to resort to the cultural conventions of how to build credibility and factuality. We address these conventions of fact making in various forms, for instance, in realistic novels, scientific publications, newspaper articles and TV news broadcasts. From the constructionist perspective, we are living our daily communal lives in the atmosphere of discussion, debate, argumentation, negotiation, criticism and justification, where the primary concerns are intelligibility and legitimization of knowledge claims (Shotter, 1993). Thus, the constructionist researcher analyzes the utilization of the cultural and rhetorical resources offered by language in various contexts: during everyday-life situations and encounters, as well as in more formal environments, such as courts of law, parliaments or scientific conferences. The researcher is not interested in any decision making or other processes that may take place inside the heads of the individuals participating in the discussion; instead, the focus is on what is public and observable at the level of discourse and the associated social, political and cultural practices and contexts.

Even though the constructionist researcher may sometimes assume a critical stance on the construction processes of factual speech or text, this does not mean that we should draw a parallel between constructionism and postmodernism or between constructionism and relativism. A methodological perspective should not be confused with ideological stands or claims about the ontological nature of the reality.

INFORMATION USE AS DISCURSIVE ACTION

Tuominen and Savolainen (1997) propose that researchers studying information use should concentrate on the way speakers utilize various external information sources when they are justifying their claims and making their arguments understandable and credible. External evidence obtained from information sources other than the speaker is used especially in situations where there is no one established interpretation of the nature of certain circumstances or a certain event; i.e., there are competing versions of the same situation or issue, and the premises of these versions may not be reconcilable with each other.

Constructing the factuality and naturalness of a certain version can be a rather troublesome task. This chore is not taken up without some kind of need: participants use stabilized and neutralized interpretations for doing and accomplishing something. If a participant in a discussion succeeds in factualizing his or her interpretations, it becomes possible to use the factual version for managing various complex discursive actions, for example, for presenting or refuting claims, refusing responsibility, legitimizing interpretations, explaining motives in sensitive situations or justifying actions. Thus, building credibility is a double activity: fact making requires active efforts, and this activity also has the goal of performing some other discursive function (Potter, 1996).

Constructionist studies have shown that, as individuals, we are morally responsible for the discursive versions we have produced. We may be asked to provide additional evidence and grounds if what we produce is actually or potentially controversial in a certain conversational context. When examining people's discursive utilization of information sources, we must take into account the fact that speakers often use information discursively for managing their *accountability* (Heritage, 1984). If the speaker presents himself or herself as the originator or source of a knowledge claim, his or her moral accountability is greater than in situations where he or she appears to be doing little more than transmitting information obtained from some other source. When utilizing information discursively, the speaker can, for instance, create the impression that he or she does not know what the truth about the topic under discussion is, but experts and studies claim that it is or is not true. As the management of accountability is associated with building factuality, information is often used as rhetorical evidence in order to back up produced versions before having to face potential counterarguments and other kinds of deconstructive attacks (Potter, 1996).

How the speaker uses information discursively depends on the *cognitive authority* attached to his or her information sources in different conversational situations. Cognitive authority refers to a person or some other information source that can be placed in a certain official or unofficial category and that is considered to possess or contain knowledge of some topic (Wilson, 1983). As Patrick Wilson (1983) has subtly observed, the need for cognitive authority stems from the fact that we do not personally have the time or the resources to check more than a tiny portion of the innumerable knowledge claims that we face. Since it is extremely expensive to acquire and equip laboratories or particle accelerators, and since it is not possible for just anyone to travel in a space shuttle, we have to make distinctions between what is true and what is either a fallacy or a lie by relying on the representations produced by others. The bulk of our knowledge inevitably remains a matter of belief and a question of trusting authority:

> We mostly depend on others for ideas as well as for information about things outside the range of direct experience. Others supply us with new theoretical perspectives as well as with information ... Much of what we think of the world is what we have second hand from the others. (Wilson, 1983, p. 10)

Cognitive authorities are often representatives of some category of experts, i.e., they are persons whose institutional status and life experience imply that they have exceptional epistemological abilities in a certain field (Potter, 1996). We think in stereotypes: doctors know about diseases and their cures and bank managers can give advice about mortgages. As Wilson puts it:

"Occupational specialization provides a basis for recognition of cognitive authority" (Wilson, 1983, p. 21). Cognitive authority is not only a feature associated with individuals; a certain book, article, instrument or organization can also be seen as a warrant of knowledge (Wilson, 1983). For instance, a university or a scientific institution is often associated with collective cognitive authority that is relatively independent of the characteristics or deeds of individual researchers. The information source used in conversation may thus be a personal source (for example, a specialist in a field relevant to the theme of the conversation) or a document source (for example, a reference book, a barometer or statistics). Sometimes references to information sources are very vague: "all researchers agree on the validity of claim X" and "statistics show that alternative Y does not support our strategic goals". This kind of vagueness creates an indisputable impression of a wide consensus concerning the topic under discussion, i.e., the presented version of the states of things and events seems to be an undeniable fact. However, the user of this kind of fact-making rhetoric might have to face critical enquiries about the specific information sources that he or she has used.

The cognitive authority of an information source may not only be rhetorically buttressed but also challenged in conversational situations. When one party to a debate relies on an outside information source to make his or her version understandable and credible, the other party may well choose a discursive strategy that does not directly criticize the produced depiction of states of things and events. Instead, he or she may attempt to undermine the cognitive authority of an information source or sources that were referred to in the opponent's speech. In such a case, the interlocutor may, for instance, refer to the general unreliability of the source, to the ambiguity of the information that has been obtained from the source, and to possible vested interests or hidden agendas of, for example, the writer of a certain document.

Discursive information use takes place in various conversational situations and contexts where speakers rely on an external information source or discuss the meaning, reliability and purpose of an information source or sources. It is essential to analyze how the information derived from various information sources is discursively utilized in debates, disputes and other kinds of conversational situations. Thus, one needs to examine (1) how discursive information use is involved in construction and deconstruction processes of factual versions and (2) what kinds of interactive, ideological and cultural functions these versions have.

COGNITIVE AUTHORITIES AND INFORMATION USE IN THE FINNISH PARLIAMENT

The Finnish parliament has been unicameral since 1907. The parliamentary reform carried out in the early 20th century made it possible to grant universal and equal suffrage to all adult Finnish citizens. Two hundred elected MPs assemble each year for the annual session consisting of the spring and autumn terms. General elections are held every 4 years, following a system of proportional representation. Both political parties and electoral organizations can nominate candidates for a general election. However, it is unusual for a candidate nominated by an electoral organization to be elected to parliament; in practice all MPs are elected from lists compiled by the various political parties. In 2005, eight parties were represented in parliament.

The current Finnish political system can be characterized as consensual democracy. Its main features include proportional representation, coalition governments and effective minority protection. The principal characteristics of parliamentary work in democracies of this type are the need to cooperate, to reconcile various views and to seek common goals (Steiner, Bächtiger, Spörndli, & Steenbergen, 2004). In this democratic model – as opposed to majority parliamentarianism of the Westminster style – the parties of the government and the parties of the opposition must reconcile their views in order to carry out extensive social reforms. Political discussions in consensual parliaments are more conciliatory and more compromise seeking than in countries with a system based on majority parliamentarianism.

By nature, political speech includes presentations of alternative interpretations. Politics as an activity ceases when there are no longer any alternatives to present (Palonen, 1997). The plenary session serves as a forum where MPs can publicly speak their minds on issues, for example, the government's actions. Presentation of these alternatives is only restricted by form, not by content. According to the constitution of Finland, a MP shall "conduct himself or herself with dignity and decorum". In practice, the members' freedom of speech is only restricted by the requirement to keep to the point and to the order of the day.

Parliamentary speech is steered by the principle of claims and counterclaims. Although in the Finnish model of democracy, parties represented in parliament usually strive to find as extensive support as possible for proposals, political issues become polarized easily as disputes between opposing views. Even in consensual democracies, parliamentary discussion follows the principle of rhetoric from the Renaissance: *in utramque partem*, issues are explored from both sides. Parliamentary practices are based on speaking for and against an issue. Parliamentary discussion involves asking questions, presenting alternatives and bringing up counterarguments (Palonen, 2005).

Even though parliamentary speech is ritualistic speech, it must be understandable to voters, i.e., political language must be recognizable and accessible to many types of people coming from various social backgrounds (Pocock, 1987). Thus, parliamentary speech can never be completely monopolized by, for example, a certain profession. However, in recent years modern parliaments have shown clear signs of the separation and professionalization of language use. For example, discussions concerning the application of natural sciences have often become so specialized that only MPs with a natural scientific education have ventured to participate in them (Turja, 2003).

Since MPs represent the people, they must be able to address their own supporters. A typical feature of parliamentary discussions is that MPs often direct their speeches to an audience outside of parliament. Although an MP is explicitly answering a claim made by another MP during a discussion, the implicit targets of the argument may be elsewhere: the speech may primarily be aimed at the supporters of the member's own party or at voters in the member's constituency.

The rhetorical situation in a debate between two MPs is never fully symmetrical, because each of them may freely utilize linguistic resources of different types or may intentionally talk past each other. Owing to the asymmetric character of political discussion, there are seldom clear winners or losers in parliamentary debates. In fact, many MPs have said that speeches given in parliament have hardly any effect on other MPs. Although MPs are able to appeal to their opponents by using rhetorical means, it is difficult for them to influence each other's real decisions and, for instance, the voting behavior that is guided by party discipline. Although the impact of rhetoric on the actual decisions made by MPs always falls short, parliamentary discussion has wider social significance. Parliamentary speech gives information about the social factors underlying decisions and defines central values and norms in society. In this sense, parliaments have been considered to be the most important arenas for social debate within nations.

From the perspective of discursive information use, MPs repeatedly refer to various cognitive authorities in order to strengthen or weaken arguments. A wide scope of rhetorical resources is a typical feature of political speech. Politicians make much more varied use of diverse cognitive authorities than, for instance, researchers and scientists, whose speech is guided by the established traditions and practices of science. In political speech, for example, the authority of natural sciences can be questioned by means of moral or religious arguments.

Political speech has many features that resemble the legal speech used at courts of law: both types of discourse are based on the evaluation of evidence from opposing views. In parliamentary discussion, MPs present various types of evidence to support their own views, and give critical accounts of the weight and credibility of their opponents' arguments. Table 1 illustrates the argument types that are conventional in parliamentary discussion. Most of the examples have been taken from discussions held during plenary sessions at the Finnish parliament.

The abundance of rhetorical resources characteristic of political language gives MPs the opportunity to present varied evidence during discussions at plenary sessions. In a debate between two MPs, one can base his argument

Table 1. Supporting and Undermining the Cognitive Authority of Different Kinds of Sources of Evidence and Information During Parliamentary Discussion.

Evidence Category	An Example in Favor of the Argument	An Example Against the Argument
Personal experience and observations	*"When visiting the countryside, I have seen how people have lost their faith in the future."*	*"My fellow Representative has been traveling in the wrong areas – where I come from, people are very optimistic."*
Personal expertise	*"As an expert in education, I know how a child should be protected."*	*"The Representative's experience of raising horses does not make him competent to evaluate the raising of children."*
Historical experience	*"History teaches us that Finland should stay outside conflicts between major powers."*	*"Times have changed; the old lessons of history no longer hold."*
Statistics	*"Statistics give an objective account of the situation: the employment rate has plummeted."*	*"Statistics can be read in any which way: we now have more people in the active workforce than at any time during the past ten years."*
Popular opinion	*"People know that prices have risen after the introduction of the euro."*	*"It's easy to use opinion polls to manipulate people; in reality, prices have fallen."*
Experts' views	*"The expert heard by the committee was against the Bill."*	*"Most experts interviewed by the committee were in favor of the Bill."*
Voters' views	*"I represent farmers; therefore I'm in favor of raising the duties on food."*	*"The interests of only one occupational group cannot decide duties."*
Moral code or moral authority	*"According to the Bible, you should obey authority – for this reason, non-military service is not a good option."*	*"Christianity is a religion of peace; non-military service should therefore be supported."*
Institutions	*"Science has proven that stem cell research will help cure many diseases in future."*	*"Scientists have made mistakes before, they are making mistakes today, and they will certainly make mistakes in future."*
General concepts	*"Economic resources must be taken into account when making major social reforms."*	*"Politics cannot be made only on the terms of the economy."*
Truisms	*"Politics is managing common affairs."*	*"For many Representatives, politics seems to be only looking after one's own affairs and interests."*

on popular opinion, the other on experts' views or on a quote from literature included in the cultural canon. The general discursive structure of parliamentary speeches is multilayered: in one and the same speech, MPs may use evidence from different categories. For instance, they may refer to truisms, moral codes, popular opinion and experts' views. In the following example, an MP refers to an important historian and peace activist, to the declarations of an international organization and to the words of a religious and political leader:

> "The human mind is built to be a missile launch pad," said E. P. Thompson, the most quoted historian of the 20th century and the leading peace activist in Europe in the 1980s. He also believed that if each person behaved as though a nuclear-weapons-free Europe were a reality, it would soon be reality. In UNESCO's words "peace begins in the minds of people" and in Gandhi's words, "there is no road to peace, peace is the road". Thus, the security and defense policy is deeply seated in culture, in people's mental images and in historical memory. (Taipale, Ilkka, Parliamentary Documents, 2001, Minutes: 2650)

The openness of parliamentary discourse distinguishes it as a linguistic type of its own, which cannot be equated with more closed linguistic systems, such as the language games of various professions. MPs are unusually free to use language: the highest cognitive authority is the law, which MPs can change with their own decisions.

SOCIAL SCIENTIFIC INFORMATION AS A COGNITIVE AUTHORITY AND AS A SOURCE OF EVIDENCE IN PARLIAMENTARY DISCUSSION

The role of science in parliamentary discussion is affected by *the dilemma of stake or interest*, which can also be seen more generally underlying interpretations or versions aiming at credibility and factuality (Potter, 1996). This dilemma stems from the fact that we must appear objective and interest-free so as to be taken at our word. The importance of objectivity and credibility is heightened if the discussion includes aspects that call them into question: competing versions or doubts about the speaker's or writer's motives. The dilemma arises from the fact that, just as the speaker or writer is most committed to the produced version and its implications, he or she must appear particularly unemotional and neutral. The main question that the participants of a discussion or debate are facing is how to produce accounts that attend to interest without being labeled or stigmatized as interested.

The deconstructing of interpretations or versions is associated with the reverse side of the dilemma described above: when undermining an interpretation, the opponent strives to show that the produced version is biased or tells only part of the truth. He or she may claim that the interpretation exposes or that some external factors reveal that the originator of the version or his or her reference group has a certain vested interest in the case or that the observations made are mistaken and the speaker has an axe to grind or that there is some other subjective factor at work (Gilbert & Mulkay, 1984; Potter, 1996).

Particularly strong expectations of objectivity and neutrality are attached to scientific knowledge: researchers should seek the truth about the circumstances or events that constitute their object of study. However, the objectivity and authority of social scientific information in parliamentary discussion can be undermined by using at least four types of arguments stressing (1) contradictions, (2) politicization of information, (3) uncertainty of information and (4) the inability of scientific knowledge to solve value conflicts.

Scientific knowledge claims are often contradictory. When compared to natural sciences, utilization of social sciences and jurisprudence in decision making is more difficult because these disciplines can only rarely produce undisputed results that the scientific community would agree on with at least some degree of unanimity. Agreement may be more widespread in natural sciences, although consensus is not always reached there either (cf., Gilbert & Mulkay, 1984; Potter, 1996). Nevertheless, irrespective of the discipline, reference to conflicts between different schools of thought or paradigms is often a useful strategy for undermining and deconstructing the cognitive authority of an information source.

Scientific information becomes politicized easily, especially in the fields of social sciences and jurisprudence. It is impossible to produce value-free social and legal research information; for this reason, some researchers even see the pursuit of science as a political activity. However, if science is understood as politics, it does not have any particular cognitive authority next to other social views and institutions. From a decision makers' perspective, the authority of a certain information source can be undermined by stressing its links with certain interests. In such situations, the findings are seen as a political comment rather than an objective account of society: "such arguments are always used by feminist researchers" or "wasn't the researcher's name on the Conservatives' list in the last election?"

Social scientific information is uncertain because social development always involves unpredictable, uncontrollable and unique factors. Among the social sciences, economics may be the closest to the natural sciences, but even economists find it hard to say anything certain about economic trends. The wider the social and political dimensions of the decision are, the less certain is any scientific information that is associated with the decision.

Although social scientific information cannot solve value conflicts, the management of these conflicts is a central factor determining political decision making. One of the main roles of parliament is to act as an institution where various group interests come together. In negotiations concerning political decision making, various opposing interests always need to be reconciled. The application of research findings to society and political decision-making calls for normative assessment where issues need to be explored from an angle wider than that used in social scientific research.

When the goal is to weaken the cognitive authority of a certain information source, MPs may utilize some or all of the above-mentioned features of social scientific information. Thus, questions about the uncertainty and contradictions inherent in information about society are always topical for MPs. For instance, Finnish MPs discussed the reliability of scientific information in 1931 during the debate on the government's bill that would amend the Prohibition Act and permit the industrial manufacture and sale of beers with low alcohol content. According to the bill, persons who had registered their business appropriately would be entitled to carry out the industrial manufacture of beer with alcohol content not exceeding 2.25% by weight. The bill aroused much heated debate between the proponents and opponents of the Prohibition Act. The central bone of contention was whether or not beer with 2.25% alcohol is an intoxicant. During committee handling, MPs heard several professors' and other researchers' views on this matter, but the opinions of scientific experts were very different from one another. Therefore, some MPs finally decided to trust only their own experiences – or their own memories of drinking beer before prohibition. As MP Väinö Kivisalo put it:

> This experience of my own means more to me than counterarguments presented by any scientists. (Parliamentary Documents 1931, Minutes: 434)

Reference to one's own experience and subjective bodily reactions is a strategy that is often used to undermine experts' knowledge when discussing issues pertaining to health and illness (Tuominen, 2001; McKenzie, 2003).

When the debate concerning the exemption of beer from the scope of prohibition was most heated, MP Bror Hannes Päivänsalo, a known temperance man, asked for the floor and presented his own opinions on the role of scientific experts in decision making:

> We respect science but we must remember that we should not always *iurare in verba magistri*. If we always follow, and had followed, scientists, we would not even be able to travel on the train. For when the first train was being designed, the French Academy was asked to give its opinion on the matter; the scientists considered it impossible that the train would be able to withstand the air resistance involved. Scientists were wrong then, and they can still be wrong. We must, therefore, remember that, if one scientist says that beer is not an intoxicant, then another will come along claiming that it is an intoxicant. If one scientist is conducting studies there, another is conducting studies here; and tomorrow all findings may be overturned. (Parliamentary Documents 1931, Minutes: 459)

More than 70 years later, the contradictions and vagueness of scientific information concerning society are brought to a discussion on education policy as follows:

> The primary goal of the Government's Bill is to ensure the availability of a highly educated workforce when the population's age structure changes. Justifications derived from employment and economic policy and the consequent logic, cannot, however, be applied to making education and university policy. A comprehensive education policy cannot be created by staring at statistics, especially in a situation where the statistics are inadequate. Discussion on the length of studies is difficult because we don't have sufficient information on factors such as interrupted studies and changing of fields; owing to lack of this information, we cannot make conclusions about the real lengths of study times. The compilation of more accurate statistics is only starting. (Ojansuu, Kirsi, Parliamentary Documents 2005, Minutes)

The discussion concerns the government's bill on amending the act on universities. The bill contains a proposal to the effect that university students would no longer have the right to prolong their studies without limit; after a certain number of years, students would risk the sanction of being denied a degree. In her comment, the MP criticizes the government's bill for "staring at statistics" and emphasizes the comprehensive nature of education and university policy. The MP also stresses that the statistics utilized in the government's bill are "inadequate": the current statistical methods do not reveal the real length of studies in different disciplines. In her speech, the MP tries to undermine the cognitive authority of the statistical data used in the government's bill in the same way as MPs criticized the contradictions and vagueness of scientists' opinions in the discussion held in 1931. Notions about uncertainty, narrowness and the contradictory nature of information concerning society are cultural resources that have a long history in political debate.

INSTRUMENTAL AND CONCEPTUAL USES OF SOCIAL SCIENTIFIC INFORMATION

Social sciences alone do not steer political decisions; nevertheless, they are not without importance, as shown by the relative abundance of social scientific information in parliamentary discussions over the years. On the other hand, it has been noted in various parliaments around the world that the expert status of social scientists has weakened while the role of natural scientists has strengthened (Turja, 2003).

For elaborating our analysis of the discursive use of social scientific information, it is useful to distinguish between instrumental and conceptual utilization of information (Lampinen, 1985). Decision makers can use social scientific information instrumentally to solve a certain social problem defined in advance, to show a causal relationship, or to justify an individual argument. Reference to certain specific statistical data during a parliamentary discussion, for instance, can be seen as instrumental use of social scientific information:

> Someone here mentioned old times, but according to statistical facts 700 people a month have been left unemployed during this Government's term; this is 100 more than a year ago. (Sirnö, Minna, Parliamentary Documents 2005, Minutes)

> The only minor comment that I think should be made to the previous discussion concerns a reference made by the chairperson of the Legal Affairs Committee who claimed that the fall in the price of alcohol has led to an increase in crime. Yesterday, I had the opportunity to listen to new statistical findings made, for example, by the alcohol researchers of STAKES [the National Research and Development Centre for Welfare and Health/KT & TT]. Accordingly, it can be said that annual variations in murders, manslaughters and even in gross cases of drunken driving are so great that it is still too early to conclude whether there has really been any increase. These were the latest findings of STAKES. (Thors, Astrid, Parliamentary Documents 2005, Minutes)

> If we want to back up this case with some statistical facts, it can be said that people who start an enterprise in Finland today are actually about 35 years of age or older. (Kantalainen, Kari, Parliamentary Documents 2002, Minutes: 174)

In addition to using statistical data, instrumental utilization of the social sciences may concern the views, interpretations or research findings of individual researchers or researcher teams:

> Since it is very widely recognized here that those bishops – or many other researchers, social scientists, who in their speeches warn about the current inequality trend – are not wrong, it is the responsibility of this Parliament to look after these people, who are the weakest of all. (Ojala, Outi, Parliamentary Documents 2000, Minutes: 5273)

According to a study made by Katariina Eskola [Finnish sociologist of literature and reading habits/KT & TT], one in six books in the showcases of our bookshops in the 1970s were still about the war. The situation has hardly changed yet, if other forms of extreme violence are also included. (Taipale, Ilkka, Parliamentary Documents 2001, Minutes: 2650)

Besides being put to instrumental use, social scientific research information can also be utilized conceptually (Lampinen, 1985). In such cases, decision makers use social scientific knowledge to provide the discussion with background information for conceptualizing social phenomena and with new perspectives for handling issues. Conceptually utilized information affects the way decision makers discuss issues and pose questions, but this kind of information does not give answers to predefined problems and does not have a direct impact on the decisions made. Slowly and almost unnoticeably, social scientific information often penetrates the symbolic definition struggles under way, and in this respect it alters social reality. When social reality is altered, the changes are reflected, sooner or later, in parliamentary discussions. These discussions may even be the first indicators of coming changes.

Parliamentary discussions abound with examples where social scientific research information is utilized instrumentally. The popularity of statistical information in parliamentary discussion is evident in the fact that when the Finnish word for statistics ("tilasto" and its derivatives) is used to search parliament's document archives between the years 1999 and 2005, altogether 1,595 speeches delivered during plenary sessions are found.

Although the instances whereby social scientific information is utilized conceptually are fewer in number, they may, however, be the most interesting cases. For instance, information derived from social and human sciences can be used to expand the perspective of the parliamentary discussion:

Some researchers, such as Anthony Clare, an English professor of education, have claimed that one reason for more violent behavior, especially among boys, is the fact that fathers have disappeared from children's lives. The reason for the missing father may be a divorce, the fact that the father is not known – or, unfortunately, also the fact that too much time is spent on career-building or hobbies. (Komi, Katri, Parliamentary Documents 2002, Minutes: 1388)

Social scientific information can also be utilized conceptually in order to alter the direction, progression or "storyline" of the discussion and the underlying symbolic struggle. This happened, for instance, in 1990 when parliament discussed the proposal to reform the way in which the president of the republic is elected: According to the proposal, the previous system of election by an electoral college chosen among MPs would be replaced by a direct popular vote conducted in two phases. Some MPs saw that the acceptance of the proposal would lead to changes in the power of parliament and MPs and alter the nature of parliamentarianism in Finland. The discussion about the nature of parliamentarianism was dominated by MPs holding a degree in law and being familiar with the details of constitutional law. Some MPs who contributed to the discussion spoke about the realization of the principles of parliamentarianism in very practical terms, based on their own experiences. When the discussion had continued for a while, the floor was taken by an MP with a degree in social sciences. Her perspective of the issue of parliamentarianism differed from that of other speakers:

> Then the next question is: how can the role of Parliament be strengthened in the political system, or structure? I think it's necessary to ponder this issue because I'm somewhat tired of people talking generally and vaguely about parliamentarianism. Let's talk about the structure now. According to sociologist Anthony Giddens, structures are mental notes taken by social actors on how things should be done. Secondly, they are social practices that are reorganized in constant interaction among actors. Thirdly, they are abilities that the implementations of operational practices require. Thus, in social practice, a structure is both an instrument for renewal and its end result. This deliberation about structure means that its nature in modifying itself is exactly the task of the structure itself.

> Of course, it is much easier to adopt the values, norms and practices that are given in the political system, so to speak as essential elements of the system. It is forgotten that structures – in this case the Constitution and many other statutes and norms – are both instruments for change and its end result. During its history, the Finnish Parliament has also undergone many phases and practices. They have all had a very strong link with nothing less than the Finnish society and its culture. (Alho, Arja, Parliamentary Documents 1990, Minutes: 127)

By using Anthony Giddens's theory of structuration, the MP was able to introduce a new perspective to the field of symbolic struggle: development of the role of parliament in the political system should not be assessed only from the angle of legal norms in the constitution or from the practical perspective of laymen's experiences. The development should be seen, above all, as a historical process that has been influenced by parliament itself – and during which parliament has also been influenced by other institutions. In other words, the MP utilizes Giddensian theory – and the cognitive authority generally associated with Anthony Giddens as a renowned sociologist – to justify why parliament itself must be active in strengthening its own role. At the same time, she raises the idea that, to strengthen the role of parliament, it is not enough to talk generally about the value of parliamentarianism or about the legal norms linked with it; what one also needs is a deeper understanding of the various practices that have affected the structures of the political system. When the speech is examined as a communicatory act, it appears as an attempt to alter the nature of symbolic struggle over the meaning of parliamentarianism in a situation where the discussion centers on the role of parliament and its relation to the reform of the presidential election system.

This type of conceptual argumentation based on social scientific information is not unusual within the Finnish parliament. The main factor affecting this trend is development of the education system, although as early as the 1920s some influential MPs, such as Rafael Erich, professor of constitutional law, Georg Schauman, Director of the Helsinki University library, and J.H. Vennola, professor of economics, began systematically to utilize social scientific research in their work as MPs. Today, an increasingly high number of MPs have a degree in the social sciences; it is, therefore, natural that these MPs know how to make use of their theoretical education. Some MPs talk fluently about concepts such as life politics, risk society and the medicalization of society; in addition to citing Finnish researchers, they also refer to other cognitive authorities such as Michel Foucault, Ulrich Beck, Manuel Castells and Anthony Giddens.

Social scientific argumentation is utilized during plenary sessions especially when the speaker wants to criticize strict legalism, the emphasis resting on legal formalities (Turja, 2003). While legal discourse refers to law mainly as a normative order, social scientific discourse focuses on empirical social practices. MPs versed in social sciences often warn against "over-emphasizing the legal perspective" (Paasio, 1999, p. 52). They may consider lawyers' viewpoint alien to practice, for instance, when foreign policy "is seen from behind paragraphs of law; not from the angle of political history, social values and insight into international politics" (Kanerva, Ilkka, Parliamentary Documents 1999, Minutes: 4357).

The minutes of parliament's sessions give a peculiar picture of the social power and role of various researchers and scientific disciplines. This picture is very different from the research results that can be found by utilizing bibliometric methods and concentrating on formal communicating patterns within and between different scientific fields. Among Finnish researchers, experts in constitutional law have the most social power, because their studies have the greatest influence on discussions within parliament and on the decisions made (Turja, 2003).

Social scientific information can be used as a means of opening up new perspectives to discussion in situations where the legalistic discourse or the layman's discourse based on personal experiences strives to monopolize the conversation. When social scientific information is utilized conceptually in parliamentary discussion, it often functions as a strategic tool in the field of symbolic struggle.

CONCLUSION

Use of information from the social sciences – and more generally, from the human sciences – in parliamentary discussion is conceptual as well as instrumental. Above, we have shown that discursive information use is a very common feature in parliamentary discussion, and that MPs can make efforts to strengthen, and to undermine, the cognitive authority of information sources brought into the discussion. However, social scientific information is not the only discursive resource available to interlocutors; it is one out of numerous instruments used for constructing, backing up and challenging argumentation, interpretations and different reality versions.

On an average, social scientific information seems to have less authority in parliamentary discussion than that of, say, natural sciences or constitutional law. However, if statistical information concerning society is regarded as social scientific information, we find that such information is used constantly. MPs prefer to base their argumentation on quantitative, standardized and internationally comparative information rather than referring to the results of, for instance, individual qualitative interview surveys (Turja, 2003). On the other hand, qualitative studies are not without significance either: they can provide conceptual innovations, new perspectives to the social reality. These innovations may have direct or indirect influence on the contents of parliamentary speech.

This article is a preliminary characterization of the roles and functions of social scientific information in parliamentary discussion. Creation of a more systematic conception of the issue is left for later studies. Since the minutes of plenary sessions are available in the Finnish parliament's electronic document archives in full-text since 1994, qualitative characterizations and case studies can easily be supplemented with various quantitative studies, for instance, on the discussion contexts where MPs lean discursively on statistical data. Besides constructionist and qualitative research approaches, the material thus enables other types of methodological perspectives.

However, it should be remembered that plenary sessions constitute only one part of the parliamentary process. As a rule, the work done by MPs in committees has a bigger impact on legislation. In the committees, MPs typically hear various experts and stakeholders before drawing up a report or a statement about a government bill. The general picture that we have given could thus be supplemented by examining discursive information use in committee work. The aspects that can be considered then are, for example, how the hearings of experts during the committee's sessions affect the committee's final report or statement and the discussions that are held about the wording of these documents. In Finland, the committees' reports and statements are publicly available in parliament's electronic document archives from the year 1991 onwards. The committees' minutes and the experts' statements can be borrowed from parliament's archives as microfiches and (since 2003) as CD-ROM discs.

Our study can help librarians to understand the serious difficulties built into their own professional position. Traditionally, librarians have embraced political neutrality and objectivity as a means of acquiring a professional status. However, in extremely politicized contexts, professional neutrality is often difficult to achieve. When the quality of information is evaluated from many angles, a situation might arise where librarians and political actors have very different opinions of, for example, what printed or electronic documents should be included in the library's collections. In such situations, there is always potential for more or less serious conflicts of interests and the "neutrality" of librarians might become the object of constant renegotiations. As librarians are not able to control the myriad discursive ways in which, for example, a specific document might be used in political decision-making processes, the professional ideal of disseminating only factual and objective information might be too rigid for many kinds of library environments.

During the plenary session of parliament in 1931, an MP asked what use scientists are to parliament and the legislative process if research findings are not exact and objective and if various experts disagree with each other. Above we have shown that social scientific research information is utilized during the plenary sessions of the Finnish parliament in colorful and diverse ways. From the perspective of parliamentary discussion, social scientific research findings and the conceptual innovations produced by social scientists continue to be important argumentation resources – and are likely to remain so as well.

REFERENCES

Bourdieu, P. (1991). *Language and symbolic power*. Cambridge: Polity Press.
Gilbert, G. N., & Mulkay, M. (1984). *Opening Pandora's box: A sociological analysis of scientists' discourse*. Cambridge: Cambridge University Press.

Heritage, J. (1984). *Garfinkel and ethnomethodology*. Cambridge: Polity Press.

Lampinen, O. (1985). *Yhteiskuntatieteellisen tiedon hyödyntäminen poliittis-hallinnollisessa päätöksenteossa [Utilization of social scientific information in politico-administrative decision-making]*. Helsinki: Valtion painatuskeskus.

McKenzie, P. J. (2003). Justifying cognitive authority decisions: Discursive strategies of information seekers. *The Library Quarterly, 73*, 261–288.

Paasio, P. (1999). Demokratian pinta ja syvänteet [The surface and depths of democracy]. *Politiikka [Politics], 41*, 52.

Palonen, K. (1997). *Kootut retoriikat: Esimerkkejä politiikan luennasta [Collected rhetorics: examples of the reading of politics]*. Jyväskylä: University of Jyväskylä.

Palonen, K. (2005). Parlamentarismi retorisena politiikkana [Parliamentarianism as rhetorical politics]. In: U. Gabrielsson (Ed.), *Suomalaisen demokratian tila ja kehittämistarpeet [Status and development needs of Finnish democracy]* (pp. 25–27). Helsinki: Tutkas Retrieved August 8, 2005 from http://www.eduskunta.fi/fakta/tutkas/tutkasjulk0105.pdf

Parliamentary Documents. (1931). Minutes of Plenary Sessions 1907 – 2004.

Parliamentary Documents. (1990). Minutes of Plenary Sessions 1907 – 2004.

Parliamentary Documents. (1999). Minutes of Plenary Sessions 1907 – 2004.

Parliamentary Documents. (2000). Minutes of Plenary Sessions 1907 – 2004.

Parliamentary Documents. (2001). Minutes of Plenary Sessions 1907 – 2004.

Parliamentary Documents. (2002). Minutes of Plenary Sessions 1907 – 2004.

Parliamentary Documents. (2005). Minutes of Plenary Sessions 2005 (www.eduskunta.fi).

Pocock, J. G. A. (1987). The concept of language and the Mètier d'historien: Some consideration on the practice. In: A. R. Pagden (Ed.), *The languages of political theory in early modern Europe* (pp. 19–38). Cambridge: Cambridge University Press.

Pollner, M. (1987). *Mundane reason: Reality in everyday and sociological discourse*. Cambridge: Cambridge University Press.

Potter, J. (1996). *Representing reality: Discourse, rhetoric and social construction*. London: Sage.

Shotter, J. (1993). *Cultural politics of everyday life: Social constructionism, rhetoric and knowing of the third kind*. Buckingham: Open University Press.

Steiner, J., Bächtiger, A., Spörndli, M., & Steenbergen, M. (2004). *Deliberative politics in action: Analysing parliamentary discourse*. Cambridge: Cambridge University Press.

Talja, S., Tuominen, K., & Savolainen, R. (2005). "Isms" in information science: Constructivism, collectivism and constructionism. *Journal of Documentation, 61*, 79–101.

Todd, R. (1999). Back to our beginnings: Information utilization, Bertram Brookes and the fundamental equation of information science. *Information Processing & Management, 35*, 851–870.

Tuominen, K. (2001). *Tiedon muodostus ja virtuaalikirjaston rakentaminen: Konstruktionistinen analyysi [Knowledge formation and digital library design: A constructionist analysis]*. Academic Dissertation. Espoo, Finland: CSC – Scientific Computing.

Tuominen, K. (2004). "Whoever increases his knowledge merely increases his heartache": Moral tensions in heart surgery patients' and their spouses' talk about information seeking. Information Research 10, paper 202. Retrieved July 26, 2005, from http://informationr.net/ir/10-1/paper202.html

Tuominen, K., & Savolainen, R. (1997). Social constructionist approach to the study of information use as discursive action. In: P. Vakkari, R. Savolainen & B. Dervin (Eds), *Information seeking in context* (pp. 81–96). London: Taylor Graham.

Tuominen, K., Talja, S., & Savolainen, R. (2002). Discourse, cognition and reality: Towards a social constructionist metatheory for library and information science. In: H. Bruce, H. R. Fidel, P. Ingwersen & P. Vakkari (Eds), *Emerging frameworks and methods COLIS 4: Proceedings of the Fourth International Conference on conceptions of library and information science* (pp. 271–283). Greenwood Village: Libraries Unlimited.

Turja, T. (2003). "Mitä me niillä tiedemiehillä sitten teemme?" yhteiskuntatieteellisen tiedon käyttö eduskunnassa ["What do we then do with all those scientists?" Use of social scientific information in Parliament]. *Tieteessä tapahtuu [Developments in Science]*, 21, 9–15.

Wilson, P. (1983). *Second-hand knowledge: An inquiry into cognitive authority*. Westport, CO: Greenwood Press.

FROM MARGINAL TO EXCELLENCE: THE DEVELOPMENT OF THE RESEARCH IN INFORMATION STUDIES IN FINLAND

Ilkka Mäkinen

ABSTRACT

The article analyzes the development of the Finnish research in library and information science into its present position of high qualitative and quantitative level (in relation to the size of the research community). A number of aspects that may explain the success of the Finnish research are presented: 1) the early academic context, i.e., the establishment of the chair in LIS at the University of Tampere in 1971, 2) the new conception of LIS that emerged in Finland in the early 1980s shifting the attention from institutions into users and actions, 3) internationalization of research including publishing in peer reviewed journals, participating in international conferences, inviting foreign top-researchers into Finland, and organizing international conferences that have become institutionalized (CoLIS and ISIC), and 4) the selection of priority areas for the research effort combined with the concentration of research and doctoral education in research groups.

Advances in Library Administration and Organization, Volume 25, 155–174
Copyright © 2007 by Elsevier Ltd.
All rights of reproduction in any form reserved
ISSN: 0732-0671/doi:10.1016/S0732-0671(07)25008-4

INTRODUCTION

Research in library and information studies (LIS) in Finland has been successful, judged by almost any standard. Ragnar Audunson (2005) has concluded that, "compared to the research output and citations, the Finnish LIS community must be one of the world's most efficient". He points to the fact that compared with LIS education institutions in other Scandinavian countries, the three Finnish departments taken together have a teaching staff of about 20 people. Compared to Denmark, Norway and Sweden this is a very low figure. But their production is impressive in both quality and quantity. A recent citation analysis of the way human information behavior researchers use each other's work showed that three Finnish articles were among the dozen most cited articles published from 1993 to 2000 in six prominent journals LIS (McKechnie, Goodall, Lajoie-Paquette, & Julien, 2005). Recently, an international panel evaluating the status of research in the University of Tampere concluded its evaluation of the Department of Information Studies of the university, the largest of the three departments in this field in Finland, by saying that "the department has been established for a long time, has a tradition of excellence and is very highly regarded internationally as an excellent research-oriented department. It operates in a number of carefully chosen niche areas, produces a considerable amount of high quality publication and a good number of doctoral graduates" (Bulletin, 2004).

All this happened in a small country with barely over five million inhabitants and a geographical position above 60° northern latitude (placing it at about the same level as Alaska and Greenland). History rarely repeats itself, and successful solutions in an environment cannot always be applied elsewhere, but it still may be of general interest to learn something about the rise of the Finnish LIS research, how it started, who were the key people behind it and what was its institutional and organizational background. What follows is more a tentative analysis of the initial stages of development than a full history of LIS research in Finland. It is written by a long-time colleague of many of the persons named in the text, and, as a result, it cannot be totally without a subjective bias, but an open sectarianism has been avoided and the sources have been documented as accurately as possible and reasonable in a publication for an audience that does not read Finnish. We shall focus our attention on a number of aspects that may explain the success of Finnish research in LIS: the early academic context, the new conception of LIS that emerged in Finland in the early 1980s, the internationalization of the research and the selection of priority areas for the research effort.

THE CHAIR IN LIS AT THE UNIVERSITY OF TAMPERE 1971

It should be plain that the Finnish situation in LIS education and research differs substantially from that of the rest of Scandinavia, the nearest cultural frame of reference, whereas there are many similarities to that of the USA. While library education in Denmark, Sweden and Norway was, until the 1990s, placed in independent library schools or attached to other similar institutions below the university level, in Finland a professor's chair in library and information science was established in 1971 at the University of Tampere, and others were established later at the Åbo Akademi University in Turku (1982) and Oulu University (1988). Before that the education of librarians had been on the sub-academic level.

The establishment of the first LIS chair at university level in 1971 was a result of both the increased expectations and demands of the library field and the educational needs and research possibilities of the technical information services. It is probable that, without the backing of information science in business, politics and academia and their appreciation of the promise of information science, the chair would not have come as soon as it did. The establishment of the LIS chair was realized in a period of qualitative and quantitative growth in Finnish academic life. New universities were established, and old ones grew fast. The support system for research underwent great changes, and new resources were poured into science, but, at the same time, the environment became more competitive than before. There was competition both for the resources offered by the newly organized Finnish Academy that channeled funds for research and for funds for new positions from the Ministry of Education. To get new positions funded by the Ministry of Education through the state budget was to a large extent a political process. The fact that the Faculty of Social Sciences of the University of Tampere applied for the chair in library and information science was itself a result of negotiations. It was positive for the faculty to get new chairs and other permanent positions, but why just library and information science? Oili Kokkonen, who was then a lecturer in librarianship of the sub-academic library education program and who was one of the people who was active in the lobbying process, believes that the dean of the Faculty, professor in political science Pertti Pesonen, strongly influenced the decision to apply for the chair in library and information science: "He had furthermore brought fresh knowledge from the USA about library and information science as an academic discipline. It is probable that just the dean's influence changed the title of the chair from library science into library and information science" (Kokkonen, 1988, p. 85; see also Iivonen, 1986 and Okko, 1986).

Once the chair and the department were established, the professor and other staff had to play primarily according to the rules of the academic world rather than those established according to the vocational interests. In the academic world, it is the academic merits that count and success in research is one of the most important of these merits, but it took years before a functioning research community in LIS matured.

One of the important decisions on the path towards the present day conception of LIS in Finland was the nomination of the first professor for the chair in LIS in Tampere. The process took many years, and the result was a shock for library and information science students and part of the staff, who preferred a candidate whose scientific merits in the field of academic library research were superior, someone who had studied the use and other aspects of public libraries in a sociological framework and who had even earned his doctorate with a dissertation on public library use. But the person who was finally nominated in 1977, Marjatta Okko, was a doctor in geology who had not published much research on any aspect of library and information science, but who had a distinguished career in information services and had participated in the construction of educational programs for information specialists. To an extent, her nomination was a political affair. At that time, university professors were nominated by the President of the Republic, and apparently there was much lobbying behind the scenes. Both right wing science activists and representatives from the academic library world preferred the solid library and information specialist over a full-blooded sociologist (about the controversies around nominating the professor in LIS, see Mäkinen, 2002). The appointment of Prof. Okko was difficult to accept for part of the department's staff and students, many of whom were political leftists. The paradigmatic controversies raged in the department years after the nomination, and they continued even after Okko's retirement. But, paradoxically, it was Marjatta Okko who in many ways opened the way into a new phase of Finnish LIS research.

During the 1970s and the 1980s, lots of energy was expended in discussing the dual character of the library science and information science field. An extra nuance was added to the discussion by the confrontation of the western and socialist conceptions of science. Even if Finland was firmly a western country, many Finnish researchers wanted to show at least a polite interest to the theory building of the Soviet Union and other socialist countries. Marxist and antipositivist conceptions of scientific research were common among the academic people in Finland from the 1960s until the 1980s. Library science in the Soviet Union was hopelessly Marxist-Leninist and could never be used as a model for the Finnish research. Information science in the Soviet Union, on the other hand, was kept relatively free from party politics. Because of this dichotomy, a socialist model of a unified library and information science was not easily constructed. Library and information science in the east was as institution-centered as in the west or more (Mäkinen, 2002).

BEGINNINGS OF RESEARCH

Professor Okko worked hard to acquire resources for the LIS Department and was successful. New positions with research responsibilities were established, and some projects got funding. During her years, two associate professor's positions and a researchers position were established (Okko, 1989). Today, there are four full professors in the department.

According to Pertti Vakkari (1986b, pp. 103–104), Finnish LIS research left the zero point behind in 1977 when the first post-graduate academic degree was awarded by the department. The degree given was the peculiar Finnish degree of Licentiate that lies between the M.A. and the doctor's degree, and the first was given to Mariam Ginman, who today is a professor at the Department of Information Management of the Åbo Akademi University, the Swedish-language university in Turku. Her Licentiate's thesis was a bibliometric analysis of the literature on alkaline pulp production (Ginman, 1977). Nevertheless, the effective start of the LIS research in Finland took place in the early 1980s when the first doctoral thesis, again Mariam Ginman's (1983), was publicly defended at the Department. Her dissertation, a study of information seeking behavior by journalists, was written in her mother tongue Swedish, which is the other official language of Finland.

During Marjatta Okko's early years in office, there followed a series of innovations that by no means can be attributed only to her but as much to ideas and discussions of students, younger staff and interested professional people. It is important in any case that she eagerly took the challenge and backed the initiatives. Among these new things were the establishment of the national scholarly association, the Finnish Association for Library and Information Science (*Kirjastotieteen ja informatiikan yhdistys*, today: *Informaatiotutkimuksen yhdistys*, the Finnish Association for Information Studies) in 1979 and the start of the national scientific journal in the field, *Kirjastotiede ja informatiikka* (Library and Information Science, today *Informaatiotutkimus*, Information Studies) in 1981. Prof. Okko became the first chair and the first editor of these institutions. The importance of the association and the journal cannot be overemphasized as the basic platforms of the early advancement of the Finnish research in LIS on the national level.

THE NEW CONCEPTION OF LIS

Even taking into account historical and structural features, it is evident that a large part of the success of Finnish research in LIS is a result of the long-time influence of a couple of individuals and their interaction with their environment on various levels. Both Kalervo Järvelin and Pertti Vakkari worked at the Department of Information Studies in Tampere before Marjatta Okko, and they both were among those who rallied against her nomination. But once she was nominated and began her work at the department, they cooperated with her. Järvelin and Vakkari who started to study together in 1972 formed an innovative duo quite early that has produced many important scientific and organizational ideas over the years, even if their profiles as researchers have differed. While Järvelin's strongest area has always been information retrieval, Vakkari's interests have been more varied, ranging from reading and user studies to the nature and history of LIS, and more recently interactive information retrieval. But the field where their interests have been united and which was revolutionary in the Finnish LIS research in the early 1980s was the study of information needs, information seeking behavior and use. In that area, they developed some theoretical ideas that still have influence both in Finland and internationally. They even anticipated some great paradigmatic shifts in the overall theoretical approach of LIS, such as Dervin and Nilan's (1986) revolution of perspective in information seeking research.

Some of their appearances together have had the character of manifestos. Already in one of their first joint academic publications, the title of which in English translation is "On the research of information needs and library use" (1981), they laid the foundation of their future work in defining the research objectives of LIS in a new way, freeing it from the direct dependency of libraries as institutions. We could cite long passages from the book, especially from the epilogue that they wrote together and titled challengingly "Toward a wider approach in the study of information needs and seeking," and acknowledge the straightforwardness and freshness of the ideas, long before they became common goods in the field of LIS:

> In the study of information needs and library use, there is often on top a pragmatic motive to seek for knowledge for developing different information service systems. That

has not led to any extensive advancement of the research in the field. Lack of advancement is evident. We can even speak of stagnation. In order to have progress, the goals of the research have to be set over the boundaries of a certain group of channels or services. We have to strive for fruitful and interesting approaches. We cannot, then, take as our point of departure institutions performing certain tasks and the presumption that they will develop. Instead, we should focus our research on the human action that serves as the basis for the use of these institutions. To move forward, we need to find new, fruitful perspectives and questions. We suggest that we should study information needs and library use from the point of view of information needs and library users.

We believe that research must start with the premise that information need, the acquisition of information, and its use should be studied as it appears in each composite system of human action, for example from work. If we pursue this tactic, we should begin by analyzing actions, where information needs arrive, and the nature of those information needs rather than the use of channels for information. Only in this way can one fruitfully think about how and from where information is acquired. [...]

We think that library and information science cannot be limited only to study library and information service institutions. The study of information seeking and needs in itself presupposes a wider approach. In another case, we cannot get a sensible picture of what affects the functioning and use of the institution. More generally, this would mean that we could not form any clear understanding of the general phenomena that incur information needs and seeking. [...] If LIS is understood only as a study of libraries and information service institutions, it would only be a set of technical skills for running these institutions. Even as such it would be incomplete, because it could not give sufficient tools for developing the work of these institutions. There is a need to depart consciously from the boundaries of library and information institutions and widén the perspective even outside them. (Järvelin & Vakkari, 1981, pp. 125–127)

It is clear that Järvelin and Vakkari did not pull their ideas out of the air. Their shift in perspective was in many ways a result of extensive reading of international research literature. It is interesting from the point of view of the history of LIS that some central sources that they cite were written in the German language by writers such as G. Wersig, W. Kunz and H. Rittel. But even with foreign sources, Järvelin's and Vakkari's view on LIS was a revolutionary shift in perspective that the Marxist-oriented and/or institution-centered Finnish LIS community had difficulty swallowing. But their approach also was, as they said, a conscious departure from the institution-centered paradigm. It was interpreted as if they turned their backs on the professional field of libraries and information services, which has caused some domestic resistance to their ideas that has followed their careers. It is possible that the existence of Finnish LIS education and research on the university level saved the new ideas from being crushed by vocational interests. Järvelin and Vakkari formulated their theoretical view as part of an academic dialogue, and that is the way it has been understood in the academic world. On the other hand, those who had different views did not value the scientific character of research less. They just had a different conception of LIS.

As the national scholarly journal in the field got on its feet, Järvelin and Vakkari started to develop their ideas further and published, now and then, new formulations and clarifications of their initial standpoint. In 1982, they again stressed that, because library and information services have no a priori value, the basis for evaluating and planning them must be sought in the actions that they serve (Järvelin & Vakkari, 1982).

Some of their theoretical formulations have influenced later researchers years after they were published; for example, Vakkari's idea of the "contact function" as a characteristic of library activity (Vakkari, 1987b) has been cited many times in studies concerning libraries and Järvelin's "two simple classifications for research on information seeking" (Järvelin, 1987) have inspired researchers of task-based information usage (e.g. Byström, 1999, pp. 44–45). The final formulation of their view on the nature of the field, "Library and information science – a science of information seeking", was published in 1988 (Järvelin & Vakkari, 1988a; see also Järvelin, 1989, where he presents, among other innovations, Dervin & Nilan, 1986 for the Finnish audience).

The discussion in Finland about the nature of LIS raged high during the 1980s, inspiring Järvelin and Vakkari to start digging into the history of LIS as a discipline and study the distribution of volumes of research in different subfields of the field. Vakkari started this line of research by writing a history of Finnish LIS research (Vakkari, 1985; Vakkari, 1986a). Järvelin and Vakkari then proceeded by developing jointly a preliminary analysis of the distribution of research in international LIS journals (Järvelin & Vakkari, 1988b) and in domestic research literature (Järvelin & Vakkari, 1989) In these articles they refined the methodology that has since been successfully used for further investigations (e.g. Aarek, Järvelin, Kajberg, Klasson, & Vakkari, 1992).

Järvelin's and Vakkari's conception of the nature of LIS has not gone unopposed in Finland. One of the most tenacious opponents of the "LIS as science of information seeking" paradigm has been Dr. Vesa Suominen. The most elaborate presentation of his views is his dissertation "Filling empty space. A treatise on semiotic structures in information retrieval, in documentation, and in related research" of 1997 (Suominen, 1997). During his career, he has defended a conception of library science as a more concretely library-oriented research field with an emphasis on documents and contents (as opposed to users) seen from an hermeneutical and semiotic angle. In a recent heated debate on the nature of LIS education and research in Finland

and its alleged alienation from the (public) library world, he even stated that, "as for me, I would claim that the greatest disaster that has met Finnish library education is just 'the science of information seeking,'" where he directly refers to Järvelin's and Vakkari's manifesto of 1988 (Suominen, 2004; see also Suominen, 1986; Suominen, 2002). Suominen's critique of "userism" in LIS has also been noted internationally (e.g. Hjørland, 2002; Noruzi, 2004), although he has published only sparingly in more well known languages.

The conception of LIS proposed by Järvelin and Vakkari got its final symbolic crowning when the official Finnish name of the department and the discipline was changed to Information Studies in 1994 (the English name had already been changed 1991 because that could be done without the blessing of the university administration). Another symbolic step was the transfer of the Tampere Department in 2001 from the Faculty of Social Sciences into the newly established Faculty of Information Sciences.

INTERNATIONALIZATION

Taking part in the international academic discussion, publishing in prestige journals and participating in scholarly conferences has characterized Finnish research in LIS since the early 1980s, but the readiness to follow this path may have older roots. There are two roots for the internationalization of LIS research in Finland. The first relates to the people involved in the information service or documentation activities who got their education in the USA during the 1940s and 1950s. The second is the desire of such researchers as Järvelin, Repo, Vakkari, etc. to earn academic recognition in the international arena, a natural part of academic life but one that was new to the LIS tradition in Finland in the early 1980s.

After the Second World War, a number of people who took central positions in Finnish academic libraries and technical documentation/ information services acquired at least part of their education in the USA (about the introduction of documentation into Finland, see Mäkinen, 2004). Many among them had been able to study in the USA thanks to the Fulbright program. Upon their return to Finland, they maintained contact with the international documentation and technical library community and participated in the work of such organizations as FID and IATUL. The first Finn to engage in research in information needs and information seeking behavior, Elin Törnudd, was one of them. She participated in a number of important conferences in the 1950s (Törnudd, 1955) and published her study of the use of information by Scandinavian scientists and engineers in the proceedings of the International Conference on Scientific Information that was held in Washington in 1958 (Törnudd, 1959). However, she was not able to pursue her research career because of her work as library director, but she continued to have influence on the plans to develop the education program for information specialists during the 1960s.

Some of the acting professors of LIS in Tampere – it took six years to fill the post permanently – also had acquired part of their education in the USA. For instance, Sinikka Koskiala (acting professor 1972–1973) earned her PhD at the University of Maryland in 1980 (Koskiala, 1980), and Ritva Sievänen-Allen (acting professor 1972–1977) received an M.A. in LIS from the University of California, Berkeley, in 1962. The first years of the department were nevertheless too chaotic with the immense flow of students and too few staff to support the development of a research program (see Tammekann, 1987).

The most important among these Fulbright veterans was, however, Marjatta Okko (1925–1995), the first permanent professor in LIS in Tampere. She valued international contacts, both as a receiving and giving partner, and urged younger researchers to publish in international journals (e.g. Okko, 1982, 1983). She herself took part in the work of the Section on Library Theory and Research of IFLA, where her successor, Pertti Vakkari, also was active. Vakkari presented one of his first international papers in a seminar on reading research organized under the auspices of the Section in Moscow in 1984 (Vakkari, 1987a).

The scholarly cooperation with Soviet Union and other socialist countries was officially endorsed and well funded during the 1970s and the 1980s. In that sense, it provided an option for Finnish researchers to step onto the international arena, but this cooperation never became as informal and extensive as did cooperation with the more open communities in the west. Some researchers in information science took part in seminars organized jointly by Finnish and Soviet scholarly bodies, e.g. Tuula Laaksovirta (1984) participated in a Finnish-Soviet seminar on communications research. Her study was in no way Marxist as were many other Finnish contributions in sociology and communication science.

Among the young researchers in Tampere, Kalervo Järvelin gained some experience in international publishing from his studies in computer science (for example Kangassalo, Jaakkola, Järvelin, Lehtonen, & Niemi, 1982; Järvelin, 1982), but his first modest contribution that can be classified as an international publication was clearly in the domain of LIS (Järvelin, 1981). His next, and decisive, international contributions were done together with

Aatto J. Repo (Järvelin & Repo, 1982, 1984a, 1984b), one of the pioneers of information science research in Finland, who has not let himself be tied in a permanent position in the academic world (except the honorary title of "docent" at the Tampere Department). He is well known internationally for his studies in the value of information. Pertti Vakkari soon also began his international publishing career with his *historia literaria* studies (Vakkari, 1986a).

The Nordic dimension has always been an option in publishing for Finnish researchers. Publishing in Swedish opens the way to the Nordic LIS community. This choice has been even more natural for those Finns who have the Swedish language as their mother tongue, such as Mariam Ginman. She has published extensively in Swedish both in Finland and in other Nordic countries, but she has also produced an extensive list of publications in English as well (see http://www.abo.fi/fak/esf/bii/mginman/publications.htm).

However, research in LIS has not been confined to LIS departments. There are a number of successful researchers who have no relationship with domestic LIS departments. Among them are, for example, the first Finnish IR researcher who has published in Information Processing and Management, Pirkko Pietiläinen (Pietiläinen, 1982, 1983) and the former chief librarian of the Helsinki University Library, Esko Häkli, a well known scholar in book and library history (for example, Häkli, 1983). Some researchers from Finland such as Leena Siitonen (Siitonen, 1984) have pursued their careers abroad.

Internationalization as practiced within the Finnish LIS community has not been unique in Scandinavia. For example, Danish LIS education and research has always had active international contacts. But even the Danes (with the exception of Peter Ingwersen and Irene Wormell) were not as visible in the 1980s and 1990s in rapidly growing areas of LIS like information retrieval and information seeking, which were just the areas where the Finns were earning their laurels.

Another aspect of the strategy of internationalization of research was to invite internationally recognized researchers to Tampere and Finland and to arrange summer schools and doctoral workshops where their talents could be made to benefit Finnish doctoral students. A number of such scholars have visited Finnish LIS departments, ranging from Marcia Bates and Nicholas Belkin, via Brenda Dervin to Paul Solomon, Diane Sonnenwald, and Tom Wilson, to name only a few. Part of the visits have been funded by the Fulbright program and part by the funds received from the Finnish Academy.

SETTING THE PRIORITY AREAS

There were during the 1970s attempts to plan rationally the direction of research in the small Finnish LIS community. The Tampere Department accepted two research programs in 1973 and 1976. Unfortunately, they were, according to Vakkari (1985, p. 18), too broad and unfocused to provide effective help in directing research, though the research program of 1976 was especially helpful in the self-analysis of the discipline (Vakkari, 1986b, pp. 103–104). In any case, the ameliorating resources for research during the 1980s started to bring results, dissertations and publications, but it was felt that decisions should be made concerning focusing of the research effort. Steps towards that end were taken in 1989, and it may not be a surprise that they more or less followed the principles set by Järvelin's and Vakkari's conception of LIS, given that Pertti Vakkari had become professor at Tampere after Marjatta Okko retired. In any case, decisions were made after discussions among the staff of the department. During that time the more serious internal controversies concerning the conception of the discipline had been resolved at the department. Many of the staff who had differing opinions had left or reorientated their approach. Some lines of research were discontinued because the people who represented them could not find a permanent position at the department. Examples of this were the research in the dissemination of scientific knowledge initiated by Tuula H. Laaksovirta (Laaksovirta, 1986) and the study of bibliography (Wiman, 1982).

Since the early 1990s, there have been three priority areas for research. Two of them, information retrieval and information seeking, have been more or less stable, although their relationship has been defined slightly differently through the years. The third area, information management or the management of information resources, has been more volatile. There was a period during the 1990s when the focus of the area shifted towards knowledge work, but some years later the original title was brought back. Information management has through the years been the most problematic area among the research priorities. There has not been a permanent professor's chair in that field and no field can develop favorably without active persons. Maija-Leena Huotari, who, after earning her doctorate at Sheffield University (1995), supervised the information management field for a long time in the Department at Tampere, is now professor at the LIS Department of the Oulu University. Today, the most strongly developing area of information management at the department is records management and archival studies, and the first dissertation in that area, written by Marjo Rita Valtonen, was accepted in November 2005 (Valtonen, 2005).

Within the framework provided by the priority areas, research and doctoral education has since the 1990s been organized into research groups, something that is a novelty outside the natural sciences. The present research groups in the priority areas are FIRE (the Finnish Information Retrieval Expert Group), REGIM (the Research Group on Information Management) and REGIS (the Research Group on Information Seeking), and the newest one among the research groups, IRiX (the Research Group on Information Retrieval in Context). The most productive groups so far have been FIRE and REGIS. FIRE has been an effective environment that has produced many mature IR scholars who are still working at the department, such as Jaana Kekäläinen, now professor, Eero Sormunen, professor and chair of the department, and Ari Pirkola. One of the most fruitful innovations in FIRE was the setting up of an information retrieval laboratory in the mid-1990s. Both FIRE and REGIS have inspired foreign doctoral students and established researchers from outside Finland to come to work in Tampere.

The setting of priority areas for teaching and research has created a strategic advantage for the Tampere Department, both compared with LIS departments in other countries and with departments in other disciplines in the domestic academic world. The priority areas and research groups are, however, not a monolithic structure that automatically produces results. Research is, in the end, always done by individuals even when those individuals are working in groups. The priority areas and research groups have survived because there have been people, leading personalities and doctoral students who are interested in working with them, or have faded away as happened with the priority area referred to as "knowledge work," when its leading personality left the department. In addition, there has been room for activity outside the priority areas. For example, there exists a research group in library history, and four dissertations in that area have been accepted since 1997.

Focusing on strengths has taken place even at the Department of Information Management of the Åbo Akademi University, where the research profile is leaning more towards information management and information seeking. The Oulu Department has a more eclectic profile because its professor's chair has only recently been filled permanently. Interest in bibliometrics-informetrics has been shared by both Åbo and Oulu Departments. But even though the Tampere Department is the oldest and largest among the LIS departments in Finland, the variety of the authors of this volume shows that the other two departments have also produced competent scholars.

CONFERENCES AS BRANDS

There is one aspect that is especially helpful in explaining the international visibility of Finnish and, especially, Tampere research in LIS. It is the innovativeness exhibited by this community in designing conferences that have become brands. There are tens of conferences even in the field of LIS, but only a few of them have acquired the status of an institution. CoLIS (Conceptions of Library and Information Science) and ISIC (Information Seeking in Context) conferences are among this small group. The origins of the first CoLIS conference in Tampere 1991 (Vakkari & Cronin, 1992) lay in the internal Finnish and international debates on the nature of LIS. The conference was a symbolic celebration of the 20th anniversary of the chair in LIS at Tampere University. The positive response to the conference proved that there was a need for a forum for discussions on the historical, theoretical and conceptual foundations of LIS. As a result, the tradition has continued, and the fifth CoLIS conference was organized in Glasgow in June 2005.

In the beginning of the 1990s, when information seeking was chosen as one of the priority areas of the Tampere Department, it became clear that there were not many conferences devoted to this important area of LIS. As stated in the Foreword of the ISIC conference proceedings, "for many reasons it was appropriate to choose information seeking and use as the topic of the conference, not least because this emphasis is among the priority areas in the research profile of the Department of Information Studies in Tampere" (Vakkari, Savolainen, & Dervin, 1997, pp. 7–9). Again, an appropriate annual celebration was appropriately at hand, this time the 50th anniversary of Finnish education in librarianship, celebrated in 1996. The theme of the conference was chosen because it represented one of the features of the discipline that in Tampere was considered to be central to the study of information seeking, namely the context. The conference also brought into the international limelight Reijo Savolainen, another father figure within Finnish information seeking studies and co-chair of the REGIS research group, along with a group of young Finnish LIS scholars, such as, Sanna Talja and Kimmo Tuominen, the initiators of social constructionist and discourse analysis types of research in the Finnish LIS community, and Katriina Byström, who has continued the task-based information seeking research initiated by Kalervo Järvelin and Pertti Vakkari. ISIC has since been followed by a series of conferences under the same title, the fifth of which was held in 2005 in Dublin.

In addition, the hosting of a third conference called the SIGIR 2002 Conference brought to Tampere the elite of the information retrieval research world and confirmed the reputation that IR research in Tampere had acquired.

CONCLUSION

There is never only one explanation for long-range developments, and we cannot know if other premises would have produced results that were different but equally successful outcomes. Even good intentions often bring disastrous results. There are no procedures that guarantee success, even if one applies them diligently. But still, there may be a lesson to be learned in the development of Finnish LIS research. If you seek academic recognition, you have to work according to the rules of the academic world. The early establishment of the chair in LIS at the University of Tampere created by itself an opportunity for the inclusion of the Finnish LIS community as independent players into the larger academic community. This process has been much more complicated in other Nordic countries where other organizational models were used (though they are progressing well today). But even if one is accepted, in principle, by the academic community, it is not enough to build an original theoretical base for your discipline. At first, the Finnish LIS community was dependent on the methodological and theoretical constructions of neighboring social sciences, especially sociology and communication studies. In that setting, LIS was regarded as a receiving partner with nothing of its own to contribute except the institution that it studied and served. The new conception that emerged in Tampere since the early 1980s freed LIS from its subordinate position and brought fresh theoretical thinking into the field. The next step was to take part in the international academic discussion in LIS using all available platforms, to include scholarly journals, conferences and international scholarly organs. That meant using English as the discipline's linguistic medium, learning the academic forms of writing and accepting the refereeing process as a measure of the quality of one's accomplishments. One has to have personal ambition to engage in an activity like this, but it is difficult to jump onto the international arena without a working academic community at home. In this sense, a domestic journal and a scholarly society were important as academic nursery gardens, as well as in creating a terminology in one's own language.

Another option taken in Tampere, the setting of priority areas for research and teaching, can be seen as a way to strengthen the home base with a strategic vision. You have to use the human and material resources available in the best possible way to produce results. This process necessarily means selection and, possibly, weeding, and cannot be accomplished without some measure of individual frustration. But once the commitment to this path is made, the concentration on carefully chosen niche areas may prove successful. The organization of research and doctoral education in research groups focusing on the priority areas has proven its value, helping to integrate and socialize new researchers effectively into the academic world.

The final step in acquiring international visibility has been the inventiveness of the community in creating and arranging conferences. The CoLIS and ISIC conferences gathered together large numbers of high-quality researchers in Finland, in general, and in Tampere in particular and imprinted the name of the place, the department and the conference as brands permanently in the mind of the international LIS community, and these brands will keep on selling the product so long as their "owners" show the kind of ambition, professionalism and vision that led to starting them.

As it was stated in the beginning of the article, the research of the Finnish LIS community can be judged successful, measured by the tools available in the academic world. People in the field are working hard to maintain this position. We may be fairly confident that progress in the core areas, information retrieval, information seeking, information management and records management, shall continue. Problems may arise from the coming generation shift when over the next ten years those who established the field leave academia and from the structural changes in the Finnish universities where small disciplines live a dangerous life. But there is nothing new in these threats. We just have to lobby harder, compete harder and work harder.

REFERENCES

Aarek, H., Järvelin, K., Kajberg, L., Klasson, M., & Vakkari, P. (1992). Library and information science research in the Nordic countries 1965–89. In: P. Vakkari & B. Cronin (Eds), *Conceptions of library and Information Science. Historical, empirical and theoretical perspectives.* Proceedings of the International Conference held for the celebration of 20th Anniversary of the Department of Information Studies, University of Tampere, Finland, 26–28 August 1991 (pp. 28–49). London & Los Angeles: Taylor Graham.

Audunson, R. (2005). *Library and information science education: Is there a Nordic perspective.* Paper at World Library and Information Congress: 71st IFLA General Conference and Council, August 14th–18th 2005, Oslo, Norway. Available at: www.ifla.org/IV/ifla71/papers/061e-Audunson.pdf

Bulletin (2004). Research evaluation: Department of Information Studies. Available at: http://www.info.uta.fi/tutkimus/evaluation2004/Research_evaluation.pdf

Byström, K. (1999). *Task complexity, information types and information sources. Examination of relationships.* University of Tampere, Tampere. Acta Universitatis Tamperensis 688.

Dervin, B., & Nilan, M. (1986). Information needs and uses. In: M. Williams (Ed.), *Annual Review of Information Science and Technology* (Vol. 21, pp. 3–33). New York: Knowledge Industries.

Ginman, M. (1977). *Bibliometrisk analys av alkalisk massframställning.* [Bibliometric analysis of the production of alcalic pulp.] Unpublished Licentiate's Thesis, University of Tampere, Tampere.

Ginman, M. (1983). En modell för journalisternas informationsanskaffning. Relationen mellan informationsflöde och -substans inom olika informationsprocesser i samhället. [A model for the seeking of information by journalists.] University of Tampere, Tampere. Acta Universitatis Tamperensis, Ser A, Vol. 154.

Häkli, E. (1983). Finnland. In: *Bibliotheken der nordischen Länder in Vergangenheit und Gegenwart* (pp. 227–283). Wiesbaden: Harrassowitz.

Hjørland, B. (2002). Domain analysis in information science. Eleven approaches – Traditional as well as innovative. *Journal of Documentation, 58,* 422–462.

Iivonen, M. (1986). Kirjasto-opista kirjastotieteeksi ja informatiikaksi [From subacademic to library and information science]. *Kirjastotiede ja informatiikka, 5,* 83–87.

Järvelin, K. (1981). Report on workshop 1: Models and theories of users' needs. In: I. Friberg (Ed.), *Proceedings of the IRFIS 4 (International Research Forum in Information Science) Conference,* September 14–16, 1981, Borås, Sweden (pp. 228–232). Borås: Högskolan i Borås. Biblioteks- och Informationsvetenskapliga Studier 1.

Järvelin, K. (1982). Finding functional dependencies for intermediate relations of relational algebra expressions. In: H. Kangassalo (Ed.), *First Scandinavian Research Seminar on Information Modelling and Data Base Management,* University of Tampere, Tampere (pp. 407–442). Acta Universitatis Tamperensis, Ser. B, Vol. 17.

Järvelin, K. (1987). Kaksi yksinkertaista jäsennystä tiedon hankinnan tutkimista varten [Two simple classifications for research on information seeking]. *Kirjastotiede ja Informatiikka, 6,* 18–24.

Järvelin, K. (1989). Tiedontarpeet ja hankinta tutkimuskohteena [Information needs and seeking as object of research]. *Kirjastotiede ja Informatiikka, 8,* 55–59.

Järvelin, K., & Repo, A. J. (1982). Knowledge work augmentation and human information seeking. *Journal of Information Science, 5,* 79–86.

Järvelin, K., & Repo, A. J. (1984a). A taxonomy of knowledge work support tools. In: B. Flood, J. Witiak & T. H. Hogan (Eds), *Challenges to an Information Society.* Proc. 47th ASIS Annual Meeting, Vol. 21, Philadelphia, PA, Oct. 21–25, 1984 (pp. 59–62). White Plains, NY: Knowledge Industry Publications, 1984.

Järvelin, K., & Repo, A. J. (1984b). On the impacts of modern information technology on information needs and seeking: A framework. In: H. J. Dietschmann (Ed.), *Representation and exchange of knowledge as a basis of information processes.* Proc. IRFIS 5 Conference, Heidelberg, Germany, September 5–7, 1983 (pp. 207–230). Amsterdam: North-Holland.

Järvelin, K., & Vakkari, P. (1981). *Tiedontarpeiden ja kirjastonkäytön tutkimisesta. Kaksi tutkielmaa* [On the research of information needs and library use. Two studies]. Helsinki: Kirjastopalvelu.

Järvelin, K., & Vakkari, P. (1982). Kirjastotieteen ja informatiikan tutkimuskohteesta: Alustava näkökulma [On the object of library and information science: A preliminary view]. *Kirjastotiede ja Informatiikka, 1*, 67–72.

Järvelin, K., & Vakkari, P. (1988a). Kirjastotiede ja informatiikka – tiedon hankinnan tiede [Library and information science – A science of information seeking]. *Kirjastotiede ja Informatiikka, 7*, 18–32.

Järvelin, K., & Vakkari, P. (1988b). Kirjastotieteen ja informatiikan tutkimusartikkelien sisällönanalyysi [A content analysis of research articles in library and information science]. *Kirjastotiede ja Informatiikka, 7*, 112–132.

Järvelin, K., & Vakkari, P. (1989). Suomalaisen kirjastotieteen ja informatiikan tutkimuksen 1970–1988 sisällönanalyysi [A content analysis of Finnish library and information science research 1970–1988]. In: M. Viljakainen-Tiittanen (Ed.), *Kirjastotiedettä ja informatiikkaa tekemässä [Doing library and information science]* (pp. 83–124). Vammala: Kirjastotieteen ja informatiikan yhdistys.

Kangassalo, H., Jaakkola, H., Järvelin, K., Lehtonen, T., & Niemi, T. (1982). System D – An integrated tool for systems design, implementation and data base management. In: H. J. Schneider & A. I. Wassermann (Eds), *Automated tools for information systems design* (pp. 67–83). Amsterdam: North-Holland.

Kokkonen, O. (1988). Muistelmia kirjastotieteen ja informatiikan syntyvaiheista [Recollections from the birth period of library and information science in Finland]. *Kirjastotiede ja Informatiikka, 7*(3), 84–87.

Koskiala, S. (1980). *Flow of technical information through the industrial information services in Finland.* Unpublished doctoral dissertation, University of Maryland, Maryland. Abstract available at: http://www.clis.umd.edu/students/dissertations/koskiala.html

Laaksovirta, T. (1984). The popularization of scientific knowledge. In: J. Jyrkiäinen (Ed.), *City – Way of life– Mass communication. Report of the 3rd Soviet-Finnish seminar*, University of Tampere, Tampere (pp. 219–234). Department of Journalism and Mass Communication. Publications. Series B 13.1984.

Laaksovirta, T. H. (1986). *Tieteellisen tiedon välittyminen yhteiskuntaan.* [Summary: Dissemination of scientific knowledge to society. A study on the dissemination of scientific knowledge (Medicine) and its transmission within the field of health policy in Finland]. Dissertation, Tampereen yliopisto, Tampere.

Mäkinen, I. (2002). Library radicalism in Finland during the 1970s and 1980s. *Journal of Swedish Library Research.* [Svensk biblioteksforskning], Special Issue, 14, 95–107.

Mäkinen, I. (2004). Finnish information services for technology during the first half of the twentieth century. In: E. B. Rayward & M. E. Bowden (Eds), *The history and heritage of scientific and technological information systems.* Proceedings of the 2002 Conference (pp. 300–309). Medford, NJ: Information Today.

McKechnie, E. F., Goodall, G. R., Lajoie-Paquette, D., & Julien, H. (2005). How human information behavior researchers use each other's work: A basic citation analysis study. *Information Research*, 10(2) Paper 220. Available at: http://InformationR.net/ir/10-2/paper220.html

Noruzi, A. (2004). Application of Ranganathan's Laws to the Web. *Webology* 1. Available at: http://www.webology.ir/2004/v1n2/a8.html

Okko, M. (1982). Provinsiaalisuus kirjastotutkimuksessa [On provinciality in library research]. *Kirjastotiede ja informatiikka, 1*, 81.

Okko, M. (1983). Suuntana kansainväliset tutkijain kontaktit [Towards international contacts for the researchers]. *Kirjastotiede ja Informatiikka, 2*, 93.

Okko, M. (1986). Dokumentaation näkökulma kirjasto- ja informaatiopalvelualan koulutusmurroksessa 1960- ja 1970-lukujen vaihteen Suomessa [Documentation and the development of education in library and information science in Finland at the turn of the 1960s to the 1970s]. *Kirjastotiede ja Informatiikka, 5*, 88–95.

Okko, M. (1989). Kirjastotieteen ja informatiikan opetuksen ja tutkimuksen kehityslinjoja Tampereen yliopistossa. Jäähyväisluenton 21.2.1989 [The development of teaching and research of library and information science in the University of Tampere. Farewell lecture February 2, 1989]. *Kirjastotiede ja Informatiikka, 8*, 21–25.

Pietiläinen, P. (1982). Relation on resemblance in information retrieval. *Information Processing and Management, 18*, 55–59.

Pietiläinen, P. (1983). Local feedback and intelligent automatic query expansion. *Information Processing and Management, 19*, 51–58.

Siitonen, L. (1984). *Online searching: Relationships between online endusers search behavior, their research results and their satisfaction with research results.* Unpublished doctoral dissertation. University of Pittsburgh.

Suominen, V. (1986). Kirjastonhoitajakoulutus ja kirjastoteoreettinen oppiaine ja tutkimusala [Education of librarians and the library-theoretical discipline]. *Kirjastotiede ja Informatiikka, 5*, 120–125.

Suominen, V. (1997). *Filling empty space. A treatise on semiotic structures in information retrieval, in documentation, and in related research.* Oulu: Oulun yliopisto (Acta Universitatis Ouluensis. B; 27).

Suominen, V. (2002). User interests as the rationale of library operations: A critique. *Scandinavian Public Library Quarterly.*

Suominen, V. (2004). Vielä informaatiotutkimuksen "refleksiivisyydestä" ja muutenkin koulutuskeskustelusta. [More about the "reflectivity" of information studies and about the debate on library education in general]. In: *Kirjastolehti.* [The Finnish Library Journal's web debate] 24.9.2004. Available at: http://www.kaapeli.fi/~fla/kirjastolehti/keskustelu/refleksi2.html

Tammekann, E.-M. (1987). Kirjastotieteen ja informatiikan professuurin ensimmäinen lukuvuosi 1971–72. [The first academic year, 1971–72, of the Department of Library and Information Science at University of Tampere]. *Kirjastotiede ja Informatiikka, 6*, 37–44.

Törnudd, E. (1955). Library and technical information services. Paper presented at International Congress on Documentation of Applied Chemistry, London 22–25 Nov., 1955 (Mimeographed).

Törnudd, E. (1959). Study on the use of scientific literature and reference services by Scandinavian scientists and engineers engaged in research and development. In: *Proceedings of the International Conference on Scientific Information* (pp. 19–76). Washington, D.C.: National Academy of Sciences – National Research Council. Available at: http://www.nap.edu/books/NI000518/html/19.html

Vakkari, P. (1985). Historia literariasta kirjastotieteeksi ja informatiikaksi. Kirjasto- ja informaatiopalvelualan tutkimustoiminnan kehityslinjoja Suomessa [From *Historia Literaria* to library and information science: On the development of the research in the library and information field in Finland]. *Kirjastotiede ja Informatiikka, 4*, 3–23.

Vakkari, P. (1986a). Roots of library science in Historia Literaria. *Wolfenbütteler Notizen zur Buchgeschichte, 11*, 72–81.

Vakkari, P. (1986b). Tutkinnonuudistuksesta tutkinnonuudistukseen. Tutkimuksen asema kirjastokoulutuksen murroksessa. [From vocational education to library and information science. The role of research in the restructuration of library education program in Finland]. *Kirjastotiede ja Informatiikka.*

Vakkari, P. (1987a). Social structure, book reading and the functions of public libraries. Paper for the international seminar "Role of Books and Reading in the Cultural Development", Moscow, May 22–24, 1984. In: N. S. Kartashov (Ed.), *Role of books and reading in cultural development. Rol' knigi i chteniia v kul'turnom razvitii.* Materialy mezhdunarodnogo seminara IFLA, Moskva, 22–24 maia 1984g. Moskva: Gos. biblioteka SSSR im. V.I. Lenina.

Vakkari, P. (1987b). Kirjasto- ja informaatiopalvelutoiminnan ominaispiirteistä [On the characteristics of library and information service]. *Kirjastotiede ja Informatiikka.*

Vakkari, P., & Cronin, B. (Eds). (1992). Conceptions of library and Information Science. Historical, empirical and theoretical perspectives. *Proceedings of the International Conference held for the celebration of 20th Anniversary of the Department of Information Studies,* University of Tampere, Finland, 26–28 August 1991. London & Los Angeles: Taylor Graham.

Vakkari, P., Savolainen, R., & Dervin, B. (Eds). (1997). Information seeking in context. *Proceedings of an international conference on research in information needs, seeking and use in different contexts 14–16 August, 1996, Tampere, Finland.* London & Los Angeles: Taylor Graham.

Valtonen, M. R. (2005). *Tapaustutkimus poliisin esitutkinnan dokumentoinnista: asiakirjahallinnan näkökulma [Summary: A case study of documentation in pre-trial investigation: a records management view].* Helsinki: Arkistoyhdistys.

Wiman, M. (1982). *Bibliografiasta informaatiojärjestelmäksi: yhteiskuntatieteiden bibliografiatoiminta Venäjällä ja Neuvostoliitossa.* [From bibliography to information system: on the bibliographical service in social sciences in Russia and the Soviet Union]. Unpublished Licentiate's thesis, University of Tampere, Tampere.

THE RESEARCH PROCESSES
OF HUMANITIES SCHOLARS

Harriet Lönnqvist

ABSTRACT

This article focuses on humanities scholars' information searching. David Ellis' model of scholars' information seeking is taking as a starting point for this study. For understanding the information needs and information seeking habits of humanities scholars, it is crucial to know about the nature of research processes within diverse humanities fields. The study at hand, therefore, starts from the premise that the information searching of humanistic researchers needs to be understood within the framework of the research process, and not as a phenomenon outside of it.

Based on 24 in-depth interviews in archaeology, art history, philosophy, and languages and linguistics, the article examines humanities scholars' research processes. The purpose of this study is to analyse the research processes, their course and different stages, and to classify these into types. The purpose is also to examine the relationships between the types of research processes and the disciplines studied. Seven types of research processes were identified among scholars working in the fields studied. The types were named the Fly, the Sphinx Moth, the Mole, the Mockingbird, and the Spider.

The findings show that the representatives of a specific humanities discipline did not always proceed in their research in similar ways. There were distinct differences according to discipline, but important differences between scholars belonging to the same discipline could also be observed.

Advances in Library Administration and Organization, Volume 25, 175–202
Copyright © 2007 by Elsevier Ltd.
ISSN: 0732-0671/doi:10.1016/S0732-0671(07)25009-6

*The findings indicate that information seeking behaviour cannot be ex-
plained by factors that lie outside the researcher and the researcher's
subject matter. Another important finding is that humanistic research
often does not proceed in linear stages. There is more variability within
the research and searching processes within humanities and among representatives of specific disciplines than is often presumed.*

INTRODUCTION

Information needs, seeking, and searching of humanities scholars have received increased attention in the 1990s (Case, 2002). However, the findings
of the studies conducted thus far can be characterised as fragmentary.
Generalizations of humanities scholars' information needs, seeking, and
searching are mainly based on studies of single fields, rather than on comparative studies across several fields. Hence, we do not know to what extent
humanities scholars' information seeking processes have similarities across
disciplinary borders or whether distinct patterns of information seeking exist
within each humanities field.

The best-known theoretical model of scholars' information seeking and
searching patterns is perhaps David Ellis' (1993) behavioural framework,
further developed by Tom Wilson (1999) into a stage process version
(Fig. 1).

David Ellis studied the information seeking patterns of academic
researchers, social scientists, and natural scientists. He also studied the information seeking of researchers in English literature. He found six main
categories among the researchers in English literature: (1) starting;

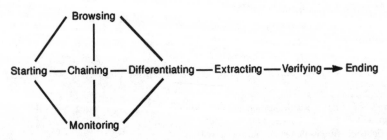

Fig. 1. A Stage Process Version of Ellis' Behavioural Framework (Wilson 1999,
pp. 254–255).

(2) surveying; (3) chaining; (4) selection and sifting; (5) monitoring; and (6) assembly and dissemination (Ellis, 1993, p. 483). A disadvantage with Ellis' model is that it is based on a study of researchers' information seeking in only one humanities field, English literature. We do not know, therefore, whether Ellis' behavioural framework is generalisable across humanities fields. We assume that it may not be possible to generalise the framework across humanities fields, because Ellis' informants did not mention browsing as an information seeking habit, whereas several studies have found that browsing is an important element in the information seeking of humanities researchers (cf. Watson-Boone, 1994, p. 206; Basker, 1984, p. 9).

Hence, although Ellis' behavioural framework is generalisable in a broad sense, and, therefore, has been widely applicable as a starting point for explorations into scholarly information seeking and searching patterns, there are also studies that suggest that it would be beneficial to take a closer look at differences within and across fields, because the information seeking behaviour of scholars within the broad disciplinary groups is not necessarily homogeneous (Lönnqvist, 1988, p. 123).

Another significant issue is that many investigations conducted thus far are somewhat limited in the scope of problems tackled. For understanding the information needs and information seeking habits of humanities scholars, it is crucial to know about the nature of research processes within diverse humanities fields. The approach used in the research at hand originates from the author's earlier investigation (Lönnqvist, 1988) showing that humanities researchers regard information searching to be a part of the research process. The study at hand, therefore, starts from the premise that the information searching of humanistic researchers needs to be understood within the framework of the research process, and not as a phenomenon outside of it. Information searching is, according to earlier research results, and according to humanistic researchers themselves, part of the research work.

Based on 24 in-depth interviews in archaeology, philosophy, art history, and languages and linguistics, this article examines humanities scholars' research processes. The purpose of the article is to describe their course and different stages, and to classify these into types. Understanding the nature of research processes within diverse humanities fields is crucial when investigating information searching of humanities scholars. The results are used to create a typology of research processes. The relationships between the types of research processes and the disciplines studied are discussed.

LITERATURE REVIEW

This section summarises earlier results from some landmark studies that are relevant to the exploration of humanities scholars' research processes. The disparity of methods used for data gathering (Chu, 1992, pp. 33–34; Case, 2002, p. 256) means that the comparison of results is difficult, and sometimes even impossible.

Sue Stone (1980) identified a series of steps in the research process of humanistic scholars. These steps took place in sequence or in parallel. These were:

- thinking and talking to people,
- reading what has already been done in the field,
- studying original sources and making notes,
- drafting the write-up, and
- revising the final draft.

Peter A. Uva (1977) studied the research processes of academic historians. His model for the research process of historians does not differ essentially from Stone's model. The five stages in historians' research process were:

- problem selection,
- detailed planning of data collection,
- data collection,
- analysis and interpretation, and
- writing and re-writing (Uva, 1977, cited in Chu, 1999, p. 268).

Clara Chu (1992) investigated the research process of literary critics, and identified six phases:

- the idea stage,
- the preparation stage,
- the elaboration stage,
- the analysis and writing stage,
- dissemination stage, and
- further writing and dissemination stage (Chu, 1992, p. 259).

All the models are very similar, and lend support to an assumption of the similarity of humanities scholars' research processes. However, in a study of information searching of historians, Raymond Vondran (1976) found that many characteristics of the information seeking behaviour of historians were associated more with the method of research used than discipline. Historians using quantitative methods searched information more like social scientists than historians who were not using quantitative methods. They also made more use of their informal communication network than histo-rians not using quantitative methods, and considered it to be of great value for their research (Vondran, 1976, p. 156).

Judith Palmer (1991) studied information styles among biochemists, en-tomologists, and statisticians working at an agricultural research station in England. She found five information styles: (1) non-seekers, (2) lone, wide rangers, (3) unsettled, self-conscious seekers, (4) confident collectors, and (5) hunters (Palmer, 1991, pp. 114–22). Lönnqvist (2003, pp. 34, 232, 188) discovered lone, wide rangers and confident collectors also among humanities scholars, which raises the question whether information searcher types are necessarily associated with discipline only. Palmer's research provides the starting point for creating a typology of research processes in this research.

RESEARCH QUESTIONS AND AIMS

This article analyses humanities scholars' research processes, their course, and different stages, and classifies these into types. The major purpose of this article is to examine the relationships between the types of research processes and the disciplines studied: archaeology, art history, philosophy, and languages and linguistics. More specifically, this article addresses two questions:

1. Does a specific type of research process exist within each discipline, or do research processes have similarities across disciplinary borders?
2. Information searching is usually considered to be important only in some stages of the research process. Is this also the case concerning researchers representing the four selected humanities disciplines? At what stages of the research process does information searching take place?

METHODOLOGY

The analysis is based on 24 in-depth interviews evenly divided between four disciplines: archaeology, philosophy, art history, and languages and lin-guistics. Each of the interviews lasted for several hours, and some partic-ipants were interviewed two or three times. The interviewees were chosen through a stratified random selection among all the researchers with connection to the university departments representing the four chosen dis-ciplines at the universities of Southern Finland. The researchers were subdivided into established (senior) and non-established (junior) researchers. Both groups were evenly represented within each. The interviews were tape-recorded and transcribed in full for analysis. The text analysis programme Ethnograph was used for processing the data, and qualitative content analysis for analysing the data.

Structured interview data and 'open-ended' interviews can be approached from what Pertti Alasuutari (1995) calls the *factist* perspective. An important characteristic of the factist perspective is "[...] that it makes a clear-cut division between the world or reality 'out there,' on the one hand, and the claims made about it, on the other" (Alasuutari, 1995, p. 47). According to Alasuutari, qualitative analysis consists of two stages: reduction of observations and solution of the problem (Alasuutari, 1995, p. 39). In broad terms, one can distinguish two types of sources or variants of the factist perspective in qualitative data. He calls them the *indicator* and *testimony* approaches (Alasuutari, 1995, pp. 50–53).

These two types of sources can be equated with two methods used to examine and increase the degree of reliability of the information received from the interviews. Alasuutari (1995) calls these two methods the *mechanistic* and the *humanistic* method. The idea of the mechanistic method is to avoid the 'reactivity of measurement', that is, "[...] the fact that the act of gathering information by bothering people with questions or other requests affects the information actually received" (Alasuutari, 1995, pp. 51–52). Reactivity can be avoided in many ways. For example, the informants may be given only limited information about the purpose of the investigation, the reason why particular questions are put, or in what way they are observed. The humanistic method can be characterised as the opposite of the mechanistic method since it aims at a close and confidential relationship with the interviewee. The implication is that, if the interviewee feels confident with the researcher, he is also honest (Alasuutari, 1995, pp. 50–52).

In this research, statements from the interviewees have been regarded as testimonies from the factist perspective, and they have been received using the humanistic method. The factist perspective plays the main role in the qualitative content analysis of the interview data. The interpretative viewpoint is applied in the explanation of informants' behaviour.

ANALYTICAL FRAMEWORK

The creation of the typology of research processes was performed according to Alasuutari's (1995) criteria for developing typologies to summarise findings. According to differences identified in humanities scholars' research processes, especially regarding whether these processes proceeded through distinct stages or in a more iterative or intuitive fashion, a typology of research processes was created. The research process types have been given metaphorical names in order to increase their comprehensibility. The development of the metaphors is based on Lakoff (1993), George Lakoff's and Mark Johnson's (1980), and Raymond Gozzi's (1999) research on metaphors. According to Lakoff and Johnson (1980), metaphors are one of the most fundamental mechanisms for making sense of the world and our experiences. Basically, a metaphor is a way of describing and understanding something in terms of something else, in terms of another domain. When we use metaphors we use the distinct expressions belonging to a "source domain" to understand and describe a "target domain" (Gozzi, 1999, p. 56). Here, the metaphors used shed light on the distinctive and outstanding features of the research processes. All metaphors are taken from the animal world, and the detailed reasons for the names are described in the following sections.

FINDINGS

Typology of Research Processes

Seven types of research processes were identified among scholars working in the fields of archaeology, art history, philosophy, and languages and linguistics. The types were named as follows:

1. The Fly
2. The Sphinx Moth
3. The Bee
4. The Geometrid Moth
5. The Mole
6. The Mockingbird
7. The Spider

Descriptions of each type will follow below. The main criteria used for developing this typology of research processes were as follows:

1. The character of the first phase: the beginning of the research. For example, research work can start by bibliographic inventory, from a theoretical framework, or collection of research material (empirical material or primary sources).

2. Whether the working of the theoretical framework took place before material collection, simultaneously with material collection, or in a later phase.
3. The phase in which the project actually began.
4. The role and importance of analysis and interpretation in the research process.
5. The nature of the research process, for instance, systematic, phase-like, philosophic, and hands-on work.

Altogether nine of the informants (9/24) shared the distinctive work practices of the "Bee". Three of them were researchers in languages and linguistics, and four art historians. Characteristics of the "Fly" were common to three researchers (3/24), one in archaeology, one in art history, and one in languages and linguistics. Characteristic for the Sphinx Moth type is broad reading of both research literature and fiction, and dislike of systematic research work. One of the art historians' research process differed in essential ways from the other types. This type is referred to as the Sphinx Moth. The Bee, as a systematic researcher, proceeds in a stepwise fashion, and the gathering of material constitutes a distinct stage.

Four researchers (4/24) in archaeology could be referred to as Geometrid Moths, who are characterised by scientific methods of analysis and theory consciousness. The Mole type, represented by one archaeologist, did archaeological research without formulating hypotheses or research questions, making instead a bibliographical inventory or preparing a theoretical frame of reference. The Mockingbird type (2/24) was found only among researchers in philosophy who analysed historic philosophical texts, returning to them repeatedly and interpreting them through logic and argument analysis. The research process of the Spider consisted of testing solutions problems one after another. This research process was also only found among researchers in philosophy, and four researchers (4/24) could be referred to this type.

Some of the types (the Bee and the Fly) were not typical to representatives of a specific discipline, whereas some of them were distinctively related to disciplines (the Sphinx Moth, the Geometrid Moth, the Spider, the Mockingbird, and the Mole). The typology underlines that the representatives of a specific discipline do not always proceed in their research in similar ways. Important differences between scholars belonging to the same discipline could be observed.

The Fly

A senior art historian, a senior researcher in archaeology, and a junior researcher in languages and linguistics have been typed as "Flies". These three researchers had the following characteristics in common: they started their research from an interesting idea, and characterised their research process as relatively unsystematic. The Fly metaphor is used to describe how these researchers' proceeded in an intuitive, dynamic, and iterative fashion rather than from stage to stage (Fig. 2). Various different solutions to research problems and direction were tried out and tested, until one solution emerged which could then be written up into a final manuscript. Material was sought and collected from different types of sources until the writing began. The Fly type is self-propelled through the research process. The movements of a fly appear random and confused, especially if it is being pursued. The Fly type researchers followed various directions in testing solutions to their research problem, and intuitively collected material from different sources, without striving for perfection. The chaos produced disturbances, which made the process dynamic and led to a final product, a whole. The chaos of the Fly was a prerequisite for creativity and in the end it produced order.

One of the researchers characterised here as type "Fly", an archaeologist, considered himself as an amateur researcher because he did not have time to do research while performing his full-time job. His research process started when an idea came to him that attracted and captured his interest. After that, the researcher defined the subject and formulated a working hypothesis based on the idea. He had a rather pragmatic approach to his research, working on it whenever opportunities arose.

The Fly had some kind of a theoretical framework at hand when the research work was started, but it could change during the research process. These researchers stressed the importance of broad reading. They began their research with an insight or research idea as a starting point, and then immersed themselves into the topic by studying literature intensively. As described by one art historian[1]:

> My research process is fairly chaotic. There are no clear stages in it except for the beginning: the insight that this is a good question. What follows thereafter is making progress in an erratic fashion. Often, I try to think of a solution and discover the direction was not very good. Then I try to find a better one. I try to get the ideas in my head somehow collected, and make others convinced that there is some sense in all this. The beginning is the insight and the end is the ready dissertation, hopefully. These are the two clear stages.

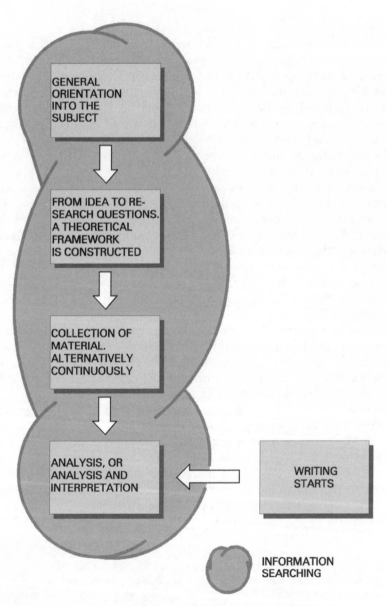

Fig. 2. The Fly.

One characteristic that was common to the researchers in the "Fly" category was that, when the research questions were formulated, the research process proceeded chaotically. They started the collection of research material without having a clear hypothesis or tightly outlined research questions. However, they did usually start with a working hypothesis. The research questions were developed and specified during the course of writing into problem formulations, which were constantly revised in dialogue with the research material. The art historian said that:

> I have problem formulations throughout, all the time. In a manner, I have the problem formulation stage all the time. I continuously try to read literature that gives me ideas. When I am reading a theoretically interesting book, I may get a new angle on the matter.

The art historian explained that models for research processes, where hypotheses are set and deductive conclusions drawn, were not applicable to humanistic disciplines, because the research material to a high degree determines the approach:

> In my view, each topic, in itself, already contains the method. I can't decide that I will use this particular model and apply it to my data. [...] The material would constantly spill over. Research models often indicate that when the hypotheses are set, the researcher already knows what is being looked for, what the outcome is going to be. And then it is unnecessary to go through the entire circle if the answer is already known.

The results of this researcher's work mostly lead to a monography. She publishes one monograph approximately every second or third year at a commercial publishing house, and can thus be regarded as being rather productive.

The archaeologist in the "Fly" category usually collected his research material over a long time span. The gathering of research material was directed by the working hypothesis. He used collections of archaeological finds and catalogues to those finds. According to him, the length of the material collection phase depended on two factors. The first was whether the research work was going to result in a monograph or an essay. The second was the personality of the researcher. The collection of printed archive material and research literature was part of the material collection phase. The archaeologist worked himself through the primary material and did reading of research literature at the same time. Because of the interaction between the primary material and the research literature, the working hypothesis was constantly revised during the process of work:

> In fact I cannot remember what my starting hypothesis was. It was something, something else than where I ended up. It lived during the process and, in fact, still lives, and

now I probably disagree with what I have written. That's what always happens. It lives
until at some phase I stop.

Several researchers stressed the difficulties associated with ending a research
project. This is probably one of the biggest dilemmas in humanistic research.
The researcher in archaeology stressed that the researcher should not lock
himself up, but should always maintain a humble attitude towards new facts
and observations that could not have been anticipated in the beginning of
the research project.

The researcher in archaeology started to write in parallel with the analysis
of the primary material. He called this phase "thinking of the problems."
The art historian started the writing process before all of the material was
collected, which she considered to be an impossible thing to do anyway. She
would never be able to collect even the most relevant material because part
of that material was "hidden" in private archives into which the researcher
did not have access. As the material she went through led to questions, she
started to write. She received associations, ideas, and new thoughts in the
sorting out process that accompanied the writing effort. Although the character of the research process was rather chaotic, it seemed somehow sensible
to the researcher.

The archaeologist gathered notes and observations on small slips of paper
and put them into an envelope or a file. Now and then he took them out to
give the observations contours and to form them further. For him, the real
analysis of the material started when the writing phase started. Up until
then, his research questions rankle in his mind, waiting to be answered.
In the analysis phase, the researcher often had to check different things, and
then went back to the primary sources and the literature for answers.

The art historian found it very easy to write and filled page after page in a
short time. For the archaeologist and the researcher in languages and linguistics, writing was a very difficult and tedious phase in the research proc-
ess.latter was sometimes engaged for a whole day formulating one sentence.
Partly, this was due to the fact that the analysis of the material and the
interpretations of the results from the analysis were not yet ready when
the writing process started. To analyse, interpret, and write at the same time
seemed to create a rather chaotic, but productive, situation for the researcher.

It is characteristic of the Fly-type researcher to follow various directions
in testing solutions to a research problem, and to intuitively collect material
from different sources during the entire research process. Information
searching did not take place within a single phase of the research process but
continued throughout. Analysis and writing were not necessarily separate

stages, either. The chaotic, erratic research process of the Fly is a prerequisite for creativity. It produces order.

The Sphinx Moth

The Sphinx Moth (Fig. 3) is a junior art historian. The research process
started when she became interested in a topic. This researcher read broadly
during a long period of time, perhaps for 2 years. She read both research
literature and fiction and let herself be influenced by the train of thought and
impressions arising from reading. She said that her way of reading also was
her way of living:

> The way I understand it, my thinking and working process, is that I have very big
> questions about people's observations and changes in them, about art and changes in
> what has been written about art and how these influence art. I read philosophy and
> fiction and almost anything. And only when I have to do the work, some work, I look at
> what I'm doing, what form I will put it in and often the questions that are the most
> important for me during the research process are not necessarily those that are visible in
> the final product, or they are merely some general atmospheres the piece of writing that
> I finally end up doing.

Fig. 3 visualises the research process of the *Sphinx Moth*. The Sphinx Moth
is a twilight butterfly that flitters along catching from time to time the smell
of this flower and that, until it finally settles upon a certain flower and enjoys
its nectar. The double meaning of the Swedish word for Sphinx Moth
(dreamer) is combined in the research process of the art historian.
A dreamer is characterised by being enamored by, carried away by someone and by surrendering to daydreaming.

This researcher got totally absorbed in her research problem, and using her
own intuitions, she daydreamed her way through the research process. This
researcher characterised herself as "not rational" and "a non-researcher"
because she read so widely and unselectively. Because her research did not
have a linear character, she was not able to start writing at the same time she
penetrated her research material. At art exhibits, she got impressions from
works of art. In this way, she formulated her "thinking material," which, for
her, constituted her research material also. The research questions were not
formulated until the research work took form and the presentation found its
contours. She analysed during the process of writing. When this creative
process had gone on for a long period of time, possibly for 2 years, she
committed her research work to paper, and a manuscript saw the light of day.

The research process of the Sphinx Moth differed from the other types
because of its longitudinal first stage, and because of its broad scope. Even
more than for the Fly type, the research found its form in writing.

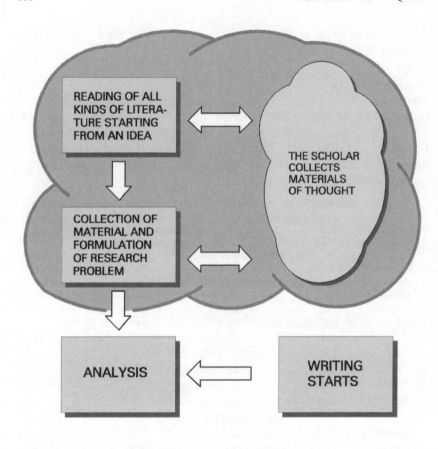

Fig. 3. The Sphinx Moth.

The Bee

The Bee (Fig. 4) has little in common with the Sphinx Moth. Four of the Bees were art historians and five were researchers in languages and linguistics. Characteristic for the Bee is the fact that the research process starts with a general orientation to the topic and a thorough literature review, or,

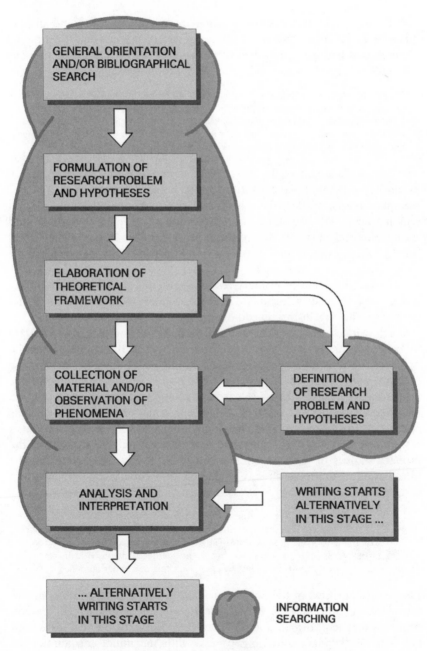

Fig. 4. The Bee.

directly with a literature review, which formed an essential and distinct phase in the research process. The Bees considered it important to gather all research that had been published on the subject and to also check to make sure that no one else was conducting research on the same topic:

> People used to be even more touchy about colliding into the same research topic than nowadays. It does not matter so much now if people are engaged in somewhat overlapping problems. But we try to avoid the situation where people are doing dissertations about the same topic, and that is why it is important to root out what others are doing and make sure that no one is doing work with exactly the same focus. (10)[2]

Another characteristic of the Bee's research process is that the gathering of primary research material constitutes another comprehensive stage. The Bee metaphor is used to describe this type of systematic and chronological research process. The Bee builds his cakes by adding one piece to another until the cake has taken shape. The research process proceeds step by step like a driving wheel, often in the form of a spiral, in which later stages influence earlier ones.

After the collection of primary research material, the researchers in languages and linguistics formulate the research problem and research hypotheses. The art historians do formulate research problems while the research work is going on. The problem formulation and the hypotheses are influenced by the gathered material, and are specified during the research process. The researchers in languages and linguistics did not start writing before results of the analysis were in hand and the interpretations of the results had been done. Those researchers whose research relied on corpora of spoken language, for instance, often represented the Bee type, whereas researchers in archaeology and philosophy were never of this type. The Bee's research process is, to a large extent, concentrated on the analysis of the primary sources or data. In comparison with the Fly type for whom the formulation of the topic already contained an approach, one art historian categorised into the Bee type stressed that:

> In aesthetics, for example, the problem is that the researcher takes a theoretical framework as a starting point. Then, the researcher tries to make the research material fit the theoretical framework and not vice versa. The starting point should be at the grass roots level, in the works of art or the artist's work and the questions posed in them, and proceed from there towards more general ideas. I see that as a better approach. (11)

The research process of the Bee is visualised in Fig. 4. As can be seen from the figure, the process involves three clearly separate stages. The first phase combines a general orientation, the literature review, theoretical ideas, and the start of the data gathering process with the initial formulation of hypotheses and problems. The second stage consists of the gathering of research material. The third stage consists of analysis and interpretation of findings and writing. The process is systematically driven, although later stages inform the initial research questions and hypotheses, and research data informs theory. Most of the Bee type researchers searched information in all three phases of the research process, though they conducted extensive searches especially in the first phase. The Bee type researchers could conduct directed subject searching, but chaining was the favourite searching method of all bees.

Not all researchers belonging to this type exhibited the pure research process of the Bee. There were some minor deviations like the art historian who preferred to leave the formulation of the theoretical framework to the last phase of the project. However, a distinct feature of the Bee's process is the systematic nature of their research work and their fixation on the primary sources.

The Geometrid Moth

The Geometrid Moth (Fig. 5) has some similarities with the Sphinx Moth. Its Swedish name "mätaren" (the measurer) also has a double linguistic meaning which is significant. The Geometrid Moth belongs to a family of butterflies (Geometrae), whose members at the larvae stage proceed forward in series of increments (the measuring worm). An individual who by profession deals with measurements such as an archaeologist who measures all the objects found at an excavation can also be called a measurer. The archaeologist measures numerous qualities in material objects with the aid of various scientific methods.

One senior and three junior archaeologists could be referred to as being Geometrid Moths, a type which is characterised by a scientific approach to research work. These researchers were typical field researchers. For them, a good researcher is always a field researcher:

> Archaeology is a discipline that collects its material in the field. The archaeologist is a field researcher, and a good archaeologist is field savvy, understands the nature of material collection, and its requirements and source criticism. It is not possible to do good archaeology otherwise. (14)

Not all archaeological research leads to scientific presentations and conclusions. Many pieces of research work never pass the collection phase, but end with field research. This is because, typically, archaeological field research work commences when a researcher receives a commission to investigate a place which is under threat of being destroyed. Because most of field

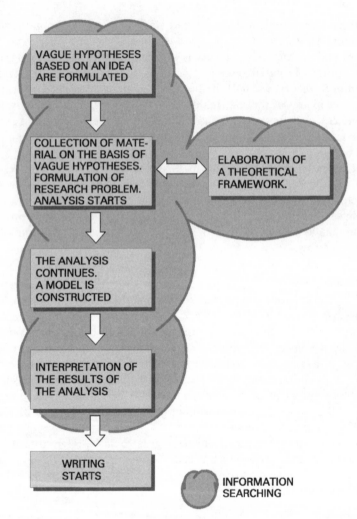

Fig. 5. The Geometrid Moth.

research is by nature rescue operations followed by reports to The National Board of Antiquity means that not all of archaeological research is led by or based on research questions. As stressed by one informant: "The research process does not have to lead very far in order to be good research."

Although the field archaeologists stressed that all archaeology is field work, it was not in fact always possible for junior researchers to stay in the field for a long period. Junior researchers often had to depend on existing collections of archaeological finds in museum collections. Existing collections of finds to a large extent defined and put limits on possible research questions. One of the junior researchers said that, after having formulated the working hypotheses, he normally started doing research in archives. The National Board of Antiquity was the most important archive used, followed by collections of archaeological finds and reports in regional museums.

Researchers belonging to the type Geometrid Moth stressed, however, that an archaeologist cannot rely on second hand sources – the researcher must always "see with her or his own eyes":

> No matter how much good literature exists, material reports, and no matter how good collections are, all these must be evaluated from a source critical viewpoint. And a researcher cannot apply evaluative skills if she does not know the field and know the field work methods. (14)

Sometimes an archaeologist has to return to the field to collect additional material in case the already collected finds are too few in number. A reason to return to the field to collect more finds might also be that the finds are not sufficient or have the qualities that allow the researcher to answer the formulated research questions.

Contacts with colleagues in other nearby disciplines, for example biologists, soil geologists, and chemists, to help conduct all kinds of analyses of the archaeological finds were very important. A typological analysis is done, and the material is grouped with the help of statistical methods. Typically, a model is constructed on the basis of the results of the analysis of the material. One of these analyses is that of provenance. The researcher makes layout plans to determine what kind of activities have there been at different places in the settlement. Where was the settling? Where were the burial-places? These hypothetical models are compared to other preexisting models. Information searching is the most intense in the stages of analysis and interpretation. The senior archaeologist stressed that the interpretations should result in a synthesis. The interpretation of finds took place by comparing them to other researchers' finds.

The archaeological research process deviates from that of the Bee in that no systematic information searching is conducted at the beginning of the process. Some preliminary hypotheses are formulated, and the phase that follows consists of the collection of research material based on vague hypotheses. The answers to the research questions can be found only through field work; therefore, in this particular type of research process unlike in

most other types of humanistic research processes, interpretation of the
results forms a separate phase.

The senior archaeologist started to write when the final results of the
analysis were ready. He then presented a description of the working process
and the final results. The research findings in archaeology are eventually
firmly anchored to theory. Scientific methods of analysis play a central part
in the research work of the typical Geometrid Moth.

The Mole

The Mole (Fig. 6) does archaeological research work in a rather traditional
manner. The research process of this female researcher could not be classified as a Bee or a Geometrid Moth because her research process had a
different beginning:

> I am in a lucky situation in that I got to explore the biggest burial ground ever found in
> Finland. There are graves from century after century, the kind that have never been
> found before. There are many centuries of continuity in the same place. I am dealing
> with a unique field and cannot build on earlier finds because there are no earlier finds.
> What is reported in the literature is without doubt more lacking than what I have been
> able to dig.

It was characteristic for her to begin her research process by putting her
hand to the shovel, by starting excavations, without formulating any hypotheses or research questions. She did not conduct a literature search in the
beginning of the research process, and differed from the Geometrid Moth in
that she did not apply theories to synthesise findings.

This researcher stressed that only when all excavations are done and all
the material has been penetrated and carefully documented will the archaeologist know what kinds of research questions the finds will be able to
answer. In the beginning of an archaeological research publication, the finds
are usually presented, the finds of other researchers and one's own. The
presentation usually contains a large collection of pictures. Before the researcher is able to present her hypotheses in a reliable manner, she must
present the material upon which the hypotheses are based. At this stage of
the research process, she thoroughly penetrates the research literature to
trace analogical finds. When the researcher starts to document the finds, she
also starts writing. When the presentation is finished, this researcher penetrates the research literature once more, but in a different way. She inves-
tigates the literature to find out if somebody else already has explored the
same idea that she is addressing, and if something was published from that
effort.

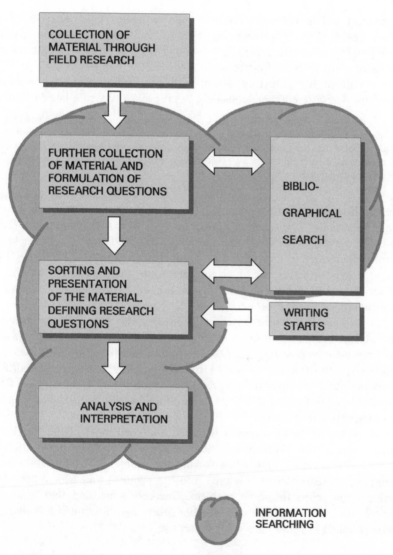

Fig. 6. The Mole.

The Mockingbird

The research process of the Mockingbird is the text-analytical one and it was found only among researchers in philosophy, one junior and one senior one. They interpret and analyse historic philosophical texts, returning to them repeatedly and interpreting them over and over again. A characteristic of the Mockingbird (Fig. 7) is its singing, which sounds like a drawn-out chatter with patterns of sounds mocking the singing of other birds. The patterns are repeated often three to four times in a row.

The philosophers' most important work tool is logic and analysis of arguments. These researchers considered that philosophy to a large extent:

> [...] deals with trying to establish what kind of a problem a problem is. Is it a problem that can be answered or is it one that goes beyond comprehension. The case often is that the problem has been badly formulated. Many problems arise because concepts have been mixed or wrong questions have been asked in wrong contexts. Much of philosophy goes out to define a useful context for a problem and pose it so that it can be answered. (16)

Researchers in philosophy claimed that they do not use methods in the traditional sense. Logic and argument analysis were their primary working tools. These researchers read relevant texts and posed questions to the texts, turning thereafter to literature that comments on the texts. Then they formulated hypotheses about which interpretations are plausible. One philosopher described his work as "[...] sitting in an abundance of diverse interpretations [...]" (16), another as "[...] reading texts not from the author's problem formulations [...]" (17) but from his own. This could mean reading against the intentions and arguments of the author, or reading a text as generously as possible "[...] to develop an interpretation that makes it [the text] as coherent as possible" (16). This type of research process differs from the other six in that interpretations come before the analysis of research material, because the texts under study cannot be analysed without an interpretive framework.

The phase where literature is searched and used most in the Mockingbird's research process is during the time when the problem under study is being defined, rather than when solving the problem. The literature gave insights to researchers of this type into the problem and how others had earlier approached the same problem. One researcher said that what she looked for in the literature was whether others had attempted to solve the same problem but had named it differently.

The Spider
The research process of the Spider (Fig. 8) is that of the problem solver. He spins a web of the right threads and tests one solution to his problem after another. This research process was found only among researchers in philosophy, that is, it was bound to a specific discipline, as was that of the Mockingbird. Four researchers, three established ones and one who was not

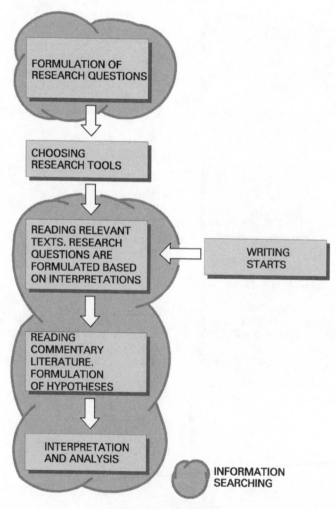

Fig. 7. The Mockingbird.

well established, could be referred to as being of this type. Problem solving has traditionally been considered characteristic of philosophic research. The researchers of this type decided on a theme that gradually got a more precise formulation. Once the problem was isolated, then the choice of research tools followed, which were the same as those of the Mockingbird (i.e., logic and argument analysis).

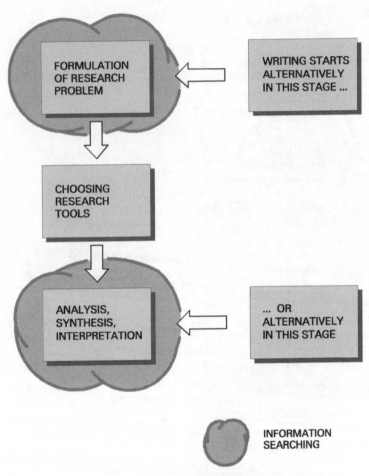

Fig. 8.   The Spider.

The character of the research material of the Mockingbird and the Spider showed notable differences, and these differences affected the development of the research process. Interpretation did not take place in the problem formulation process, since the Spider interprets the research results of others, not those of his own. Writing could start either in the last phase, when these philosophers had reached an overall view of how to synthesise their ideas, or earlier in the problem formulation phase (see Fig. 8).

The Spider's research process did not lean on historical texts of philosophy, read over and over again, like that used by the Mockingbird's. The Mockingbird had to arrive at an interpretation before starting the analysis, whereas the Spider read literature and weaved a web around it that resulted in the solving of the research problem.

SUMMARY

The article at hand focused on differences in humanities scholars' research processes. Seven types of research processes were identified among scholars doing research in the fields of archaeology, art history, philosophy, and languages and linguistics. The types of research processes found were: *the Fly, the Sphinx Moth, the Bee, the Geometrid Moth, the Mole, the Mockingbird*, and *the Spider*.

The Fly's research process was intuitive and dynamic. Characteristic of the Sphinx Moth type was a total absorption in the research problem and a dislike of systematic research work, and broad reading of both research literature and fiction. The Bee, as a systematic researcher, proceeded step by step, and the gathering of material constituted a comprehensive stage. Four researchers in archaeology could be referred to the Geometrid Moth type which was characterised by scientific methods of analysis and a consciousness of theory. The Mole type did archaeological research without formulating hypotheses or research questions, making a literature review or preparing a theoretical frame of reference. The Mockingbird type was found only among researchers in philosophy. These researchers analysed historic philosophical texts, returning to them repeatedly and interpreting them using logic and argument analysis. The research process of the Spider consisted of testing solutions to problems one after another. This research process was also only found among researchers in philosophy, and four researchers could be referred to as being of this type.

CONCLUSIONS

The representatives of a specific humanities discipline did not always proceed in their research in similar ways. There were distinct differences according to discipline, but important differences between scholars belonging to the same discipline could also be observed. Various research models such as those by Stone, Uva, and Chu tend to assume that types of research

processes and phases are connected to disciplines in a clear and unambiguous manner, but this assumption has not previously been systematically
tested by comparing various humanities disciplines to one another. This
study has addressed this gap and found this hypothesis to be only partly
true.

The findings indicate that information seeking behaviour cannot be explained by factors that lie outside the researcher and the researcher's subject
matter. The research processes of philosophers (Spider and Mockingbird)
and archaeologists (Mole and Geometrid Moth) were not similar to those of
representatives of other disciplines. This can be explained by the nature of
the research problems with which the scholars dealt. The research questions,
research materials, and research methods varied greatly among the humanities disciplines studied, and research processes varied accordingly to these
aspects of the research process.

Another important finding is that humanistic research often does not
proceed in linear stages. There is more variability within the research and
searching processes within humanities and among representatives of specific
disciplines than is often presumed. In this light, the models of humanistic
researchers' research processes presented earlier (Uva, 1977; Stone, 1980;
Ellis, 1993; Chu, 1999) can be regarded as preliminary in nature and
sketchy. These models may be said to form a general background for developing a typology of all research processes. But as shown here, it is not
necessarily possible to generalise or to apply them in all humanities fields.
Nor do they account for differences within fields, differences that can be as
great as those between fields.

A third important finding is that the humanities scholars interviewed
often did not consider information searching as a specific or clearly identifiable stage in their research process. Only the Bee's research process
closely resembled the "textbook" version with an identifiable literature
searching phase. According to the findings of this study, many humanities
scholars interact with literature during the entire research process and can
use literature for different purposes at different stages, for instance, in
problem formulation and in synthesis. The "Sphinx Moth" was an extreme
case in her broad reading and literature use, and her habits were very different from the archaeologists' precise "hands-on" work processes that involved digging that was similar for finds in literature as in field excavations.
The findings reported here contribute to the existing body of research by
bringing into view subtle but essential variations and diversity in the
research processes of humanities scholars.

NOTES

1. The quotes have been translated from Swedish by Sanna Talja.
2. Informants within the same type are distinguished from each other by interview numbers. Numbers are not used when there is only one informant representing a category.

REFERENCES

Alasuutari, P. (1995). *Researching culture. Qualitative method and cultural studies*. London: Sage.

Basker, J. (1984). Philosophers' information habits. *Library and Information Research News, 1*, 1–10.

Case, D. O. (2002). *Looking for information. A survey of research on information seeking, needs, and behavior*. Amsterdam: Academic Press.

Chu, C. M. (1992). *The scholarly process and the nature of information needs of the literary critic: A descriptive model*. Unpublished doctoral dissertation. London, Ontario: The University of Western Ontario.

Chu, C. M. (1999). Literary critics at work and their information needs: A research-phases model. *Library & Information Science Research, 21*, 247–273.

Ellis, D. (1993). Modeling the information-seeking patterns of academic researchers. A grounded theory approach. *Library Quarterly, 63*, 469–486.

Gozzi, R. (1999). *The power of metaphor in the age of electronic media*. Cresskill, NJ: Hampton Press.

Lakoff, G. (1993). The contemporary theory of metaphor. In: A. Ortony (Ed.), *Metaphor and Thought*, (2nd ed., pp. 202–251). Cambridge: Cambridge University Press.

Lakoff, G., & Johnson, M. (1980). *Metaphors we live by*. Chicago and London: The University of Chicago Press.

Lönnqvist, H. (1988). *Humanister söker information eller "Mötet med den litauiske skoputsaren" [Humanities scholars seek information, or "Meeting with the Lithuanian shoepolisher"]*. Esbo: NORDINFO.

Lönnqvist, H. (2003). *Humanistiska forskningsprocesser och informationssökare. Typologier för informationssökande forskare. [Humanistic research processes and information searchers. Typologies for researchers searching information]*. Doctoral dissertation. Tampere: Juvenes Print. Available at: http://acta.uta.fi

Palmer, J. (1991). Scientists and information: I. Using cluster analysis to identify information style. *Journal of Documentation, 47*, 105–129.

Stone, S. (1980). CRUS humanities research programme. In: S. Stone (Ed.), *Humanities Information Research: Proceedings of a Seminar* (pp. 15–24). Sheffield: Centre for Research on User Studies, Sheffield.

Uva, P. A. (1977). *Information-gathering habits of academic historians: Report of the pilot study*. Syracuse, NY: SUNY Upstate Medical Center (ERIC Document Reproduction Service No. ED 142 483).

202   HARRIET LÖNNQVIST

Vondran, R.F. (1976). *The effect of method of research on the information seeking behavior of academic historians.* Unpublished doctoral dissertation. The University of Wisconsin-Madison.

Watson-Boone, R. (1994). The information needs and habits of humanities scholars. *RQ, 34,* 203–216.

Wilson, T. D. (1999). Models in information behaviour research. *Journal of Documentation, 55,* 249–270.

INFORMATION LITERACY IN MEDICAL EDUCATION: RELATIONSHIPS WITH CONCEPTIONS OF LEARNING AND LEARNING METHODS

Eeva-Liisa Eskola

ABSTRACT

This paper reports on part of a dissertation project on the relationships between learning methods and students' information behavior in Finland. In this qualitative study, information behavior is studied in the contexts of a problem-based learning curriculum and a traditional curriculum. In 1998, 16 theme interviews were conducted at the Tampere University Medical School, which applied the problem-based learning curriculum and 15 interviews at the Turku University Medical School, in which the traditional curriculum with an early patient contact program was implemented. The focus of this paper is on the concept of information literacy as a part of the students' information behavior and its relationships with students' conceptions of learning. The findings indicate that students' information literacy is developed, on the one hand, through active use of information and sources in connection with real information needs, and, on the other hand, through an educational context which offers opportunities to get different viewpoints on issues. Following the same tendency, the more

Advances in Library Administration and Organization, Volume 25, 203–238
© 2007 Published by Elsevier Ltd.
ISSN: 0732-0671/doi:10.1016/S0732-0671(07)25010-2

developed conceptions of learning were mostly held by the students be-
longing to the problem-based group with simple or developed skills in
information literacy, although there were exceptions from this pattern.

1. INTRODUCTION

The movement from teacher-centered to student-centered methods in higher
education supposes independent information seeking. Students have to independently locate and gather information for their studies, and to use and
evaluate information critically, i.e., they need to be information literate (Fridén,
1996). According to research, the need to use different information sources and
channels increases in problem-based learning (e.g., Rankin, 1992; Fridén &
Oker-Blom, 1995). On the other hand, the research results show that students
have undeveloped skills in seeking and managing information (e.g., Dunn,
2002). In the present study, information literacy including information seeking
is explored in the broader context of learning. The learning process is influenced by many different factors including conceptions of learning. By conceptions of learning are understood people's different ways to conceive learning
(Säljö, 1979). In general, conceptions affect the learning process and study
behavior including the outcomes of learning (Lindblom-Ylänne, Nevgi, &
Kaivola, 2003; Entwistle & Peterson, 2004). In this research, information behavior and information literacy are considered as related to students' study
behavior and study practices. Thus, the aim is to explore the possible relationships between students' conceptions of learning and information behavior
as manifested in their information literacy in the two different learning contexts, the problem-based learning curriculum and the traditional curriculum.

2. DIFFERENT KINDS OF MEDICAL CURRICULA

Barrows and Tamblyn (1980) categorize the teaching and learning methods
in medicine in two ways. The first categorization is based on the person who
is responsible for learning, either the teacher or the student. The other
categorization is based on how knowledge is organized for learning, either
on subject areas or on problem areas. A medical curriculum can thus be
teacher-centered and subject-based, student-centered and subject-based,
teacher-centered and problem-based, or student-centered and problem-
based. The teacher-centered and subject- or discipline-based curriculum has

been the most common combination in medical schools as well as in other educational institutions until the latter part of 19th century when the development towards alternative methods began due to advancements in psychology and learning research (Barrows & Tamblyn, 1980).

The traditional teacher-centered and discipline-based education, for example, lecturing without students' active participation, is an efficient method to cover the content to be learned, but while it ignores the variation in students' own knowledge and learning abilities, the learning may remain unsatisfactory. Subject-based learning offers a convenient way to define the extent and knowledge to be learned by the subject areas. It provides the teacher and the students with a feeling of security that learning has occurred when the specified concepts and knowledge of the area are memorized and recalled in tests. Disadvantageous is that memorized discipline-based knowledge is not applicable as such to the complex real-life situations, such as patient problems, which need integrated knowledge from different subject areas (Barrows & Tamblyn, 1980). Teacher-centered and subject-based teaching is based theoretically on behaviorism which argues for the external regulation of individual's behavior (e.g., Rauste-von Wright, von Wright, & Soini, 2003).

The implementations of student-centered and problem-based methods in medical education (e.g., the problem-based learning approach and programs with early patient contacts) started after 1960s because of: rapidly growing medical information, need for the integration of knowledge in basic sciences and clinical practice, lack of motivation of students in the pre-clinical speriod, and medical doctors' poor skills in communication with patients (Vainiomäki, 1995; Barrows, 1996; Boud & Feletti, 1997). The theoretical framework corresponding the ideas of learning and knowledge in problem-based learning approach is constructivism according to which learning is seen as an active process in which learners construct new ideas based upon their prior knowledge (Ryan, 1997).

Contemporary problem-based learning medical programs usually employ three fundamental principles: basic sciences are learnt in the process of problem-solving by analyzing typical cases, learning is motivated by student curiosity and self-direction, and small-group tutorial meetings serve as the center of learning while the role of the teacher becomes one of guide, facilitator, and resource (Barrows, 1996). In analyzing a case, the students come to a point where more information is needed to continue. This results in the generation of an issue. An issue specifies an item of information that must be learned to complete the case. Once an issue has been identified, it becomes a learning goal for the next meeting. Each student must then independently find an answer to this question and be prepared to share it with other students. Thus, problem-based learning employs students' initiative as a driving force. The students generate the issues, provide the answers, and teach fellow students (Schmidt, 1983; Donner & Bickley, 1993; Silén, Normann, & Sandén, 1995; Engel, 1997).

Medical educational programs called early patient contact and early community exposure were developed in the 1960s and 1970s to better meet the needs of patients and the community. The goals of the programs are to let the students become acquainted with practitioners' work and patients in the early stage of their education, learn interaction skills, motivate basic science studies, and combine theory and practice (Vainiomäki, 1995).

2.1. Information Seeking in Problem-Based and Traditional Learning

In a problem-based learning (PBL) approach, it is assumed that the students are gathering information from different sources while working with the problems (Barrows, 1996). Information sources such as libraries, databases, different textbooks, journal articles, experts, other students, faculty members, field trips, and laboratory work are mentioned as possible sources. Although lectures are not regarded as a primary source of instruction, they are used also in problem-based learning and form a source of information for students (Rankin, 1992; Blake, 1994; Nikkarinen & Hoppu, 1994). Members of the tutorial group function naturally as information sources for each other (e.g., Engel, 1997).

In a traditional curriculum, the teacher determines the learning needs of the students and transfers the disciplinary knowledge to them. Also learning resources can then be specified easily for the students, for example, as relevant chapters in textbooks to be read for examinations (Barrows & Tamblyn, 1980; Rauste-von Wright et al., 2003). It can be assumed that while the learners are seen more as passive recipients of knowledge than active learners, a traditional learning approach may not contribute to the independent information seeking as a matter of course.

According to studies exploring the differences in PBL students' and traditional students' information seeking and library use, the way the library and its services are used changes, and the use of the library and library services increases when the PBL method is applied in the curriculum. PBL students are more frequent library users and they use a greater variety of sources more frequently than students taught with traditional methods (Marshall, Fitzgerald, Busby, & Heaton, 1993; Saunders, Northup, & Mennin, 1985; Fridén & Oker-Blom, 1995). After the implementation of PBL, the student book loan increases, as well as the use of the reference collection (Taylor & Lande, 1996). The studies suggest that PBL students self-select the resources (Saunders et al., 1985), choose sources which support independent learning, and learn how to seek information on an early stage of education (Rankin, 1992). Students in the problem-based curriculum use MEDLINE searching more often and they use the library as a place to study and meet other students more than the students in conventional curriculum (Marshall et al., 1993).

Information seeking is one factor in the concept of information literacy, and in the following section, this concept and some related research are reviewed.

3. INFORMATION LITERACY

The concept of information literacy, which describes the knowledge and skills needed in all areas (e.g., in studies, in the workplace, and in the every-day life of people in the information-rich society of today), was introduced in the United States at the beginning of the 1970s (Limberg, Hultgren, & Jarneving, 2002; Webber & Johnston, 2000). At the end of the 1980s, the American Library Association defined information literacy as follows:

> Ultimately information literate people are those who have learned how to learn. They know how to learn because they know how information is organized, how to find information, and how to use information in such way that others can learn from them. (American Library Association, 1989, p. 1)

An extensive amount of literature has been published on information literacy during the last three decades and the concept is defined differently by different authors; also, related terms such as information competency, computer literacy, library literacy, mediacy, media literacy, network or Internet literacy, and digital (information) literacy have been created to emphasize different aspects of the phenomenon (Webber & Johnston, 2000; Bawden, 2001).

In the information literacy competency standards for higher education of the Association of College & Research Libraries (2000), it is concluded that an information literate individual is able to: "Determine the extent of information needed, access the needed information effectively and efficiently, evaluate information and its sources critically, incorporate selected information into one's knowledge base, use information effectively to accomplish a specific purpose, understand the economic, legal, and social issues surrounding the use of information, and access and use information ethically and legally."

Webber and Johnston (2000) pay attention to the way the definitions listing skills reduce the complex set of skills and knowledge to small, discrete units that fragment the field of knowledge and may encourage a surface learning approach instead of a deep learning approach. Bruce (1997) categorizes different models of and approaches to information literacy in two categories based on whether information literacy is described through people's characteristics or their conceptions. To the former category belong behavioristic and constructivistic approaches. In the behavioristic approach, an information literate person shall show that he/she owns certain characteristics, and abilities defined outside the person and thus the measurable skills are emphasized. In the constructivist approaches, information literacy is also described through characteristics but the role of the person is more active and his/her own knowledge and understanding become important in the process. As an alternative to these approaches, Bruce presents her relational approach, which is based on hermeneutic and phenomenological thinking and describes information literacy through people's own conceptions, not their characteristics. In the relational approach, information literacy is described through a combination of individuals' different ways to experience and understand the phenomenon (Bruce, 1997).

Bruce (1997) identified seven different categories or ways in which educators in higher education experienced information literacy. The seven different ways of understanding information literacy, also called the "seven faces of information literacy," are:

1. Using information technology
2. Finding information
3. Executing a process, i.e., recognizing a need for information and using the accessed information to meet the original need
4. Controlling information
5. Building up a personal knowledge base
6. Working with knowledge and personal perspectives in such a way that novel insights are gained
7. Using information wisely for the benefit of others

The seven categories can be seen as hierarchically related to each other so that the topmost conceptions five, six, and seven are more complex and powerful regarding information use than the lower conceptions (Bruce, 1997).

The advantage of the relational approach is that learners and teachers become aware of the existing different conceptions of information literacy. This helps them understand which kind of information literacy is appropriate in different situations. The awareness of different existing conceptions enables also the development of information literacy (Bruce, 1997; Limberg et al., 2002).

In the present study, information literacy is approached through examination of students' own perceptions of the instruction and guidance given in information searching and the critical judgment of information, their actual use of databases and other information sources, and their skills in the critical judgment of information and its sources. While approaching information literacy partly through students' own perceptions, Bruce's study forms a relevant theoretical framework for reflecting the results.

3.1. Related Research in Information Literacy

Empirical studies in information literacy have been conducted in educational contexts in order to get knowledge of the problems and issues crucial in planning and enhancing instructional programs in information literacy.

Webber and Johnston (2000) studied students' conceptions of information literacy and compared them with Bruce's seven faces of information literacy. They found that students identified information seeking and sources in their conception of information literacy, and the role of information technology was emphasized. Thus Bruce's first three categories, (1) using information technology, (2) finding information, and (3) executing a process, were present in the conceptions. The students' conceptions developed during the course in information literacy from information-technology-related conceptions towards a conception of information literacy that implies evaluation, application, and organization of information. A transition was seen towards Bruce's latter four categories, (4) controlling information, (5) building up a personal knowledge base, (6) working with knowledge and personal perspectives in such a way that novel insights are gained, and (7) using information wisely for the benefit of others. Students considered also that active, constructivist methods of teaching and learning information literacy enhance understanding and learning compared to lecturing, although lectures are experienced as easier. In the recent research of Julien and Boon (2004) in which the instructional outcomes in Canadian academic libraries were studied, the statements related to the seven faces of information literacy were found in the student interviews.

McGowen (1995) studied practicing physicians' attitudes towards lifelong learning, defined in the study as ability to identify a need, access and retrieve information, evaluate and use it appropriately (cf. definitions of information literacy). It was assumed that the graduates of problem-based learning curriculum and traditional curriculum should have different conceptions of lifelong learning. The study showed that such differences did not exist. It was concluded that in order to enhance the retention of the knowledge and skills in information literacy and lifelong learning, the skills should be taught throughout the entire medical education, not only during the first two years. Novice academic library users in a study by Kasesniemi and Talja (1997) brought up the need for education in information seeking skills also to take place later in studies.

Studies by Schilling, Ginn, Mickelson, and Roth (1995), Minchow (1995), and Saarti and MacDonald (2003) emphasize the importance of integration of information literacy skills and activities into existing courses. Students' attitudes towards integrated courses were positive and their skills improved significantly during the courses.

To sum up, the studies established the essential factors in successful development and instruction in information literacy: the knowledge of students' perceptions of information literacy, the pedagogically appropriate teaching and learning methods, integration into curricula, and timely instruction. Cooperation between faculty and the persons responsible for information literacy instruction, usually librarians, in planning the courses is considered important (e.g., Schilling et al., 1995).

4. CONCEPTIONS OF LEARNING

In order to enhance understanding of the phenomenon of learning, research has been conducted on how people conceive learning and what kind of beliefs they have of knowledge. Conceptions of learning and knowledge refer to individuals' ways of thinking about what learning and knowledge is, i.e., how they define them, their ideas about how knowledge is created and evaluated, and how knowing occurs. In general, conceptions of learning and knowledge direct how people experience and interpret learning situations and affect the learning process and study behavior including the outcomes of learning (Hofer, 2002; Lindblom-Ylänne et al., 2003; Entwistle & Peterson, 2004).

The research into conceptions associated with student learning originates in Perry's (1970) work of students' epistemological development (Eklund-Myrskog, 1996). Perry (1970) identified a developmental pattern in students' conceptions of knowledge during their college years. Students' reasoning developed from dualistic thinking in which knowledge is conceived as either right or wrong gradually through acceptance of the existence of different views to relativistic thinking. In relativistic thinking, students perceived knowledge and values as contextual and relativistic and developed finally a personal commitment on issues (Perry, 1970).

The phenomenographic research approach developed in 1970s in Gothenburg has had a strong influence on thinking about students' learning (Entwistle & Peterson, 2004). Säljö (1979) distinguished five qualitatively different conceptions of learning among adults: (1) learning as increase of knowledge, (2) learning as memorizing, (3) learning as acquisition of facts or procedures which can be retained and/or utilized in practice, (4) learning as abstraction of meaning, and (5) learning as an interpretative process aiming at the understanding of reality.

Entwistle and Peterson (2004) compare Perry's and Säljö's categories of conceptions as follows: The dualistic thinking is parallel with Säljö's first three reproducing conceptions of learning, and relativistic thinking is parallel with the latter two conceptions of learning, which imply seeking meaning. According to Entwistle and Peterson (2004, p. 410), "the most important theoretical aspect of Perry's work was the recognition that the developmental process involved an expanding awareness of the nature of knowledge, created through a broader conception of learning that integrated earlier conceptions within a more meaningful whole."

Conceptions of learning and knowledge or epistemological beliefs are intertwined; beliefs about learning and teaching are closely related to how knowledge is acquired (Lonka, 1997; Hofer & Pintrich, 1997). According to Lonka (1997, p. 19), conceptions of learning "provide a window for looking at epistemologies, because they implicitly include conceptions of the origin of knowledge." On the other hand, they seem to be separated; conception of knowledge deals with the nature of knowledge and the process of knowing, while conception of learning is more related to the activity of studying. Also in terms of conceptual clarity, they should be treated as separate constructs in research (Hofer & Pintrich, 1997; Entwistle & Peterson, 2004).

After Perry and Säljö, several researchers have identified and developed conceptions of learning and knowledge in their research in both qualitative and quantitative methods. According to reviews of Hofer and Pintrich (1997) and Entwistle and Peterson (2004), research has focused on the interrelationships of the two conceptions, relationships between these and learning orientations, motivation, and attitudes as well as connections to the other concepts describing students' study behavior, such as approaches to learning and studying and study strategies. Also, contextuality, domain specificity of the conceptions, and gender differences have been explored.

In the following section, some of the research studies conducted in the field of learning and psychology of learning exploring the conceptions of learning among medical students and conceptions in different educational contexts are presented in more detailed. The categorizations of conceptions in these studies as well as Säljö's (1979) categorization form a framework against which the analysis of the conceptions of learning in the present study is reflected. Also, some previous research on the conceptions of knowledge and information seeking behavior in the domain of library and information science is reviewed.

4.1. Related Research in Conceptions of Learning

Lonka and Lindblom-Ylänne (1996) were studying epistemologies, conceptions of learning, and study practices of freshmen and fifth-year students in psychology and medicine in a non-PBL curriculum through a task-booklet with open-ended and Likert-type questions. In an open-ended question, the students were asked to give their own subjective definitions of learning. Additionally, the conception of learning was studied through statements which described five conceptions of learning adopted from the Inventory of Learning Styles of Vermunt and van Rijswijk (1988). Those five conceptions of learning were as follows: intake of knowledge, construction of knowledge, use of knowledge, stimulating education, and cooperation with fellow students.

Intake of knowledge means that learning is viewed as taking in knowledge provided by education through memorizing and reproducing. Other learning activities are tasks of teachers. Construction of knowledge implies the view of learning as constructing one's own knowledge and insights. Most learning activities are seen as task to students. In the conception use of knowledge, learning is viewed as acquiring knowledge that can be used through concretizing and applying, which are seen as tasks for both students and teachers. Stimulating education includes that learning activities are seen as tasks of students, but teachers and textbook authors should all the time stimulate students to use these activities. Cooperative learning conception lays stress to learning in cooperation with other students and to sharing the tasks of learning with them (Vermunt & van Rijswijk, 1988).

The students' subjective definitions of learning were classified on three different scales adopted from Lonka, Joram, and Bryson (1990): active epistemology scale, constructivity scale, and representation scale (Lonka et al., 1990 in: Lonka & Lindblom-Ylänne, 1996). Active epistemology refers to beliefs about learners' active role in the learning process; constructivity refers to the idea that knowledge is constructed by the learner. On the representation scale, the use of the terminology of mental representation (i.e., schemata, knowledge structure) as a means for explaining learning was observed. Statements concerning the students' epistemological beliefs were included in the booklet, and the answers were used to classify the students as dualists or relativists according to Perry (1970) (Lonka & Lindblom-Ylänne, 1996).

It was found that constructivist conceptions of learning were most typical of advanced psychology students and these conceptions were negatively related to Perry's dualism scale. Learning was seen as intake of knowledge more often by medical students than by psychology students. Highest dualism scores were obtained by the freshmen, especially medical students, and the dualists' conceptions of learning were more passive than were the relativists. On the other hand, all the students, especially the advanced medical students, emphasized the students' active role in learning. The results support the idea that conception of learning may be domain-specific (Lonka & Lindblom-Ylänne, 1996).

In order to explore the influence of learning context on students' learning process, Eklund-Myrskog (1996) investigated students' conceptions of learning, approaches to learning, and outcomes of learning in two different educational contexts, i.e., among student nurses and car mechanic students. The different phenomena were explored at the beginning of and at the end of the educational programs and the comparisons were made within and between the programs. In the interviews, the students were asked to explain how they knew they had learnt something as a part of the discussion of how they usually learn.

The analysis of student nurses' ways of experiencing learning resulted in five different conceptions which were classified into the following categories of description:

A. Learning in terms of remembering and keeping something in mind
B. Learning in terms of understanding
C. Learning in terms of applying knowledge, based on understanding
D. Learning in terms of getting a new perspective
E. Learning in terms of forming a conception of one's own

Conceptions A, B, C, and D could be identified both at the beginning and at the end of the program. Conception E could be identified only at the end of the program.

The four categories describing car mechanic students' conceptions of learning were:

A. Learning in terms of remembering
B. Learning in terms of applying knowledge, based on knowing how to do something

C. Learning in terms of understanding
D. Learning in terms of forming a conception of one's own

Categories B and C were found both at the beginning and at the end of the program. Category A could only be identified at the beginning, and category D at the end of the program.

In comparison of student nurses' and car mechanic students' conceptions of learning, only two of the conceptions found could be identified in both groups, i.e., learning in terms of understanding and learning in terms of forming a conception of one's own. Differences found in the conceptions of learning were fewer within a program than among the students in different programs, and thus it is concluded that conceptions are to some extent contextually dependent.

In addition to an educational program and the field of study, context also embraces teaching and learning methods, which affect learning and conceptions of learning (Entwistle & Peterson, 2004). Martin and Ramsden (1987) studied the influence of two differently taught and organized study programs on students' conceptions of learning. One program, called the study skills program, used lectures while the other program, called learning to learn program, used group-discussion methods. The aim of the both study programs was to help the students to learn more effectively through learning the general study techniques, such as note-taking, reading, writing, and organization of time. In the learning to learn program, the study techniques and methods were integrated to the curriculum, and in the study skills program, the students were supposed to learn the study techniques independently of other courses. The results showed that students' conceptions of learning developed more among those students who had attended the learning to learn program than among the students who participated in the study skills program. The results indicate that integration of learning skills programs to curriculum and teaching methods based on interaction between the students and the teachers enhances development of students; conceptions of learning.

In the field of information behavior research, a few studies have explored the relationship between students' epistemological beliefs and their information seeking behavior (Whitmire, 2003, 2004). Whitmire (2003) interviewed the undergraduate students about their search process while they completed a major research paper. Some of the interview questions concentrated on epistemological beliefs. As a result of a content analysis of the interviews, the study subjects were placed into three different epistemological development categories based on their ability to recognize authoritative information sources and whether or not they believed that knowledge was contextual. The categories were: medium–low level, medium–high level, and high level. The categories of the epistemological development levels were related to the stages of Kuhlthau's (1993) information search process (ISP) model: (1) task initiation, (2) topic selection, (3) prefocus exploration, (4) focus formulation, (5) collection, and (6) presentation. The results of the study indicated that epistemological beliefs affected the topic, the use of mediators, search techniques, the evaluation of information, and the ability to recognize authority. The following stages of the ISP-model were affected by the epistemological beliefs: topic selection, prefocus formulation, focus formulation, and collection. Medium–low epistemological believers tended to allow the faculty member to select an essay topic for them, and when they searched for information, they did not apply different search techniques, such as browsing, reading the table of contents of journal issues, or following citations in bibliographies. Medium–high and high epistemological believers used a variety of search techniques and variety of individuals as mediators during the search process. They were able to recognize authoritative sources and also considered themselves capable of critically judging information.

In another study of Whitmire (2004), the relationship between under-graduates' epistemological beliefs, reflective judgment, and information seeking behavior was explored. The study results were consistent with Whitmire (2003). Students at higher stages of epistemological development could handle conflicting information sources and recognize authoritative sources better than the students at lower stages, who rejected information sources that were opposite to their own views and asked faculty for help to determine the authority of sources instead of doing the judgment them-selves.

In Limberg's (1998) study, the interaction between information seeking and learning is approached through students' conceptions. High school seniors' experiences of information seeking process and their conceptions of information seeking and subject matter were explored while they were con-ducting a learning assignment of the consequences of Swedish membership in the European Union (EU) which implied independent information seek-ing and use.

Limberg (1998) found three major ways of experiencing information seeking and use:

A. Fact-finding
B. Balancing information in order to make correct choices
C. Scrutinizing and analyzing

Also three different categories describing students' different ways of understanding the subject matter of the assignment were identified:

A. Fragmentary knowledge of EU
B. An understanding of the EU as mainly economic cooperation
C. A conception of the EU membership as a matter of ethical or political decision or commitment

It was found that the different conceptions of information seeking and use interacted closely with students' conceptions of the content of information. The students experiencing information seeking as fact-finding had fragmentary knowledge of the EU and thought that consequences of EU membership cannot be assessed due to a lack of facts. Those students who experienced information seeking as balancing information in order to make correct choices were holding the conception B. They related the possible consequences of the EU membership to their subtopics such as labor market, industry and competition, education and research, and environment. Students' weak prior knowledge of the subtopics made information seeking and use more difficult. The students experiencing information seeking as scrutinizing and analyzing held the conception C. They related the EU membership to large context and considered that political and moral values were at stake. The findings indicate that variation in information seeking and use interact closely with variation in ways of understanding the content of information. It's concluded that information seeking is not independent of the content of information, as experienced by the users. The results show the same kind of developmental pattern as in Perry's (1970) scheme of epistemological development (Limberg, 1998).

To sum up, the research results show that students' conceptions of learning, knowledge, and information seeking vary and develop during the learning process and in different contexts and learning environments. Epistemological beliefs affect various stages in information seeking process and how individuals make judgments about information, whereas conceptions of information seeking and use affect the search process and learning about the information content.

5. PROCEDURES AND METHODS

The following section describes the research questions, the study contexts and subjects, and data analysis technique.

5.1. Research Questions

The overall research questions of the dissertation project were:

– Which factors, connected to the learning/teaching methods, affect information seeking and use and in what way?
– What kind of information is needed for learning purposes?
– Which kind of sources and channels are used, in what way, and why?
– How is the information used in the purpose of learning?

5.2. Traditional Medical Curriculum Complemented with the Early Patient Contact Program

In Finland, the time needed to complete the degree of licentiate in medicine is six years. At the Turku University Medical School, the degree studies were at the time of the research divided into pre-clinical and clinical studies and practical training. The degree entails a Master's thesis as part of the advanced studies. Study modules were classified as obligatory core studies or elective studies. Lectures were the main method of instruction during pre-clinical studies, complemented with teaching in groups and laboratory sessions. The curriculum implemented an early patient contact program during the first four semesters of the studies. The extent of those studies was 2.5 credits from the total 240.0 credits. After the fourth semester, the program was included in the elective studies. The system of evaluation was in the form of written tests during the pre-clinical stage. Clinical skills were learned at the Turku University Central Hospital. After the first semester, medical students could seek admission to a special program providing basic research skills, which proceeded in parallel with the medical curriculum. The objective of this program is to familiarize the students with methods used in medical research (Opinto-opas, 1997).

5.3. The Problem-Based Medical Curriculum

In 1994, the University of Tampere Medical School became the first medical school in Finland to implement the problem-based learning approach in the education of medical doctors. The first three to four years of the degree course was divided into 25 phases in which the theory and practical substance of several disciplines were integrated. The last two to three years of the education were spent mostly in full-time supervised work with patients in various hospital clinics and in health centers. The degree course includes practical periods, which may be completed during vacations, and a six-week training period for all students. The studies consist of obligatory and elective studies. The Master's thesis is included. There was no separate research track program, but it was possible for the students take part in the research program of the faculty from the beginning of their studies. The greater part of the study was undertaken in groups of eight undergraduates, each guided by a member of faculty as a tutor. Lectures average one a day. Other forms of instruction used were group work in clinical skills and different disciplines, including laboratory sessions, and study visits. Clinical skills were learned and practiced in a special clinical skills laboratory, which was equipped with training models, physician's equipment, literature, and audio-visual materials. Evaluation methods formed part of the learning process. Knowledge, skills, attitudes, and the learning process as a whole were evaluated. Self-evaluation and feedback were included in the evaluation. After every phase, written examinations took place. Progress tests which embraced all disciplines were organized several times a year. They gave information to both the students and the faculty about the progress made in the studies (Lääketieteen koulutus, 1997).

5.4. Instruction in Information Searching in the Traditional Curriculum

In the traditional curriculum, the instruction was given in a course called Electronically Mediated Information and Library Use, which included a unit of Introduction to University Studies. Students were attending the course in the beginning of their first study year. It consisted of three hours of lessons and a minimum of one-hour practice for every student. The content of the course was introduction to electronic resources and search systems in networked databases and CD-ROM databases. The lessons were held by the medical librarian in the auditorium with equipment to demonstrate the use of databases. To get the course accepted, all students were required, in cooperation with the librarian, to conduct information searches in databases on the subject area of their theses. The practical information searches were conducted using the library's computers (Opinto-opas, 1997).

5.5. Instruction in Information Searching in the Problem-Based Learning Curriculum

In the problem-based learning curriculum, the course in information searching was organized as small group instruction on three occasions. In the beginning of the first semester, in connection with the study phase called Introduction, the students were instructed in the use of domestic databases through two classes, each of two-hour duration. During the second semester, the students were given instruction in the use of the MEDLINE database in the connection with a course called Research Basics. The instructions were given in small groups, with 8–10 students and the practices were tutored by two library personnel in a room specifically equipped for the purpose with six computers and a data projector. The medical librarian was responsible for planning the course in cooperation with faculty in the planning group for the Introduction phase (Ongelmakeskeinen, 1998).

5.6. Information Resources

Finnish universities are equipped with computer laboratories connected to the Internet. The university library's task is to acquire both printed and electronic material for studies and research. Access to the network and resources is free of charge for students and staff. Concerning the access to databases, it can be concluded that from this point of view, the contexts were in principle similar to each other. It can be assumed that the bigger classes in the traditional curriculum (an intake of 70 students a year compared with about 40 students a year in the problem-based learning curriculum) affected the access of printed course materials available in libraries. On the other hand, medical students tended to buy the elementary textbooks in following either curriculum.

5.7. Methods and Subjects

Qualitative methods were used for the collection and analysis of the data. The study subjects were 16 second-year medical students in the problem-based learning education and 15 second-year medical students studying according to the traditional curriculum, complemented by an early patient contact program.

The methods for collecting data were theme interviews (with open-ended questions), students' diaries, observation, and relevant documents, the interview transcriptions forming the main source of information.

5.8. Data Analysis

The data were analyzed following the principles of qualitative analysis for finding differences related to the research questions in the interviews and building categories that formed the basis for the analysis (cf. Alasuutari, 1994). In the categorization process, the coding paradigm (Strauss & Corbin, 1990) was applied. In the coding paradigm, data are analyzed in terms of conditions, interactions, strategies, tactics, and consequences. Data processing used manual methods initially, but in order to assist in managing the material, a computer program for qualitative data analysis (NUD*IST) was later employed.

The data analysis proceeded in two phases. In the first phase, different empirical categories were established on the basis of variations and differences in the interviews. The starting point for exploration of the categories were the two main interview themes: learning and studies, and information seeking and use in the context of learning and studies.

Issues or sub-themes under the first theme, which were discussed and which became the initial empirical categories, were: the role of different learning situations and teaching, including instruction in information seeking; students' ways of studying; problems in learning; studies, and information gathering; and conceptions of learning. The second main theme included aspects connected with information needs: choice, evaluation, and use of information, and different sources and channels of information. During the second phase of the analysis, the meaning of the empirical categories established in the first phase was interpreted in the light of the existing research literature. Thereafter, the categories were synthesized and new main categories were developed. Information literacy is one of the main categories in the overall research.

6. RESULTS

Following the analysis procedure described earlier, the medical students' information literacy was built up from the following initial categories:

1. Students' conceptions of the instruction in the use of databases organized by the library and of information searching,
2. Students' actual use of databases,
3. Students' conceptions of how instruction in critical judgment of information appears in the medical education generally,
4. Students' use of different information sources, and
5. Students' evaluation of information.

The analysis of information literacy proceeded in two parts. The first part considered the two first initial categories: (1) students' ideas of the instruction in the use of databases organized by the library and of information searching and (2) students' actual use of databases. The second part implied the initial empirical categories three, four, and five. Finally, to get an overall understanding of students' information literacy, the analysis of the both parts was synthesized and as a result three combination categories describing the medical students' information literacy emerged. Those combination categories are:

1. undeveloped information literacy skills,
2. simple information literacy skills, and
3. developed information literacy skills.

In the following, the results are given through descriptions of these combination categories. The schematic description of the analysis is presented in the appendix. Before the descriptions of the combination categories, the results of the analysis of the initial categories are given with the main characteristics of the categories. The detailed descriptions of the initial categories are presented in Eskola (2005).

6.1. Information Literacy – Part 1

1. Students' ideas of the instruction in the use of databases organized by the library and of information searching and
2. students' actual use of databases.

The examination of students' information literacy through their conceptions of the instruction given in the use of databases, their ideas of information searching, and their actual use of databases resulted in categorization of the students in three initial categories:

1. No problems
2. No motivation
3. Learning by doing

1. No problems. Typical for the students in the initial category, No problems meant that they experienced information searching relatively problem-free. Problem-based learning students seemed to have a neutral attitude to the given instruction in the use of databases. They stated that they did not have any problems in using databases because they had been taught how to use them. Traditional students appeared critical of lecturing. Variations were found among the students in the actual use of databases and in information retrieval skills, as reported by them. On the one hand, there were students who conducted searches for their Master's theses, and on the other hand, there were students who had not started their theses project and conducted searches occasionally for their course papers. Some students were obviously interested in computers generally and relied on their own skills. Those students who did not regard themselves as active and qualified users, although not finding information retrieval difficult, relied on getting help, for example, from the library personnel or printed instructions usually found near computers.

2. *No motivation.* The main characteristic of the category No motivation was that its members emphasized that they did not have any need to use databases. The given instruction in the use of databases was considered, in principle, as important; but when students did not need databases, they forgot how to use them. Students wanted more instruction at a more suitable moment, that is, when there was a real need to use the databases. Lectures as a method of instruction were criticized by traditional students. Students reported use of databases mostly in connection with course papers. It was common that searches were conducted together with some other, more qualified student. The reason for searching together also depended on the fact that assignments and papers were often written in pairs.

3. *Learning by doing.* The main characteristic of the initial category Learning by doing group was the conception that information searching is something which should be learned in connection with real information needs. Sometimes this meant that one learned with difficulty using the trial end error method. The group included students from both curricula. Problem-based learning students had attended the course in information search and in their opinion it was useful and gave basic skills for using databases. Traditional students either had not attended the instruction or criticized the method, i.e., lectures. It is important that all the students except one had started to work on their theses. This meant that the students had at least conducted information searches in databases for literature reviews in the research area of their own thesis subject. Students also used databases in connection with writing papers for some courses. Problem-based learning students occasionally searched in databases for solving the problem-based learning problems. This was the case with the only student in this group who had not begun to write the thesis. Although the students highlighted the personal involvement in learning to use databases, they got assistance from other students, friends, and senior researchers. Among the students, there was also consciousness that information searching can be complicated and requires knowledge and skills.

6.2. Information Literacy – Part 2

The second part implied the initial empirical categories three, four, and five, i.e., (3) students' conceptions of how instruction in critical judgment of information appears in the medical education generally, (4) students' use of different information sources, and (5) students' evaluation of information.

3. Students' conceptions of how instruction in critical judgment of information appears in the medical education generally. In addition to the instruction in the use of databases organized by the medical libraries, students were asked how instruction in critical thinking and critical judgment of medical information and information sources was brought up in the medical education generally. Students answered by describing different courses and learning situations, which they considered to be organized in order to give this kind of guidance. Students in the traditional group considered that there was little or no instruction of this kind in the curriculum more often than students in the problem-based learning group. The problem-based learning students mentioned tutorial meetings and special seminars as examples which gave an opportunity for them to change their ideas or to present different views, while the traditional students mentioned reading circles included in some elective courses. Thus the instruction in critical thinking and the critical judgment of medical information and information sources tended to appear as a more visible and tendentious function in the problem-based curriculum than in the traditional curriculum.

Students' critical judgment of information and sources was analyzed through the following issues:

4. students' use of different information sources, and
5. students' evaluation of information.

One of the research questions in the dissertation project was: Which kind of sources and channels are used, in what way, and why? The analysis explored the use of printed sources (books, journals) electronic resources (databases, Internet) media sources (TV, radio, newspapers), and people. The wide use of many information sources has been connected to a critical approach to information (Heinström, 2002; Ford, 1986). Jacobs, Ott, Sullivan, Ulrich, and Short (1997) have generated from research literature the following indicators for critical thinking: obtaining data from all sources, distinguishing relevant from irrelevant data, validating data obtained, identifying missing data, recognizing assumptions, detecting bias, identifying unstated assumptions, identifying relationships or patterns, recognizing logical inconsistencies, and determining generalizations.

In the analysis, three different initial categories of using information sources were found: (1) slight use of sources, (2) simple use of sources, and (3) rich use of sources. In order to explore students' evaluation of information, they were asked if they paid any attention to the critical judgment of information and sources. The issue was additionally brought up spontaneously by the students under various themes, including the use of media sources and the Internet and the selection of different sources. The overall analysis of critical judgment was made on the basis of the students' use of information sources, whether they used to evaluate information and sources, and how advanced the judgment was. Students were considered to have a more critical approach to information when they expressed or applied various appropriate criteria than the students who either did not question the information and sources or commented in general terms on the reliability of information. Below are listed the criteria used in the categorization of students' critical judgment.

Less critical approach to information:

– use of only few sources of information
– nonexistent or slight judgment such as:
  – general comments on the reliability and/or age of the
  – information in the Internet
  – general comments on the reliability of the information in the mass media
  – not questioning authorities
  – some discussion of the type and the age of the information source

Critical approach to information:

– use of several different sources of information
– more and more advanced judgment of information and sources such as:
  – distinguishing relevant from irrelevant information
  – observing that information can be bound up with situation and/or time
  – approving uncertainty of information
  – questioning the authorities
  – demanding for arguments for information
  – discussing the type and age of the information source

Also this analysis resulted in three categories:

1. Slight use of sources and undeveloped critical judgment.
2. Simple use of sources and simple critical judgment.
3. Rich use of sources and developed critical judgment.

6.3. The Combination Categories of Information Literacy

Finally, to get an overall understanding of students' information literacy, the analysis of both parts was synthesized, and as a result, the three combination categories describing the medical students' information literacy emerged. Those combination categories are:

1. undeveloped information literacy skills,
2. simple information literacy skills, and
3. developed information literacy skills.

1. Undeveloped information literacy skills. Students' use of different information sources in their studies was slight. They seldom consulted sources other than those mentioned in the study guides and did use electronic sources practically not at all. In connection with course papers, printed sources other than textbooks were consulted. In these cases they often got tips about the resources needed from the faculty member who had given the assignment.

Compared to the students in the two following categories, the students in this category evaluated information and sources least. They considered that either critical judgment was not needed, or they did not master how to judge information and sources critically. When the students referred to the judgment of information and sources, they were likely to mention the type of source.

Examination of the students' division in the initial categories, formed on the basis of their conceptions of the instruction given in the use of databases, their ideas of information searching, and their actual use of databases, revealed that they belong to the categories No motivation and No problems.

In the category Undeveloped information literacy skills, the majority of the students came from the traditional curriculum and no one had started to write the thesis.

2. Simple information literacy skills. This was the largest combination category and consisted primarily of students whose use of information sources can be characterized as simplified, with the nuance of straightforwardness. Students consulted mainly the resources mentioned in study guides and handbooks. Occasionally, other sources could be selected, for example, in connection with writing course papers. Electronic sources were seldom used. Only one student had started to write the thesis.

Students did not usually question the information they read in textbooks or heard in lectures. They did not ponder very much over the reliability of information and sources and, when they did, they paid attention to type of

source and age of information in addition to the common remarks on the
reliability of information in mass media and/or on the Internet versus textbooks and the fast-aging and chancing character of information.

The students in this combination category belonged to the initial categories No motivation and No problems. They came from the both curricula
and most of them had not started to work on the thesis.

3. *Developed information literacy skills.* This category included the students whose use of information sources can be characterized as wide and
rich. Students tended to consult many different sources in various situations.
In addition to the use in connection with thesis preparation and course
papers, the different sources were also consulted during the ongoing course
or phase of study.

Their approach to the critical judgment of information can be characterized as awake and conscious. In the critical judgment of information, they
used more advanced criteria. They referred to the topical relevance of
information in choosing information and sources in addition to bringing up
issues concerning the type of document and its age. Typical for these
students was that they did not only consider the information in textbooks or
from authorities as unchanging facts but also highlighted the influence of
situation and time. The students also wanted grounds for the claims
appearing in the information sources they found.

Examination of the students' division in the categories formed on the
basis of their conceptions of the instruction given in the use of databases,
their ideas of information searching, and their actual use of databases
revealed that all the students belonging to the initial category Learning by
doing were categorized to this combination category.

In addition to the students in the category Learning by doing, this combination category included problem-based learning students from the initial
category No motivation, who had not started the thesis, and one traditional
student from the initial category No problems, who had started the thesis
writing. The majority of the students came from the problem-based learning
curriculum.

6.4. Students' Conceptions of Learning

In order to get knowledge about the medical students' conceptions of
learning, all students were asked to explain what they mean by learning
(cf. Säljö, 1979), and how the students knew they had learnt something
(cf. Eklund-Myrskog, 1996).

The analysis of students' utterances concerning learning resulted in four different categories of conceptions:

1. Learning as an intake of knowledge and/or memorizing.
2. Learning as an application of knowledge in practice.
3. Learning as an (constructive) activity aimed at understanding.
4. Learning as a formulation of a conception of one's own.

In the following, the categories of conceptions are described and exemplified with quotations. The quotations are identified with the following abbreviations of the curriculum: PBL (problem-based learning) and TRAD (traditional learning), with the number of the interviewee.

1. Learning as an intake of knowledge and/or memorizing. In this category, students emphasized intake of existing knowledge and/or memorizing. Some of the students were referring to intake of knowledge in different ways, through reading or through working in groups in practical courses. In the utterances were often referred to exams and examination questions and rote learning. For example, some students explained that they had learnt something when they had acquired new knowledge and could remember and reproduce it in the written exam. Although the students tended to describe learning as rote learning, they expressed the desire to retain the knowledge in their memory for a longer time, not only until the exam is over.

Two students from the PBL group and six from the traditional learning group held this conception.

What do you mean by learning? How do you know when you have learnt something?

> (PBL 27)/.../ I have read a lot of things, but it does not stay, sort of, in my mind and of course learning is that it stays in your mind and when it [something you have studied/read] comes up so you remember it, you remember how many percents of them died and how serious that was, and, what I have been thinking is that learning is not merely that I read it's also that I remember the most of it lets say after one week.

What do you mean by learning? How do you know when you have learnt something?

> (TRAD 14) Well it means that, in some subjects, such as pharmacology, you learn a lot from the lectures and practical courses, and then the reading is like that you really learn. That's when you read the area for the examination, you remember that this was said and then you learn. But in some other [subjects] such as in biochemistry it's learning by heart on the basis of old examination questions.

2. Learning as an application of knowledge in practice. Those students who described learning in terms of applying knowledge were easily identified from the others. They explained clearly that they have learnt when they know how to use and apply knowledge in practice in the future. Most of the students commented generally that learning is identical with using or applying knowledge, while one student exemplified his conception by mentioning a situation in the medical education and clinical work. Some students referred to reading and texts as examples of those contexts when the learning does not occur.

Four students from the problem-based learning (PBL) group and three from the traditional learning group held this conception.

What do you mean by learning? How do you know when you have learnt something?

> (PBL 2) Well, in a way it's to adopt [the knowledge] so that I can use the knowledge also in future.

> (TRAD 3) Well, learning ... that's when you can internalize a new thing and you try to, or you are able to use it. When for example you learn how to listen heart sounds and after that you really can listen to those heart sounds, and you are able to on that account later recognize how the different heart diseases sounds.

3. Learning as an (constructive) activity aimed at understanding. In this category, learning was explained with references to processing of knowledge or activity connected to acquisition or creation of knowledge in some way in order to understand and by that means learn. Some of the students said that learning implies assimilation of new knowledge to prior knowledge. Others described that they have noticed that they have learned and understood something in discussion with others when they could explain the subject matter to somebody with their own words. One of the students took up a need for critical evaluation when encountering new knowledge and infor- mation before internalizing it. Also in this category was mentioned that learning can occur in many ways, such as through reading, listening, explaining, or thinking. The difference between the first and third category was that in the third category, the emphasis was on the active processing of knowledge not on the intake of existing knowledge as in the first category. In the second category, Learning as an application of knowledge in practice, the students also referred to understanding while explaining their conception of learning. However, the difference between the second and this category was in the different emphasis on applying of knowledge and understanding of knowledge, the emphasis being in this category clearly on understanding.

Ten students from the problem-based learning group and two from the traditional learning group held this conception.

What do you mean by learning?

(PBL 15) Well it's usually so that when you have to think about something so then you [learn] and something which you don't understand is when you just read it for the first time. Just reading the subject matter from the book does not definitely mean that you learn something if you don't remember anything on the next day. But when you have to think about something, because you don't understand it, and you have to think about it and then you realize it. And from it [the difference] you notice you have learned because it is not a proof of learning a content of a book although you have read it. /.../

How do you know that you have learned something?

(PBL 15) When you have to think about the same thing or read it many times before you understand what you read from the book of somewhere else, you notice it [that you have learned] when reading. Although it does not have to happen only when you read, you can understand the same thing while listening a lecture. You may not have understood the subject matter when you were reading but you understand it there [on the lecture], or in the tutorial meeting somebody is explaining and if something remains unclear you can always ask.

What do you mean by learning?

(TRAD 12) Well, of course, when you can't for the moment yet apply [the knowledge], it will maybe be on the next autumn for the first time when we begin to seriously practice applying, it's in some way when you realize that you have learnt something in those moments when you have for example read an article, which have been written for physicians and you understand it, the ideas from it. When it's discussed some medicines or diseases you now the vocabulary and understand what is it all about as a whole.

4. Learning as a formulation of a conception of one's own. In this category, learning was seen in terms of forming a conception of one's own. The two students, both from the traditional learning program, described learning as one's own perception or insight or something which earlier has been strange and suddenly has become familiar to oneself to one's own knowledge.

This conception was similar to the third conception. Also, in the third category, the students used expressions such as "you know you have learned when you can explain it with your own words, which you could not do without understanding." However, the emphasis in the fourth conception was even more on the ability to form one's own conception of the subject matter.

What do mean by learning? How do you know that you have learned something?

(TRAD 4) Well, it means that you yourself can explain the thing which you have been studying and although it consisted of large amounts of different kinds of knowledge so there is the connecting thought and you have yourself become aware of it. You must yourself invent the thing otherwise its just rote learning and you forget it as soon as you have read it.

6.5. Relationships Between the Categories of Conceptions of Learning and the Categories of Information Literacy

In the following, the division of the students in the categories of conceptions of learning and categories of information literacy is presented.

1. Learning as an intake of knowledge and/or memorizing (Table 1). Six students from the traditional group and two from the problem-based learning (PBL) group held this conception. The two traditional students having developed information literacy (IL) skills and the one having simple IL skills had started to work on their theses and one of them attended the special learning program in research basics, while the remaining students had not started their thesis projects.

2. Learning as an application of knowledge in practice (Table 2). The one PBL student who held this conception and belonged to the category developed IL had started to work on thesis. All the other students had not started to work on their theses.

3. Learning as an (constructive) activity aimed at understanding (Table 3). This conception was held by 10 PBL students, of which two students in the

Table 1. Learning as an Intake of Knowledge and/or Memorizing.

Undeveloped IL	Simple IL	Developed IL
Three traditional students Two PBL students	One traditional student	Two traditional students

Table 2. Learning as an Application of Knowledge in Practice.

Undeveloped IL	Simple IL	Developed IL
Two traditional students	One traditional student Three PBL students	One PBL student

Table 3. Learning as an (Constructive) Activity Aimed at Understanding.

Undeveloped IL	Simple IL	Developed IL
Two traditional students	One traditional student Three PBL students	One traditional student Seven PBL students

Table 4. Learning as a Formulation of a Conception of One's Own.

Undeveloped IL	Simple IL	Developed IL
	Two traditional students	

category developed IL skills had started to work on their theses. The one student from the traditional group belonging to the category developed IL skills attended the special learning program in research basics and worked in a research group with plans to write the thesis in the same area.

4. Learning as a formulation of a conception of one's own (Table 4). Only two students held this conception, both of them came from the traditional curriculum and belonged to the category of simple IL skills. One of them had started to work on thesis and attended the special learning program in research basics, while the other student had not started the thesis writing and was not involved in the separate program.

7. DISCUSSION AND CONCLUSIONS

The study investigated the relationships between students' information literacy, conceptions of learning, and methods of learning. Firstly, three categories describing the information literacy of the medical students have been found: (1) undeveloped information literacy skills, (2) simple information literacy, and (3) developed information literacy skills. When the categories are examined in relation to Bruce's seven faces of information literacy (Bruce, 1997), it is observed that the categories (1) undeveloped information literacy skills and (2) simple information literacy skills are related to Bruce's faces 1 to 4, i.e., using information technology, finding information, executing a process, and controlling information. Critical analysis of information is not included in these categories and information is perceived as objective, a part of the external environment. In the present study, this became apparent from the fact that students did not question information and authorities. Category 3, developed information literacy skills, comes near to Bruce's conceptions, (5) building up a personal knowledge base and (6) working with knowledge and personal perspectives in such a way that novel insights are gained. In those categories, critical analysis of information and subjective or transformational conception of information are present. Bruce underlines that none of the conceptions is wrong but simply a different way of understanding information literacy, which can be used appropriately in different situations. However, she proposes that the hierarchical nature should be taken into account in information literacy education as the conceptions at the lower levels may reflect inadequate educational outcomes. Although there were more students from the PBL group than from the traditional group in the category Developed information literacy skills, any conclusions from the educational outcomes cannot be drawn while the educational outcomes did not belong to the scope of this study. However, the reflection of the categories in this study and Bruce's seven faces of information literacy supports the idea that there are relationships between the different learning environments and development of students' information literacy. In the problem-based learning curriculum, the guidance given in critical judgment of information was more visible and conscious than in the traditional curriculum. The problem-based learning curriculum also offered more situations than the traditional curriculum for the students to get different viewpoints on ideas. The results indicate also that real information needs, such as finding information for a thesis or course papers, trigger development in information literacy in addition to the educational context.

Secondly, in the analysis, four categories describing students' conceptions of learning were found: (1) learning as an intake of knowledge and/or memorizing, (2) learning as an application of knowledge in practice, (3) learning as an (constructive) activity aimed at understanding, and (4) learning as a formulation of a conception of one's own.

As the tables above show, 10 of the 16 PBL students saw learning in terms of understanding. The PBL students belonged to the categories Simple and Developed Information Literacy (IL) skills and two of them had started to write their theses. In the traditional group, the division of the students in the categories of conceptions was more even, although six of the total fifteen students experienced learning as intake of knowledge and/or memorizing. Of those six students, four were involved in research either through their own thesis project or through involvement in a separate learning program in research basics. Three of the traditional students holding this conception of learning belonged to the category Undeveloped IL skills, one student in Simple IL, and two students in developed IL skills. This result is consistent with results of Lonka and Lindblom-Ylänne (1996) and Martin and Ramsden (1987) according to which the traditional medical students tend to view learning as intake of knowledge and student-centered learning methods enhance the development of conceptions of learning. The PBL students had discussed the concept of learning in connection with introduction to problem-based learning, which may have made them more conscious about the variations in conceptions of learning.

Medical students tend to appreciate unambiguous information and ready answers to questions because they imagine that this kind of information helps them to manage the different patient situations. The more practical advice the teacher can give, the better the students feel (Nuutinen, Kokkonen, Rantala, Vainionpää, & Uhari, 1998). Thus, it could have been assumed that medical students in the both curriculum would more often have seen learning as applying knowledge in practice. However, this conception was held only by three traditional and four problem-based students. This may be explained by the fact that the traditional students were at the moment of the interviews attending the basic science courses, such as microbiology, which they experienced as very theoretical.

Interesting result is that the topmost conception of learning, learning as a formulation of a conception of one's own, was held by two students from the traditional group, both of whom belonged to the category of Simple IL skills. One of them had started to work on thesis and attended the special learning program in research basics, which may have influenced the development of the conception, while the other student had not started the thesis writing and was not involved in the separate program.

It can be concluded that the relationships between the categories of information literacy, conceptions of learning, and the two curricula are not clear, although the results indicate that the problem-based learning environment may enhance the development of students' conceptions of learning and information literacy. More research is thus needed in the relationships of conception of learning and knowledge, i.e., epistemological beliefs and information behavior in educational and other contexts (cf. Whitmire, 2003, 2004).

Although the scope of the study is restricted, the findings demonstrate that in order to enhance the development of students' information literacy, some aspects should be taken into account in planning learning situations in medical education. While the developed information literacy skills and developed conceptions of learning tended to appear more among the problem-based learning students than the traditional students, the study suggests that more situations where the students come into contact with different viewpoints on issues and where they themselves have to motivate their choices of information and its sources should be included in the curriculum. The fact that the students' own motivation, manifested in the study as real information needs, triggers the development in information literacy and underlines the importance of integrating learning information literacy with other appropriate learning goals and assignments in the curriculum. This relates also to correct timing of the instruction in database searching and use of other information sources. When the students need information and have to use databases and other sources to find it, they are motivated to learn how to use them. A rough comparison of the categories in this study against Bruce's seven faces of information literacy indicates the need to organize information literacy instruction according to students' different conceptions, which means increased investments of human and financial resources in the instruction.

REFERENCES

Alasuutari, P. (1994). Laadullinen tutkimus. 2 uud.p. [Qualitative research.] 2. rev. ed. Tampere: Vastapaino.

American Library Association (1989). *Presidential Committee on Information Literacy: Final Report*. Chicago: American Library Association. [Available at http://www.ala.org./ala/ acrl/acrlpubs/whitepapers/presidential.htm].

Association of College & Research Libraries (2000). *Information Literacy Competency Standards for Higher Education*. Chicago: ACRL. [Available at http://www.ala.org./acrl/ ilcomstan.html].

Barrows, H. S. (1996). Problem-based learning in medicine and beyond: a brief overview. In: L. Wilkerson & W. Gijselaers (Eds), Bringing problem-based learning to higher education: Theory and practice. *New Directions for Teaching and Learning*, 68, 3–12.

Barrows, H. S., & Tamblyn, R. M. (1980). *Problem-based learning. An approach to medical education*. New York: Springer.

Bawden, D. (2001). Information and digital literacies: A review of concepts. *Journal of Documentation, 57*, 218–252.

Blake, J. (1994). Library resources for problem-based learning. The programme perspective. *Computer Methods and Programs in Biomedicine, 44*, 167–173.

Boud, D., & Feletti, G. (1997). What is problem-based learning? In: D. Boud & G. Feletti (Eds), *The challenge of problem-based learning* (2nd ed., pp. 1–14). London: Kogan Page.

Bruce, C. (1997). *The seven faces of information literacy*. Adelaide: Auslib Press.

Donner, R. S., & Bickley, H. (1993). Problem-based learning in American medical education: An overview. *Bulletin of the Medical Library Association, 81*, 294–298.

Dunn, K. (2002). Assessing information literacy skills in the California State University: A progress report. Journal of Academic Librarianship, Jan/Mar. [Available at http:// search.epnet.com/direct.asp?an = 6174801&db = afh].

Eklund-Myrskog, G. (1996). *Students' ideas of learning. Conceptions, approaches, and outcomes in different educational contexts*. Doctoral dissertation. Åbo: Åbo Akademi University Press.

Engel, C. E. (1997). Not just a method but a way of learning. In: D. Boud & G. Feletti (Eds), *The challenge of problem-based learning* (2nd ed., pp. 17–27). London: Kogan Page.

Entwistle, N. J., & Peterson, E. R. (2004). Conceptions of learning and knowledge in higher education: Relationships with study behaviour and influences of learning environments. *International Journal of Educational Research, 41*, 407–428.

Eskola, E.-L. (2005). Information literacy of medical students studying in the problem-based and traditional curriculum. *Information research*, 10(2), paper 221 [Available at http:// InformationR.net/ir-10-2/paper221.html].

Ford, N. (1986). Psychological determinants of information needs. A small-scale study of higher education students. *Journal of Librarianship, 18*, 47–61.

Fridén, K. (1996). The librarian as a teacher: Experiences from a problem-based setting. *Health Libraries Review, 13*, 3–7.

Fridén, K., & Oker-Blom, T. (1995). *Påverkar problembaserad inlärning studenternas informationsvanor och biblioteksanvändning? [Does the problem-based learning influence students' information behavior and library use?]*. Linköping: Linköpings universitet.

Heinström, J. (2002). *Fast surfers, broad scanners and deep divers: personality and information-seeking behaviour*. Doctoral dissertation. Åbo: Åbo Akademi University Press.

Hofer, B. K. (2002). Personal epistemology as a psychological and educational construct: An introduction. In: B. K. Hofer & P. R. Printrich (Eds), *Personal epistemology: The psychology of beliefs about knowledge and knowing* (pp. 3–14). Mahwah, NJ: Lawrence Erlbaum Associates.

Hofer, B. K., & Pintrich, P. R. (1997). The development of epistemological theories: Beliefs about knowledge and knowing and their relation to learning. *Review of Educational Research, 67*, 88–140.

Jacobs, P., Ott, B., Sullivan, B., Ulrich, Y., & Short, L. (1997). An approach to defining and operationalizing critical thinking. *Journal of Nursing Education, 36*, 19–22.

Julien, H., & Boon, S. (2004). Assessing instructional outcomes in Canadian academic libraries. *Library & Information Science Research, 26*, 121–139.

Kasesniemi, E-L., & Talja, S. (1997). Sisälle kirjastosysteemiin: kirjastonkäyttäjän noviisiongelmat ja käyttäjäkoulutuksen merkitys [Understanding the library system: Novice problems in academic library use and the meaning of user education]. *Informaatiotutkimus [Information Research], 16*, 75–84.

Kuhlthau, C. C. (1993). *Seeking meaning. A process approach to library and information services*. Norwood, NJ: Ablex.

Limberg, L. (1998). *Att söka information för att lära. En studie av samspel mellan informationssökning och lärande. [Experiencing information seeking and learning. A study of the interaction between two phenomena]*. Doctoral dissertation. Göteborg: Valfrid.

Limberg, L., Hultgren, F., & Jarneving, B. (2002). *Informationssökning och lärande – en forskningsöversikt [Information seeking and learning – A research review]*. Stockholm: Skolverket.

Lindblom-Ylänne, S., Nevgi, A., & Kaivola, T. (2003). Opiskelu yliopistossa [University studying]. In: S. Lindblom-Ylänne & A. Nevgi (Eds), *Yliopisto- ja korkeakouluopettajan käsikirja [Handbook of university and college teachers]*. Helsinki: WSOY.

Lonka, K. (1997). *Explorations of constructive processes in student learning*. Doctoral dissertation. Helsinki: University of Helsinki.

Lonka, K., Joram, E., & Bryson, M. (1990). Students' changing conceptions of knowledge and learning. A poster presented at AERA annual meeting, April 16-20 Boston, MA.

Lonka, K., & Lindblom-Ylänne, S. (1996). Epistemologies, conceptions of learning, and study practices in medicine and psychology. *Higher Education, 31*, 5–24.

Lääketieteen koulutus (1997). *Lääketieteen koulutus Tampereen yliopistossa [Medical education at the Tampere University]*. Tampere: Tampere University (Booklet).

Marshall, J. G., Fitzgerald, D., Busby, L., & Heaton, G. (1993). A study of library use in a problem-based and traditional curriculum. *Bulletin of the Medical Library Association, 81*, 299–305.

Martin, E., & Ramsden, P. (1987). Learning skills or skills in learning? In: J. Richardson, M. Eysenck & D. Piper (Eds), *Student learning research on education and cognitive psychology* (pp. 155–167). Milton Keynes: Open University Press.

McGowen, J. J. (1995). The role of health science librarians in the teaching and retention of the knowledge, skills, and attitudes of lifelong learning. *Bulletin of the Medical Library Association, 81*, 184–189.

Minchow, R. (1995). Changes in information-seeking patterns of medical students: Second-year students' perceptions of information management instruction as a component of a problem-based learning curriculum. *Medical Reference Services Quarterly, 15*(1), 15–40.

Nikkarinen, T., & Hoppu, K. (1994). Ongelmakeskeinen opetus, ongelmalähtöinen oppiminen ja aktivoivat opetusmenetelmät [Problem-oriented education, problem-based learning, and activating teaching methods]. *Duodecim, 110*, 1548–1555.

Nuutinen, M., Kokkonen, J., Rantala, H., Vainionpää, L., & Uhari, M. (1998). Tiedon etsinnän opettaminen ja ristiriitaisen tiedon käsittely korkeakouluopetuksessa [Teaching information seeking and managing unumbiguous knowledge in higher education]. In: A. Nuutinen & H. Kumpula (Eds), *Opetus ja oppiminen tiedeyhteisössä [Teaching and learning in the scientific community]* (pp. 129–133). Jyväskylä: Jyväskylän yliopisto.

Ongelmakeskeinen. (1998). Ongelmakeskeinen opetus ja kirjasto [Problem-based learning and library]. *Signum, 31*(2), 39–40.

Opinto-opas. (1997–98). *Opinto-opas 1997–98. Lääketieteen lisensiaatin tutkinto. Turun yliopisto. Lääketieteellinen tiedekunta [Study guide 1997–98. Degree of licentiate in medicine. Turku University. Medical faculty]*. Turku: Turun yliopisto

Perry, W. G., Jr. (1970). *Forms of intellectual and ethical development in the college years. A scheme*. New York: Holt, Rinehart & Winston.

Rankin, J. A. (1992). Problem-based medical education: Effect on library use. *Bulletin of the Medical Library Association, 80*, 36–43.

Rauste-von Wright, M., von Wright, J., & Soini, T. (2003). *Oppiminen ja koulutus [Learning and Education]*. Helsinki: WSOY.

Ryan, G. (1997). Ensuring that students develop an adequate, and well-structured, knowledge base. In: D. Boud & G. Feletti (Eds), *The challenge of problem-based learning*, (2nd ed., pp. 125–136). London: Kogan Page.

Säljö, R. (1979). *Learning in the learner's perspective 1. Some common-sense conceptions*. Reports from the Institute of Education. No 76. Gothenburg: University of Gothenburg.

Saarti, J., & MacDonald, E. (2003). Farmasian verkkotiedonlähteiden arviointi osana farmasian verkko-opetusta [Evaluating pharmacy web resources as a part of pharmacy web teaching]. *Informaatiotutkimus [Information Research], 22*, 42–51.

Saunders, K., Northup, D. E., & Mennin, S. P. (1985). The library in a problem-based curriculum. In: A. Kaufman (Ed.), *Implementing problem-based medical education. Lessons from successful innovations* (pp. 71–88). New York: Springer.

Schmidt, H. G. (1983). Problem-based learning: Rationale and description. *Medical Education, 17*, 11–16.

Schilling, K., Ginn, D., Mickelson, P., & Roth, L. (1995). Integration of information-seeking skills and activities into problem-based curriculum. *Bulletin of the Medical Library Association, 83*, 176–183.

Silén, C., Normann, S., & Sandén, I. (1995). *Problembaserad inlärning – en beskrivning av ideologi och pedagogisk referensram [Problem-based learning – A description of ideology and pedagogical framework]*. Linköping: Hälsouniversitet, Vårdhögskolan i Östergötland.

Strauss, A., & Corbin, J. (1990). *Basics of qualitative research. Grounded theory procedures and techniques.* Newbury Park: Sage.

Taylor, S. I., & Lande, R. E. (1996). A library for problem-based learning (PBL). *Health Libraries Review, 13,* 9–12.

Vainiomäki, P. (1995). *Kasvamassa lääkäriksi: tutkimus juonneopetuksen suunnittelusta, toteutumisesta ja vaikutuksista Turun yliopiston lääketieteellisessä tiedekunnassa vuosina 1989-1993. [Growing up to be a doctor: A study of planning, implementation and outcomes of an early patient contact programme at the Faculty of Medicine of University of Turku in 1989-1993].* Doctoral dissertation. Turku: University of Turku.

Vermunt, J. D. H. M., & van Rijswijk, F. A. W. M. (1988). Analysis and development of students' skill in selfregulated learning. *Higher Education, 17,* 647–682.

Webber, S., & Johnston, B. (2000). Conceptions of information literacy: New perspectives and implications. *Journal of Information Science, 26,* 381–397.

Whitmire, E. (2003). Epistemological beliefs and the information-seeking behavior of undergraduates. *Library & Information Science Research, 25,* 127–142.

Whitmire, E. (2004). The relationship between undergraduates' epistemological beliefs, reflective judgement, and their information-seeking behavior. *Information Processing & Management, 40,* 97–111.

APPENDIX: INFORMATION LITERACY (IL) OF
MEDICAL STUDENTS: SYNTHESIS OF PARTS 1 AND 2

UNDEVELOPED IL	SIMPLE IL	DEVELOPED IL
Slight use of sources and undeveloped judgment No motivation No problems	Simple use of sources and judgment No motivation No problems	Rich use of sources and developed judgment No motivation No problems Learning by doing

Students' conceptions of how instruction in critical judgment of information appears in the medical education generally

TTTTTTTTTTTTTTTTT	EXISTING "BETWEEN THE LINES"
PPPPPPPPPPPPPPPPPPP	VISIBLE, SYSTEMATICAL

LESS DEVELOPED	MORE DEVELOPED
INFORMATION LITERACY	INFORMATION LITERACY

---- + ---+ ---+ ---+--+--+ -+ -+ -+-+-+-+-+-+-+-+- +- + -+ -+- ++-++-+++ - +++

TT– TT – TP – TP – TP – TP – TP – TP – TP – TP- TP - TP – TP –PP - PP

T = TRADITIONAL STUDENTS
P = PROBLEM-BASED STUDENTS

SHARING EXPERTISE AND INNOVATION: COMMUNITIES OF PRACTICE IN THE DEVELOPMENT OF SMALL LIBRARIES

Terttu Kortelainen and Päivi Rasinkangas

ABSTRACT

Ways of sharing information as part of the development and implementation of new evaluation methods were studied in a project involving thirteen public libraries, one polytechnic library, and one university library. The purpose of the project was to initiate collaboration in evaluation and to develop qualitative evaluation tools that would be easy to use. Communities of practice, comprising of representatives of the different libraries, had a focal role in the development work, in which sharing of information was elemental. Qualitative tools consisted of portfolios and various forms for collecting information. In addition, informal consortium benchmarking was applied to evaluate different library tasks. Although small units have rarely been studied with regard to the sharing of knowledge or information or benchmarking, they should be. Moreover, small units may even be able to contribute to development. The study is based on information gathered from participants using interviews and questionnaires as well as project documentation, the contents of which have been analyzed qualitatively.

Advances in Library Administration and Organization, Volume 25, 239–257
Copyright © 2007 by Elsevier Ltd.
ISSN: 0732-0671/doi:10.1016/S0732-0671(07)25011-4

INTRODUCTION

The sharing of knowledge is a crucial part of innovation and development, not only in industrial innovation, but also in the public sector and in numerous different tasks. A need for development may arise from insufficient working tools or methods, as pointed out by a group of northern Finnish libraries concerning qualitative evaluation of library work. There was a desire to describe the diversity of library work and to evaluate it without devoting excessive human resources to it. The reason for this limitation was the small size of several units whose staff was needed in actual library work and had no time for large-scale development efforts. Fifteen libraries started a joint development project with three targets:

- to find methods to describe library work in its full diversity,
- to conduct evaluations in a practical manner without imposing too much extra work that would take time from primary library work. The evaluations were expected to give utilizable results, to be exact, fair, flexible, feasible to carry out, and responsive to the situation, and to not unnecessarily infringe on the primary work (Patton, 1982), and
- to strengthen regional library work through joint development and evaluation.

Evaluation focused on the collections, the contents of different library functions, and the competence required to do the work as well as on the need for staff education. Portfolios were developed as one evaluation method applied in the project. Other tools such as evaluation forms were also developed by cross-library teams consisting of librarians or assistant librarians from the different participant libraries. Their task was to develop the evaluation tools, to compile data from the libraries, to compare resource and performance factors and to evaluate the contents and practices of library work (Rasinkangas, 2001). The teams' work included elements of benchmarking, as the resources and performance of different units were compared in order to find good solutions for each unit, but also innovative elements that resulted from the development work implemented in the libraries. Therefore, the following account of the theoretical background describes the characteristics of both benchmarking and innovation processes. The following research questions are posed:

1. How was information shared by the cooperating library units?
2. What was the impact of participation in the communities of practice on the implementation of new evaluation methods in very small library units?

THEORETICAL BACKGROUND

When adopting new working processes or implementing new technologies, knowledge concerning them is crucial. New knowledge is most often created through the cooperation, socialization, and externalization of knowledge, by combining knowledge with earlier knowledge structures and through internalization (Nonaka & Takeuchi, 1995). In most studies on knowledge management and sharing, the cases represent big organizations where the problem is how to share information between all partners. However, development is also needed in smaller units where the problem may be how to introduce progressive influences and applicable ideas for advancement rather than how to share existing information. Below, benchmarking and diffusion processes are viewed specifically from the viewpoint of information transfer and sharing.

Benchmarking Process

Benchmarking can be defined as a tool for improvement based on comparisons with other organizations that are recognized as the best within the area (Cross & Iqbal, 1995, p. 4) or through comparison with a relative or local optimum (Kouzmin, Loffer, Klages, & Korac-Kakabadse, 1999). Its end product is positive change. Benchmarking has been regularly applied to evaluation in the industrial (Dattakumar & Jagadeesh, 2003) and public sectors (Dorsch & Yasin, 1998). In the library field, benchmarking studies have been reported from public (e.g., Creaser, 2001; Favret, 2000) and academic libraries (e.g. Laeven & Smith, 2003; Deutsche & Silcox, 2003; Charbonneau, 2005). Both in industry and in libraries, the participants are usually big units, and the targets of benchmarking studies pertain to performance and quantitative indicators (e.g., Creaser, 2001).

Benchmarking may be focused on performance, processes, or strategies, and the comparison can be internal, competitive, functional, or generic (Andersen & Pettersen, 1996). Performance benchmarking means a comparison of performance measures, financial or operational, to determine how well one's own organization fares when compared to others. Process benchmarking consists of a comparison of the methods and practices used in performing business processes to learn from the best actors, whereas strategic benchmarking means a comparison of the strategic choices made by organizations in order to collect information to improve one's strategic planning. Benchmarking can also be divided into internal, competitive, and functional benchmarking categories. Internal benchmarking involves the comparison of departments or units within the same organization, while competitive benchmarking involves comparisons of one's own performance against the best competitor, i.e., an organization that provides the same service or product. Functional benchmarking consists of comparisons of processes or functions against non-competitor companies within the same technological area or industry, and generic benchmarking involves a comparison of one's processes against the best processes available regardless of industry (Andersen & Pettersen, 1996). The approach that the organization takes to benchmarking may range from informal to formal. A formal approach is defined as the use of a disciplined and structured methodology, whereas informal is defined as "common sense" comparison (Cross & Ibqal, 1995, pp. 5–6).

Consortium benchmarking differs somewhat from the benchmarking of two partners. De Vito and Morrison (2000) described a case of several partners that focused on a target, the benchmarking of which would most likely benefit all participants but in which nobody would be exceptionally poor or outstandingly excellent. In this case, the participants gradually learned to work as a team and, hence, to benefit from the opportunity to learn from one another and to share practices in order to improve their own processes rather than to force every participant's processes into the same mold. The participant organizations exchanged documentary information, and this was followed by an informal exchange of information on how each participant does the process. Data from each participant's measures were submitted to the benchmarking facilitator who compiled and blinded the data to preserve confidentiality. After the best practices had been documented and verified by the team, each participant could adapt and implement the practices in a way that was best suited to improve the organization's process. After this, benchmarking was continued with partners outside the consortium. In this process, the consortium participants acted as a single unit. While this formal benchmarking process was being developed, "continued informal benchmarking among the consortium process owners has had a synergistic benefit. In addition to exchanging benchmarking skills among participant members, the approach strengthens a culture that values continual improvement and teamwork to achieve excellence. It builds a foundation for continued benchmarking, formal and/or informal, through the use of common terminology, tools, and techniques." In the authors' opinion, consortium benchmarking is a technique for any organization, public or private (De Vito & Morrison, 2000).

In the literature, benchmarking is divided into at least five phases (Andersen & Pettersen, 1996; Cross & Ibqal, 1995):

1. Planning: Select the process for benchmarking, document the process, and develop performance measures.
2. Searching: Find a benchmarking partner.
3. Observation or collecting data: Understand and document the partner's process, including both performance and practice.
4. Analysis: Identify gaps in performance and find the root causes for the performance gaps.
5. Adapting, integrating, or changing: Choose the best practice, adapt to the company's conditions, and implement changes.

Some authors combine phases 1 and 2, while others combine phases 3 and 4 and label them jointly as analysis. Still others add recycling, verification or maturity cycles after the adaptation phase (Fernandez, McCarty, & Rakotobe-Joel, 2001).

The Innovation Process

Diffusion is a process by which an innovation is communicated through certain channels over time to the members of a social system. It is a special type of communication concerned with the spreading of messages that are perceived as new ideas. Through communication, participants in the system create and share information with one another in order to reach a mutual understanding. Diffusion has a special character because of the novelty of the idea (Rogers, 1995). According to earlier studies, a process of innovation consists of the following phases:

I. Beginning
  1. Agenda setting
  2. Matching
II. Implementation
  3. Redefining/restructuring
  4. Clarifying
  5. Routinizing (Rogers, 1995, pp. 391–400).

Agenda setting is an ongoing process in all systems. It occurs when a general organizational problem that may create a perceived need for an innovation is defined (Rogers, 1995, p. 391). Agenda setting identifies and prioritizes needs and problems and enables a search of the organization's environment to locate innovations that can address the problems at hand. Setting the agenda may take a long time. A performance gap, defined as a discrepancy between the organization's expectations and its actual performance, can trigger the innovation process (Rogers, 1995, p. 393). However, the presence of an innovation may also launch the innovation process without any initial recognition that there is a problem or a need.

At the matching stage, the organization's problem is conceptually matched with an innovation to determine how likely it is that the innovation can solve the problem (Rogers, 1995, p. 394). Agenda setting and matching constitute the initiation, defined as the information gathering, conceptualization, and planning that leads up to the decision to adopt an innovation.

Redefining/restructuring occurs when the innovation is re-invented to more exactly address the organization's needs and structure or when the organization's structure is modified to fit the innovation. Both the innovation and the organization are expected to change at least to a certain degree during the redefining/restructuring stage (Rogers, 1995, p. 304).

Clarification is used to gradually develop a better understanding of new ideas among the members of the organization when innovations are put into more widespread use in that organization. Routines emerge after the innovation has become incorporated into the regular activities of the organization, and the innovation loses its separate identity (Rogers, 1995, p. 399).

In the innovation process, participation includes the participant's active work (operating), including information sharing, joint goal setting, and participation in the innovative decisions (Johnson, Donohue, Atkin, & Johnson, 2001). In numerous studies, participation has been positively associated with the diffusion and application of innovations (Leonard-Barton, 1988; Leonard-Barton & Sinha, 1993; Rogers, 1995; Clayton, 1997).

Recapitulation of the Common Phases

Diffusion of innovations and benchmarking overlap in that they both are connected with finding new solutions to problems. Fundamentally, both processes involve the sharing of information and knowledge.

The processes are initiated with phases devoted to *planning* or *agenda setting*, which include the notion that there is a need for change or improvement, and also possible agreement or discussion about the definition of the need. In benchmarking, this means the compilation of preparatory information, a definition of the need for development or documentation of the process, and the development of performance measures. In an innovation process, this may mean prioritization of needs and problems and a search for information about a possible solution. In either case, there must be a recognition that something new is required.

These phases are followed by the *observation and analysis* phases in benchmarking, which include getting acquainted with the partner's processes and analyzing the gaps in the participant's own process in order to close them using what has been learned from the partner. Then, *matching* is used in the innovation process to apply a conceptual application of the innovation to address observed needs.

Another common phase is the *adaptation* or *integration* or *routine development* phases, in which the innovation is implemented and information is shared between its future users in the adopting organization.

The sharing of information is crucial in both processes. In benchmarking, it must be emphasized that the participants must be thoroughly familiar with their work processes to be able to share information concerning it and to adopt innovative ideas from the partner's processes. Respectively, in the diffusion of an innovation, sharing information between the change agent or other source of information and the adopter is crucial to the adoption process. The innovation decision is based on this information, as is also its possible redefinition or restructuring.

The difference in the processes is that, in the innovation process, the adopter's search for an innovation to address perceived needs (or find it without searching), whereas in the benchmarking process, the partner is chosen first and information concerning the work process is shared only after that. However, the choice of the partner is based on his or her expertise relating to the specific needs that are being addressed.

Library units with scant human resources are unable to assign anybody to merely carry out evaluation or development. This paper describes some working methods of information sharing by the representatives of such libraries in a development project. According to Rogers, more effective communication occurs when two or more individuals are homophilous, i.e., share common meanings and a mutual subcultural language and are alike in personal and social characteristics. The ideal situation would be to have two individuals homophilous on all other variables (education and social status), even though they are heterophilous regarding the innovation (1995, p. 19). In the following chapters, the sharing of information in the project is studied in three phases of the project: *initiation, analysis,* and *adaptation.* The names of these phases were derived from the innovation and benchmarking processes.

MATERIAL AND METHOD

This study is based on documents that describe the course of the project, the procedures implemented during it, records of meetings, evaluative data, and feedback from the participants. Part of this data has been collected through structured questionnaires and qualitative interviews conducted by Rasinkangas for her licentiate thesis concerning the implementation of evaluation methods. Some questionnaires were answered only by members of different teams, while others were addressed by all participants in the project, the number varying from 52 to 65 persons annually. The targets of the project were qualitative, and so also is the descriptive material to be presented here. The general representation of the processes is based on the contents of these records, which have been analyzed qualitatively.

RESULTS

The participants in the project consisted of librarians and assistant librarians in one university library, one polytechnic library, and 13 public libraries, including two regional central libraries. The libraries are located in three different areas of Finland. The Department of Information Studies at the University of Oulu was involved in the project as consultant. The project lasted three years, from 2000 to 2003. This paper, however, only describes the work done by the information service team in one area, i.e., at five libraries in the Oulu region. The task of the team was to evaluate each information service unit and to create qualitative evaluation tools for this purpose. Participation was voluntary, and, therefore, not all libraries of the region were represented on each five-person team.

In this project, a "team" can be characterized as a community of practice, which consists of people responsible for the same task in different departments of the same organization (Ståhle & Grönroos, 1999). The purpose of communities of practice is to share expertise, information, and best practices and to create common practices. Their meetings consist of discussions in small groups and sharing of information. In most reported studies, the participants have come from different parts of the same large organization. In this case, however, they represented different, mostly small, public libraries, where they were responsible for the same tasks. Below, the communities of practice are also called teams, a term used by the participants themselves.

Initiation

In the initiation phase, the information service team, i.e., the community of practice, had to decide about the specific areas of its work it wanted to target and to identify the methods it wanted to use to evaluate those areas. To be able to evaluate an information service unit, it seemed necessary to specify the composition of its tasks. There was some degree of structural variation between the units, due to both the resources available to them and the requirements placed upon them by the surrounding community. Taking all of this into account, the team produced a form itemizing the elements, resources, and competencies necessary for an information service unit.

The information service team combined the work required to document their work process and to develop standards for those processes. The members of the team together described the fields of expertise necessary in the information service of a public library such as the competence to use both domestic and international databases and web services, as well as printed sources of information. Other competencies were also described in detail in the form created by the team. One unit may not need them all. On the other hand, a broader repertoire of competencies may provoke ideas for development. This document (see Appendix 1) can be regarded as a "qualitative measure of competence" and a description of the contents of the work done in the information service in a public library. The form was used as a comparative reference in the evaluation of resources and competencies of the information service units. The compilation of this list of competencies entailed a lot of discussion about information service and its preconditions. This was perceived as a good way to work. As one participant put it,

> I think that this kind of activity will only enhance collaboration, because there are
> several people from different libraries with new ideas about the ways to do things.

Analysis

The sharing of information was connected with a number of activities, one of which was informal consortium benchmarking (De Vito & Morrison, 2000). The team visited each of the five participating units. The hosting librarian introduced the visitors to her information service unit, its resources, work practices, problems, and success stories. The team learned about the good practices and provided its expertise to solve possible problems or to further develop the information service. A record of each meeting was developed by the hosting librarian (Rasinkangas, 2001).

The task of the team, i.e., the task to develop qualitative evaluation tools, was complicated, and the competence and knowledge of every participant was urgently needed. Simultaneously, cooperation provided a possibility to compare the resources, working practices, and results of their units as they related to other libraries about the same size. For this purpose, each participant library compiled statistics about its performance and resources.

The form describing the components of information service served as a qualitative evaluation tool. It helped the librarians to document their competencies and the resources enabling their use, while demonstrating what other possible competencies or information resources were needed elsewhere, thereby suggesting possible needs for development. The filling in and even reading of the qualitative measure form of information service was felt to be a way to develop one's work. The form also served as a tool for informal, qualitative benchmarking.

A portfolio was also used for evaluation purposes. It included a library philosophy and the targets of work, a short history, a description of resources and performance, feedback from various sources and plans for the future (see Appendix 2). Two teachers from the Department of Information Studies and the secretary of the project contributed to the development of the tools by discussing the principles and reasons for evaluation and the construction of the portfolio during the lessons attended by all project participants. However, the practical development work and adaptation of the tools were done by the teams of librarians.

The tools were redefined by the libraries. The forms and portfolios were introduced and tested by the team members in the libraries and slightly modified as they gained experience. As changes were made, these modifications were shared among the team members.

Oral transfer of information has been found to be less stressful than written information. Information transfer in this community of practice was oral, concerned relevant topics, was current, comprehensible, and often unique, and its contents had been tested in surroundings resembling the unit where the information would be used.

Feedback from the project indicated that the major benefits were the learning of good practices from other participants and the encouragement given by the team to actually adopt new working methods. However, the participant's own contribution was also considered important.

Teamwork gave me courage for my own work.

It was nice to be able to contribute the team, not only to be a receiving partner.

Fulfilling the project's complicated tasks familiarized the team members with each other and made it possible not only to share information and expertise but also to admit the lack of it. Cooperation generated the trust necessary for the participants to take up problems relating to their work.

In addition to this, it was informative to compare resources and their allocation and to compare the performance of like units. The enablers of library work such as libraries' partners in and outside the municipality are also an interesting topic. Even with equal resources, functions can be organized differently. Sharing of such information helped the participants to "place" themselves in their work and environment.

One of the major difficulties in the project was the lack of time. Every participant was responsible for her information service during the period when they were also participating in the evaluation project. Finding time for joint meetings of the team was not easy, because the participants came from small units and had no one to fill in for them when they were away from the library.

Adaptation

It has been two years since the project ended, and it is now possible to see which evaluation methods have become part of library work in the region. The advantage of having the team members acting as change agents was that they were familiar with the rest of the staff and the needs of their respective libraries. However, to make an evaluation tool part of real everyday life, the person must be convinced of its usefulness. In fact, this means that the employee should be concerned about evaluating his or her resources and performance to motivate herself to adopt new working methods. The diffusion of the tools was perceived to be somewhat difficult. Also, the attitude of the organization may have an impact on the adoption of evaluation tools. If everyone is told to complete a form, every employee will complete it, and this implies that person can use part of his or her working time for this purpose. Administrative support of such efforts is crucial.

Another influential factor is user involvement in the planning of a method of low transferability (Leonard-Barton, 1988, p. 619). The portfolio comprises several components whose contents may not be totally approachable at first glance. Its application in the evaluation of information services required its adaptation for this purpose, i.e., conversation and agreement between the team members. Three years after the end of the project, all those who now use portfolios for their own work had participated in teamwork either in the information service or in some other team. They accounted for a third of all those who filled in the questionnaire (33 persons). No one without experience of teamwork had adopted this evaluation tool. This confirms Leonard-Barton's view of the importance of user involvement in the adoption of innovations. One third of the team members also utilized a library level portfolio, whereas only one (7%) of those without teamwork experience did so. Respectively, after the end of the project, 42% of the team participants continued to use the evaluation form of information services, whereas only one person outside the teams had adopted it. In learning and adopting the use of a new tool, it seems to be important to be able to contribute to its planning and application. This was stated by one interviewee concerning the ease of adoption of the new evaluation tool:

> Because I participated in making it, it was inside me.

Benchmarking should not be a one-time event, but rather a continuous process of improving the organization's performance. This includes the introduction of the benchmarking process into new areas and the dissemination of the experiences and lessons learned (Andersen & Pettersen, 1996, p. 19). Some teams have continued their work after the project ended by meeting at least yearly to discuss this effort. The community of practice has found its function in the support and development of work and the sharing of best practices. Working in a community of practice is close to informal consortium benchmarking, because it serves as a point of reference for an individual librarian wanting to place herself among the others in her field. A concrete and important result of the project was the "discovery" of local expertise. Collegial support encouraged the librarians to trust in their own ideas and competence.

The experiences have been disseminated in a published project report (Kortelainen, 2003). Cross-library cooperation currently involves more libraries than at the beginning. The qualitative form describing the components of information service has been adapted to the needs of the libraries of the whole region, to be used in a regional evaluation of both competencies and needs for education.

EXPERIENCES OF AND FEEDBACK BY THE PARTICIPANTS

A general theme in the feedback was the importance of professional discussions and mutual learning stimulated by teamwork. Discussion in a general meeting is not as useful as conversations that take place in communities of practice where the participants are responsible for the same type of work. This was a major aspect of development in the project.

Another theme in the feedback was that the project still caused a lot of work, even though it aimed to design evaluation methods that would be easy to use. It is natural that a development phase requires time. Hopefully, the use of the methods is not equally difficult. Still, working in these communities of practice – or teams – was not felt to be hard, but rather inspiring and supportive.

CONCLUSIONS: METHODS OF SHARING KNOWLEDGE AND INFORMATION

Sharing information and knowledge is an essential element in the development of both products and processes. According to Nonaka and Takeuchi (1995), the basic condition required for sharing and creating information is the abundance or even chaotic availability of information. Discussions and collaboration are necessary in making tacit information explicit and in forging agreement about the contents of different concepts. However, a discussion group may not reach the same results as a team that uses everyone's knowledge to solve a complicated task. At the start of the work, a clear definition of the task is needed to start the work and to provide a focus for the allocation of time by the team members. Time is a necessary resource in any development work.

Functional benchmarking is defined as learning from those closest to you (Andersen & Pettersen, 1996). A change agent is an individual who influences the client's innovation–decision in a direction deemed desirable by a change agent, usually seeking to obtain the adoption of new ideas. More effective communication between change agents and their clients occurs when they are homophilous with each other, which means that they resemble each other with respect to education, experiences, attitudes, etc. (Rogers, 1995, pp. 27, 346). The team members in this case can be regarded as change agents charged with evaluating their libraries, and they had the advantage of homophily, meaning that the sharing of information involved no terminological barriers between the change agent and other employees in the service unit. However, user involvement was crucial in the implementation of new working methods or tools, as was also pointed out by Leonard-Barton (1988). User involvement enhances understanding of the innovation, its

purpose, and utilization. It is also advantageous for the organization to utilize the professional employees' expertise in the adaptation of an innovation.
The project took three years to complete, and now, two years after its
termination, it is possible to see that some evaluation methods or new
practices have been adopted in the libraries involved. Portfolios are used by
some librarians for planning and evaluation purposes in their personal
work. All except one of these users were members of the teams adopting the
portfolio model. Evaluation forms are used for regional evaluation by the
regional central library. Some teams continue their work and have included
more libraries in their discussions than during the project.

Both knowledge management and benchmarking issues have previously
been studied, but mostly in big organizations. They should, however, be
considered and utilized even in small units, especially in mutual cooperation.

REFERENCES

Andersen, B., & Pettersen, P.-G. (1996). *The benchmarking handbook. Step-by-step instructions.*
London: Chapman and Hall.
Charbonneau, M. (2005). Production benchmarks for catalogers in academic libraries. Are we
there yet? *Library Resources and Technical Services, 49*(1), 40–48.
Clayton, P. (1997). *Implementation of organizational innovation.* California: Academic Press.
Creaser, C. (2001). Comparing performance of service points in public libraries. *Performance
measurement and metrics, 2*(2), 109–135.
Cross, R., & Iqbal, A. (1995). The rank xerox experience: Benchmarking ten years on. In:
R. Asbjorn (Ed.), *Benchmarking – Theory and Practice.* London: Chapman and Hall.
Dattakumar, R., & Jagadeesh, R. (2003). A review of literature on benchmarking. *Benchmark-
ing: An International Journal, 10*(3), 176–209.
Deutsche, P., & Silcox, B. (2003). Learning from other libraries: Benchmarking to assess library
performance. *Information Outlook, 7*(7), 18–20.
DeVito, D., & Morrison, S. (2000). Benchmarking: A tool for sharing and cooperation. *The
Journal of Quality and Participation, 23*(4), 56–62.
Dorsch, J. J., & Yasin, M. M. (1998). A framework for benchmarking in the public sector:
Literature review and directions for future research. *International Journal of Public
Sector Management, 11*(2/3), 91–115.
Favret, L. (2000). Benchmarking, annual library plans and best value: The implications for
public libraries. *Library Management, 21*(7), 340–348.
Fernandez, P., McCarthy, I. P., & Rakotobe-Joel, T. (2001). An evolutionary approach to
benchmarking. *Benchmarking: An International Journal, 8*(4), 281–305.
Johnson, J. D., Donohue, W. A., Atkin, C. K., & Johnson, S. (2001). Communication,
involvement, and perceived innovativeness. Tests of a model with two contrasting
innovations. *Group and Organization Management, 26*(1) 24/52.
Kortelainen, T. (2003). *Kirjastojen arviointi ja osaamisen jakaminen seutuyhteistyönä. [The evaluation and sharing of information as regional cooperation].* Helsinki: BTJ Kirjastopalvelu.

Kouzmin, A., Loffer, E., Klages, H., & Korac-Kakabadse, N. (1999). Benchmarking and performance measurement in public sectors. Towards learning for agency effectiveness. *The International Journal for Public Sector Management, 12*(2), 121.

Laeven, H., & Smith, A. (2003). A project to benchmark university libraries in the Netherlands. *Library Management, 24*(6/7), 291–304.

Leonard-Barton, D. (1988). Implementation characteristics of organizational innovations. Limits and opportunities for management strategies. *Communication Research, 15*(5), s.603–s.631.

Leonard-Barton, D., & Sinha, D. K. (1993). Developer-user interaction and user satisfaction in internal technology transfer. *Academy of Management Journal, 36*, 1125–1139.

Nonaka, I., & Takeuchi, H. (1995). *The knowledge-creating company. How Japanese companies create the dynamics of innovation.* New York: Oxford University Press.

Patton, M. Q. (1982). *Practical evaluation.* Newbury Park, CA: Sage Publications.

Rasinkangas, P. (2001). *Parkki. Pohjoisten kirjastojen tutkimus- ja kehittämisprojekti. [Parkki. The research and development project of Northern libraries].* Oulu.

Rogers, E. M. (1995). *Diffusion of innovations* (p. 4). New York: Free Press.

Ståhle, P., & Grönroos, M. (1999). *Knowledge management – tieto yrityksen kilpailutekijänä.* Helsinki: WSOY.

APPENDIX 1. QUALITATIVE DESCRIPTION OF SKILLS NECESSARY IN AN INFORMATION SERVICE

Evaluation of expertise in an information service
5 = Excellent expertise (all current and potential clients can be served and all colleagues can be trained in advanced use of the tool or service)
4 =
3 = Adequate expertise (all clients can be either served locally or directed to a more adequate source; colleagues can be advised in the use of the tool or service)
2 =
1 = Minimal expertise (there is a need for improvement in expertise; clients cannot be sufficiently served; external training is needed)

Description of the degree of urgency of needed improvement
3 = Urgent need for improvement
2 = A need for improvement has been noted
1 = No current need for improvement

Expertise Necessary in an Information Service	Level of Expertise					Need for Education or Development		
	5	4	3	2	1	3	2	1

1. *Basics*
1.1. An understanding of the theoretical basics of the information service (education and following the development of the field)
1.2. Utilizing one's own and others' experience

2. *Tools of an information service*
2.1. Familiarity with manual or traditional tools: card catalogues, printed sources
2.2. Familiarity with the contents or scope of databases and search languages and electronic sources
   2.2.1. Library's own database
   2.2.2. Fennica (Finnish national catalogue)
   2.2.3. Aleksi (Finnish article catalogue)
   2.2.4. Ebsco
   2.2.5. Finnish law CD
   2.2.6. Internet searches
   2.2.6.1. Finlex database
2.3. Familiarity with the classification system

APPENDIX 1. (*Continued*)

Expertise Necessary in an Information Service	Level of Expertise					Need for Education or Development		
	5	4	3	2	1	3	2	1

3. Collections/contents
3.1. Knowledge of non-fiction
   3.1.1. Maps
   3.1.2. Statistics
   3.1.3. Official publications (blue book)
   3.1.4. Others
3.2. Knowledge of fiction
   3.2.1. Fiction
   3.2.1.1. Domestic fiction
   3.2.1.2. Foreign fiction
   3.2.2. Poetry
3.3. Ability to describe the contents of different
   material categories
3.4. Identification of relevant material

4. Expertise in information retrieval
4.1. Analyzing the topics of information searches
   and choosing different search methods
4.2. Knowledge of sources that are worth
   searching

5. Teaching library use and information retrieval
5.1. Teaching library use and information retrieval
   to groups
   5.1.1. Sufficient mastery of the above-
     mentioned skills to be able to teach them
   5.1.2. Presenting the topic according to the
     needs of different groups
   5.1.3. Ability as a public performer
5.2. Personal training in library use and
   information retrieval
5.3 Producing material for user education
   5.3.1 In Finnish
   5.3.2. In Swedish
   5.3.3. In English

6. Language proficiency
6.1. Swedish
6.2. English
6.3. German
6.4. User education can be provided in the
   following languages
   6.4.1. Swedish
   6.4.2. English
   6.4.3. German

APPENDIX 1. (*Continued*)

Expertise Necessary in an Information Service	Level of Expertise					Need for Education or Development		
	5	4	3	2	1	3	2	1

7. *IT skills*
7.1. Basic skills in Windows use and ability to use a personal computer
    7.1.1. Word processing
7.2. Using e-mail
7.3. Use of the Internet
7.4. Solving minor problems with IT equipment or printing
7.5. Advising clients in the use of IT
    7.5.1. Advising in the use of the Internet
    7.5.2. Advising in the use of word processing

Qualitative Evaluation
The skills needed in an information service also include important abilities such as meeting the client. Consider these items without a numerical evaluation.
Information needs of the client.
- Knowing or anticipating the client's information needs
- Ability to help the client focus his/her information needs
- Ability to define the degree of reception of the client
- Advising the client in evaluating sources of information
- Recommending journals or books according to the client's needs

Utilizing a Network of Experts
- Courage to ask a colleague for advise
- Courage and possibility to contact other libraries
- Delimiting the scope of the service: guiding the client to another place of service

Skills in Customer Service
- Patience, natural friendliness, situational sensitivity
- Speed of service
- Tolerance of disparity

APPENDIX 2. CONTENTS OF A LIBRARY PORTFOLIO

A library portfolio includes the following parts:

1 Library philosophy: the principles guiding library work and the agreed objectives of library work.
2 A short history: how the library has reached its current circumstances.
3 Resources
4 Performance: activities and functions of the library.
5 Feedback from various sources.
6 Cooperation and partners.
7 Plans for the future.

A portfolio can be a document including the above-mentioned chapters and appendices documenting the contents of the text. In addition to this, the partners of the project also produced a folder in which each page represented one part of the portfolio and included a pocket in which authentic material describing resources, activities, etc. could be placed.

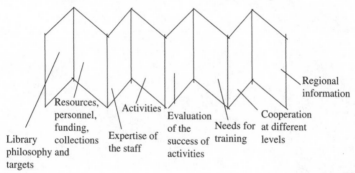

SCHOLARLY COMMUNITIES AND COMPUTING EXPERTISE: THE ROLE OF FORMAL AND INFORMAL LEARNING

Sanna Talja

ABSTRACT

Based on in-depth interviews of forty-four scholars across four specialist fields, this article explores the role of formal and informal learning in scholars' adoption of computing expertise. In the light of the findings, formal courses had a minor role in the development of scholars' computing expertise. Patterns of collaborative work and information sharing at the workplace, professional role and identity, available time resources, the nature of work tasks, place(s) of work, and existing social ties and networks, were the most important factors at play. It is argued that considerations such as interconnectedness of professional identities and ICT, the mutually shaping relationships between ICT and the sociocultural context in which working and learning takes place, and the importance of social networks for development ICT expertise, are rarely foregrounded in information society initiatives. The findings may thus inform efforts to support professional development not only in academia but other workplaces as well.

Advances in Library Administration and Organization, Volume 25, 259–279
Copyright © 2007 by Elsevier Ltd.
ISSN: 0732-0671/doi:10.1016/S0732-0671(07)25012-6

INTRODUCTION

The importance of studying informal learning in workplaces is increasingly being acknowledged. Explorations into workplace learning can provide insights into issues that deserve greater attention, and into the ways in which workplace learning could be facilitated and supported. As noted by Hara (2007), professional education has a long tradition of supporting learning and performance through formal training. In a study of information retrieval instruction, Halttunen (2004) argued for a shift from traditional training and formal courses to designing effective learning environments. Workplaces can be seen as such environments. People often informally help each other in using computer applications and share knowledge and expertise. To help in fostering workplaces as effective learning environments, it is important to analyze and understand the issues at play in workplace learning. As stressed by Twidale (2005), it may well turn out that informal workplace learning is not merely one of several possible learning activities, but that it is a significant part in the learning of many people. This article explores the role of formal and informal learning in scholars' use of information and communication technologies (ICT).[1]

Based on in-depth discussions with 44 scholars on computing at academic work, this paper seeks to bring into view contextual considerations that have a crucial impact on ICT learning. Among the issues that arose from the interviews are: the interconnectedness of scholarly and professional identities and ICT, the mutually shaping relationships between ICT and the sociocultural contexts in which working and learning takes place, and the importance of social networks for development of ICT expertise. Although the study is contextualized in the academic work community, the results may inform efforts to support professional development in other workplaces such as libraries as well.

RELATED WORK

In the research literature, there exist two diverse streams of research on learning to use computer applications. These can be called the cognitive and user-psychological viewpoint, and the sociocultural viewpoint (Talja, 2005). Studies undertaken from the psychological and cognitive viewpoint have generally aimed at predicting and explaining user acceptance, and at developing measures of IT attitudes and skills (cf. Eastin & LaRose, 2000; Hargittai, 2002; Jerabek, Meyer, & Kordinak, 2001; Kay, 1993; Munro, Huff, Marcolin, & Compeau, 1997). The user-psychological viewpoint views the growth of IT knowledge as a process that takes place within individual minds, and involves the learning of concepts. The user-psychological perspective embraces the belief that IT skills and knowledge are best adopted in courses that provide a conceptual model of programs and IT innovations (Talja, 2005).

The sociocultural viewpoint, often relying on the theory of situated learning developed by Lave and Wenger (1991), approaches the development of computing expertise as a process that takes place within specific social and institutional contexts, or "communities of practice." Studies undertaken from the sociocultural viewpoint typically aim at gaining an in-depth understanding of situated work practices and user communities (cf. Orr, 1996; Orlikowski, 2002; Star & Ruhleder, 1996).

A classic example of ethnographic research into work practices is the study by Orr (1996) on photocopier repair technicians. Orr (1996) discovered that formal training courses and manuals offered very little help beyond the simplest technical problems. In principle, the technicians worked on their own but in practice they built up their expertise by exchanging "war stories" about the problems they had encountered during lunch breaks (Orr, 1996). They threw different ideas around and tried in this way to figure out what the problem might be and how it could be resolved (Orr, 1996). It was not uncommon that no one, not even the tool planners, had any set answers to the technical problems; sometimes they were new even to the tool manufacturers. Orr's (1996) insight that expertise is gained through problem solving in connection with practical work tasks, has since received further support.

Sharrock and Button (1997) studied the work practices of engineers. They found that engineers' work expertise developed in a process of negotiation and interaction with the computer and with other professionals. IT professionals resolved emerging problems and built up their expertise by establishing apprentice relationships with one another, by consulting one another, and by thinking things through together (Lyman, 1995). Håpnes and Sörensen (1995) observed that young men interested in computing often had a circle of friends and networks where they could exchange experiences and where they informally built up their knowledge and expertise. Nardi and Miller (1991), in a study of spreadsheet use, found that spreadsheet work flows across different users in fluid, informal ways, and that cooperation among spreadsheet users has a spontaneous, self-directed character. Spreadsheets were often co-developed as users having a strong basis of domain knowledge asked users with more programming expertise and interest in technology about advanced spreadsheet features (Nardi & Miller, 1991).

These studies indicate that informal learning not only takes place in formally designated teams, but that actors often informally train and help each other in

ICT use and problem solving. The traditional view of computing assumed that the knowledge needed for using computer applications is formally "designed into" a program, outlined in its key features and characteristics, and that learning to use a computer application involves an introduction into its features in a logical order. Yet, the informal learning processes described in the studies reviewed above suggest that this is a too limited view of both learning and information technology.

THEORY OF SITUATED LEARNING

Lave's and Wenger's (1991) situated theory of learning has in recent years gained momentum within the field of knowledge management, especially within theories of organizational knowledge and learning (Davenport & Hall, 2002; Cox, 2005).[2] Lave's and Wenger's sociocultural learning theory has it that learning is grounded in contexts of action and that learning is a dimension of practical action. They developed the well-known "communities of practice" (CoP) concept to argue that all knowledge creation and learning is deeply *embedded* within concrete work tasks and interpersonal exchanges. Learning, for Lave and Wenger (1991), is not a cognitive process that takes place in the closed space that is the individual's head, but rather a practical activity that happens in and through social interaction.

Originally, Lave's and Wenger's CoP concept referred to the process of how newcomers learn their professions through moving from "legitimate peripheral participation" (LPP) to full community membership. The LPP concept emphasized that learning takes place not by internalizing a "received" (abstract) body of knowledge and a set of (predetermined) work procedures, but by taking part in the execution of specific work tasks, through observing co-workers, and in interaction with specific tools and technologies. In other words, the theory holds that learning does not take place through the assimilation of information that is transmitted to the individual in a formal process, but only becomes possible through participation in a professional or some other productive, goal-oriented activity. Lave's (1988) learning theory originally developed as a critique of school exams and laboratory tests that measured individuals' knowledge levels and competencies in isolation from the concrete practices of everyday life and the world of work (Vann & Bowker, 2001). According to Lave, school exams measure the extra-contextual success of individuals detached from their social relations and their lived and experienced world in relation to an abstract and formal knowledge package that schools have created all by themselves (Vann & Bowker, 2001). Studying different occupational groups, Lave and Wenger (1991) set out to demonstrate that success in working life is dependent on access to and adoption of the cultural and practical knowledge possessed by more experienced co-workers. The CoP concept conveys an idea of the fundamental sociality of all work tasks, and the reliance of any social practice upon interactions of people interested in similar issues.

Traditional thinking about learning assumes that the knowledge and skills learned in one context, say on a training course, can readily be exported to and applied in another context. Lave and Wenger (1991), by contrast, emphasize the existence of discontinuities between sociocultural contexts and situations. They maintain that all action is necessarily conditional upon the situation. We do not learn about the world, we learn in the world. According to Lave and Wenger (1991), learning always involves social relations, the definition and (re)formation of professional identities, and the construction and reinforcement of workplace communities. In their learning theory, identity, knowing/ learning, and social membership determine and presuppose one another. The question they lead us to ask is therefore not what kind of knowledge and skills should be transmitted by means of IT education, but *what kinds of social ties and commitments make learning possible.*

The choice to use the viewpoint provided by Lave's and Wenger's theory in my work was influenced by the empirical results. As often is the case in qualitative research, the choice of research perspective was a hermeneutic circle: I chose to frame my interpretation in the theory developed by Lave and Wenger because of its close match with the insights gained through interviews.

DESIGN AND IMPLEMENTATION OF THE STUDY

The 44 researchers interviewed represent four different disciplines and two different universities in Finland. The informants include 10 environmental biologists, 12 nursing scientists, 11 literature and cultural studies scholars, and 11 historians. I wanted to have a good cross section of different disciplines, departments, and researchers with different kinds of ICT expertise and work practices. I made my choices by studying the homepages of university departments and individual researchers. The humanities are represented by two disciplines, history, and literature and cultural studies, because my initial familiarization showed that in these two fields it would be easy to find both researchers engaged in ICT development through their research or publishing projects, and researchers who wished to be only minimally involved with ICT.

In each department, one-third of the recruited participants were professors, one-third lecturers and assistants, and one-third doctoral students. For those who had not completed their doctorate, I use the term junior researchers, while referring to those who had the degree in hand as senior researchers. Half of the interviewees were men, and the other half women. Lasting about 90 min each, the interviews were conducted in May–August 2000.[3] The interviews were tape-recorded and transcribed in full for analysis. They were structured around the following themes: (1) personal IT history and relationship; (2) IT resources, support, and training; (3) use of electronic resources; (4) the work community and ICT. We[4] asked the researchers detailed questions about their use of ICT applications, how they had learned to use them, the courses they had attended, and the difficulties and successes experienced with ICT. The informants were asked also to complete a questionnaire in connection with the interviews. This covered the use of various applications, and the interviews focused more on learning experiences and work community issues.[5]

RESULTS

ICT and Academic Work

The IT experience of the interviewees ranged from 3 to more than 30 years. The majority had used PCs for about 15 years. Most of the informants had experience of different kinds of learning situations and were in a position to view the development of ICT over a longer time perspective. In one sense, researchers may be described as a pioneering group in the design and use of ICT. Many applications currently in everyday use, such as e-mail, mailing lists, and discussion groups, were initially created in and for distinct types of research work. Most of the interviewed researchers described themselves as ordinary IT users or typical workplace users, however. Only a minority of the informants identified themselves as having a deeper interest in ICT. Thus, the informants as a rule did not see themselves as ICT experts, despite their long experience, and despite the way many were also involved in development of the web, for instance, in the form of homepages, web-based services, pure electronic journals, and book-like web publications. ICT was conventionally talked about as something "already designed," as something given, even "imposed."[6]

This is explained by the fact that for most scholars, efficient work means being able to concentrate on the contents of scholarly work, and the need to take care of and focus on "technical issues" is often experienced as a stop in the flow of work (see also Lyman, 1995). Many scholars said that they were constantly having to draw boundaries between which applications belong to the category of "have to know," essential for carrying out core work tasks, and what kind of learning belongs to the category "useful to know." One literature scholar remarked that "every time new tools arrive, work efficiency vanishes and the idea of what was the idea here, to do this work or to learn to use these tools."

Many of the interviewed scholars had, due to their long careers in computing, experienced that changes in ICT affect the resources and infrastructures of work tasks. The informants offered many examples of how work tasks are also shaped by the capabilities offered by ICT. Where some applications such as aggregated e-journal databases were experienced as generally improving the ease and speed of carrying out core work tasks, some applications were experienced as invisibly raising and changing general expectations regarding secondary aspects of work, like the graphic and technical quality of presentations. One senior historian remarked that "my work is mentally complicated enough, so tools should be very simple."

However, the definitions of core of work tasks and "core competencies" tended to vary depending on the researchers' overall work situation. Those who were already using a specific application tended to rate it as more important than those who had not yet taken it into use. How the boundaries of core competencies were drawn depended a great deal on the amount of time, opportunities, and social resources available for ICT learning, as illustrated by the following interview excerpt:

> When you have to get a presentation done, it's too late to start learning. For me it's been an achievement that I've been able to organize things here in such a way that I can get the help I need. (Senior researcher, nursing science, female)

Distinctive features of academic work that have an impact on ICT learning and expertise include: the constant pressures posed by deadlines, the need to "safeguard" research time from other work tasks such as teaching and administration (see also Ylijoki & Mäntylä, 2003), and the blurring of home-work boundaries. Many of the interviewed scholars chose to do the research work requiring the most intense and uninterrupted concentration, such as writing, at home, and divided their work tasks into those to be done at the workplace, and those to be done at home (see also Noble & Lupton, 1998).

The following factors emerged as having significant impact on the development of scholars' ICT expertise:

- differences between work communities and between disciplines in the sharing of ICT expertise,
- professional role and identity,

- time resources,
- the nature of work tasks and specialist fields,
- place(s) of work,
- existing social ties and networks,
- gaps between the language of work and ICT language.

Differences between and within Disciplinary Communities in Sharing ICT
Expertise

Lie (1998) showed in her study of social workers that the growth of ICT
expertise is not simply a matter of learning how to use computer applications. Learning also presupposes that social actors share interpretations of
the uses of various applications and their role in work tasks. Vehviläinen
(1997), in a study of female office workers, observed that with the introduction of new programs, the female office workers first jointly developed
an understanding of how certain programs were suited to their specific tasks
and their organizational context.

   The importance of having access to others with whom to read and interpret
a program's uses surfaced also in this study. As long as scholars only knew the
name of a new program and its general purpose, they tended to estimate that
there was no pressing need for them to start using it. Before making a decision
on taking up a new application, they had talked with their colleagues or other
trusted contacts about the program in order to hear their views about its
features and advantages. As noted above, the main source of satisfaction for
researchers is the sense that they have made real progress with their science.
Therefore, the interviewed scholars stressed the importance of carefully
estimating the "right moment" for taking up a new application:

> In history, it seems to be hard to strike the right kind of balance in terms of where
> information technology really is useful, and where it is unnecessary to try to take it on
> board. Where it will just take too much time to start learning it, or where it will do
> something that is completely unnecessary. (Senior researcher, history, male)

As noted earlier, many researchers experienced that it was difficult to draw a
line between what kinds of computing expertise could be considered as
relevant to their professional competence, and what kind of learning could
be counted more as hobby-like or a distraction from core work tasks. Some
of the humanities scholars described themselves as slow starters preferring
to adopt new applications later than others. Humanities scholars do not
work in teams or co-author articles as often as natural scientists, so the
compatibility of programs and applications is not so important to them.

Some humanities scholars stressed that they wished to improve their skills only to the extent and at the rate required by their work tasks. These scholars preferred to work with the programs they were accustomed to and that they felt did the job. They could, for instance, stress that a major part of their work "is still to read books" (senior researcher, literature, male), or to do "basic archive work." They stressed that the usefulness of applications such as spreadsheets and web-based resources vary greatly according to research topics and specialties:

> ICT use, and how much use the Internet is, really varies according to the subject matter. Some may be able to use materials directly from the net, others will follow the discussions there, and others still rely primarily on printed literature. For a traditional political historian like myself, the Internet's not much use because I won't find materials I need there. (Senior researcher, history, male)

> I'm sure most others are more interested in information technology than I am and use more of the existing variations of it. Many of these other people specialize in social and economic history and need to use quite a lot of bar graphs and statistics and what have you. I specialize in political history, and using graphs and the like is much less common there; you don't have the same kinds of needs because the things we cover, you can't really describe them in statistics or in graphics. (Senior researcher, history, male)

As noted also by Massey-Burzio (1999), humanities researchers are often reflexive and critical in discussing the development of ICT. Humanities scholars tended to critique the general expectation that the emergence of new applications mandates that they be adopted. In addition to the researcher's specialty and topic, the access to interpretations of ICT applications depend on the cultural traditions of a disciplinary community or "tribe" (Becher, 1989). It is an integral part of the humanist's professional identity to suggest alternative ways of thinking. This does not mean that ICT and aspects of humanities scholarship should in any way be at variance with each other, or that humanities scholars would contrast ICT and book culture, for instance. When two humanists meet over coffee, they are more disposed to talk about matters other than everyday ICT use. For humanists who are less interested in ICT, this means limited access to ICT interpretations. Without a social context of everyday conversations related to ICT use, it is quite difficult for users to develop their expertise (see also Brown & Duguid, 2000). As pointed out earlier, researchers need and want information about what ICT can do for them in the particular context in which they use computers. Mostly, they learn about the advantages of programs when they hear and see how other researchers use them:

> I really think it's important that someone shows you concretely how it works. That way, I might become interested myself. I rarely start using a new program without having seen or heard about someone else using it. (Junior researcher, nursing science, female)

I haven't really studied the use of these programs at all, just looked at others using them. I've seen someone do something and then asked, 'hey, how did you do that?'; and then, 'oh you can do that with the program, I'll try that as well.' It is like this that I've learned about these things. (Junior researcher, nursing science, female)

Environmental biologists frequently discuss ICT use in their workplace community. The environmental biologists and also many of the nursing scientists I interviewed typically gather large volumes of data for their studies, processed with statistical software. For these researchers, a good working knowledge of statistical and graphics software is an integral part of professional competence. In these fields, researchers also work more closely with one another than is the case in the humanities. Therefore, it is important that they use compatible programs and talk with one another about the use of programs. It follows that their computing skills are comparatively similar, whereas there is greater variation in the ICT expertise of humanities scholars.

For environmental biologists, the department community provides the kind of community of practice (Lave & Wenger, 1991) where computing skills are passed on and where they constitute a shared social resource.[4] People in that community will know who is the best expert when it comes to using a specific program, and they can take advantage of one another's strengths and areas of expertise. Environmental biologists referred to the development of computing expertise as a "group effort:"

In a sense it's been a group effort in which we've learned how to use these applications. Someone learns and then helps others out. (Senior researcher, environmental biology, female)

It was just last week, I was having a problem with Photoshop. There's always someone who knows something, so when you're in the coffee room you'll say that I can't do this or that and then someone will come round and show you. They'll know how to do it, so it's all there amongst ourselves. (Junior researcher, environmental biology, female)

Because the problems we have they're pretty much the same amongst colleagues, people will run into a problem that someone else has figured out earlier, and the other way round. (Junior researcher, environmental biology, male)

It was also quite common for nursing scientists working on the same research teams to share the same programs and to develop their competencies when working together on a research project. The collective development of computing expertise requires not only shared work tasks and practices but also a common framework of interpretation, however. Within nursing science, computing expertise did not necessarily travel across the boundaries of research groups, since the groups could have divergent interests and goals. Nursing science as a research field is less unified than environmental biology in its views of what are the central problems to study and how to study them (Fry & Talja, 2007).

Computing expertise does not cumulate in the same way as a "group effort" in work communities where researchers typically work alone and pursue divergent topics and research tracks. In history and literature and cultural studies, some informants shared a mutual interest in ICT. There were typically "circles of young men" (Håpnes & Sörensen, 1995) who liked to play with ICT, talk about ICT, and were generally good at resolving ICT problems. The humanities scholars who counted themselves as having an uneasy relationship with computers, in turn, reported that they did not want to trouble colleagues with their computing problems or reveal their ignorance to others:

> At least in the 1980s we saw younger teaching staff come in and use these concepts and terms and in general, we had this sense among older staff that these youngsters were sort of taking over, so I did tend to think that I'm sure not going to ask their advice, you do quickly get this sort of thing. (Senior researcher, history, male)

As noted by Brown and Duguid (2000), individuals are often inclined to think that others are more proficient with ICT unless they have the chance to observe other users and see how they too need help and advice when they encounter novel situations.

The Significance of Place of Work

Star and Ruhleder (1996), in their study of the introduction of an Internet-based Worm Community System intended for worm biologists, described how researchers took it for granted that they would start using the service "quite soon" and that its adoption would be a smooth and easy process – so much so that some researchers even said they were using the service although they had never actually tried it. The biologists did not question the usefulness of the service, but when they tried to gain access, starting to use the service turned out to be such a complex process that in the end most biologists failed to climb the first hurdle. Taking the system into use required researchers to acquire competencies about systems compatibilities, and protocols that were familiar and transparent to the system developers but for the biologists unfamiliar terrain (Star & Ruhleder, 1996).

The prevailing assumption about computing expertise is that users who have attended formal courses and received training will also be able to cope independently with the problems they encounter in everyday computer use (Talja, 2005). Star and Ruhleder's (1996) study showed how ICTs are entangled not only with specific types of expertise and work tasks, but also involve a complex configuration of interrelated technologies. The biologists did not lack motivation, but they could not take up the task of solving infrastructure level problems.[7]

A similar gap between motivation and existing social and time resources surfaced in this study. For instance, many researchers recognized the value of homepages to research and teaching but could not find the time for learning the entire process of building and maintaining web pages. Most of the researchers who had personal homepages had not created them on their own. The homepages had been set up either as a joint department project with help from PC support staff or with the help of colleagues, family members, or friends with web design skills. At technical infrastructure level, most researchers – as indeed other users (Brown & Duguid, 2000) – needed help. Even most researchers taking a deep interest in ICT preferred to leave the setup of websites to others.

At work, infrastructure level tasks such as program installations and network connections were handled by PC support staff. Half of the researchers I interviewed preferred not to update their computers by themselves and were reluctant to take up such tasks. In their view, such tasks were too far removed from the content of research work and the core competencies of a researcher.

For those scholars who also worked at home, social resources such as relatives and family members and even weak social ties (Granovetter, 1973)[8] such as neighbors were often crucial sources of help and expertise in dealing with infrastructure level problems:

> I needed to install SPSS and virus protection on my PC at home. I didn't dare try by myself. So I had to ask our neighbours. Their son is good with computers so he came round and helped me out. (Junior researcher, nursing science, female)

The researchers who conducted a lot of their work at home and had no family members or friends who could help at infrastructure level tasks experienced considerable difficulties in having their needs for ICT support met. These scholars found "keeping up" with ICT development overwhelming, regardless of whether they had taken courses and training in computing.

Time

In Finnish universities, the acquisition and updating of computing expertise is generally organized so that courses in various computer applications are offered, but these are typically prescheduled to take place only a few times a year. The courses are usually for all university employees and not departmentally based.

Many of the researchers I interviewed said it would make sense to attend IT courses:

> I only use the most basic functions, I notice it all the time that I am not using all the features of this program. That would require a more determined approach, going to courses. (Senior researcher, history, male)

These researchers anticipated that by taking courses, they would learn how to make the best of programs' functionalities and features. However, statements such as these also express consciousness of cultural norms, and expectations (Silverman, 1985). In cultural interpretations of IT competence, people who take courses and who are keen to take on board new applications rapidly, who have a positive attitude toward learning, will also use ICT more efficiently (Talja, 2005). The researchers I interviewed thus expressed an awareness of cultural expectations by saying that "I really should attend courses." However, there was again a gap between time resources and motivation.

Researchers rarely could manage to fit ICT courses in their schedules. Typically, such "windows of opportunity" (Tyre & Orlikowski, 1994) were open in early phases of doctoral studies and immediately after earning the doctorate. Otherwise, researchers typically resolved ICT problems as they emerged. They took up new applications at the moment when new work tasks threw up new competence requirements. When taking up a new application emerged as an absolute necessity, researchers did not hesitate to rely on colleagues, office staff, and whichever sources of help they could reach. As noted earlier, informal learning interactions mostly take place with people nearby. Family members, office staff, and closest colleagues were the first people researchers usually turned to. Participants also gave accounts of help-seeking instances where they had engaged in a behavior that can best be called "over the phone learning," calling up some trusted colleague or friend to get help in starting to use a new application:

> It was quite difficult to start with because I didn't really know how. But then my friends helped me out. I phoned different people, you know, 'how do I use this?' I mainly asked my brother when I needed to know like "what do I do when I need to do that." (Junior researcher, nursing science, female)

The interviewed researchers stressed that when they acquired the information they needed to resolve a current computing problem, the acquired competence immediately got integrated into their work routine. In contrast, taking courses in computer applications in anticipation of a future need to use the application had, for many, turned out to be a waste of time and effort:

> I think I've taken a couple of courses, on setting up websites and Excel. But the courses really were no use at all. Even though the courses covered everything, I did not get a real sense that I understood it at all. And it didn't stick with me. I didn't understand how things really worked. (Junior researcher, history, male)

One researcher had attended several IT courses in school and during her studies at the university. She had learned, among other things, "what kinds of components there are in the PC and what kinds of PCs there are, and wordprocessing" (junior researcher, nursing science, female). In her case, the courses were taken at a stage and in a context (compulsory studies) where she had no specific work-related tasks. Another researcher had taken several IT courses both on her own time outside the university and during office hours at the workplace, and she concluded that:

> I'd need private tutoring. I have no doubt I can learn, but on the kinds of courses that I've been able to attend, there's no way to learn properly. (Senior researcher, history, female)

The common assumption is that training courses teach skills that will be useful later on regardless of what kind of work people do. In the light of the interviews, however, the knowledge and skills taught at school and on general training courses did not easily "travel" from one context to another. The researchers quoted above saw that the courses they had attended did not add to their skills and expertise because they lacked a direct connection with a specific work task.

Researchers who had attended courses rarely felt that the courses had met their needs. A training course is necessarily designed with certain uses and users in mind. The lessons learned from the courses were difficult to put into practice if the examples and the assumptions on which they were based were not applicable in the context in which the researchers carried out their own work. For instance, a historian uses Excel for different purposes than a plant researcher.

The researchers benefited from the courses most when they did not attend them in order to learn a new program, but to learn more about the functions of a program that they were already using. It emerged clearly from the interviews, however, that researchers wanted to learn at their own place of work, at their own desk. They wanted to anchor the things they were learning to their own PC, to the order of things in their own computer – which also is the order of their own work process.

I wouldn't go on a course any more. For me the best way to learn is here in research cooperation. When we're working together to develop a figure or something, you know, we discuss how shall we do this, what should we use here, and so on. I also have doctoral students. When we work together, they observe my style of working and they'll say they'll help me create new folders and things like that. We look at them together, what to do and how to organize them. This is the best way to learn, looking at these things and doing them together. That way leaves out all the snobbery (Senior researcher, nursing science, female)

In the excerpt above, a senior nursing scientist states that she "would not go on a course any more," reflecting that a natural way to learn is in everyday research work that involves communication and collaboration with doctoral students and colleagues. She also makes a point that the kind informal learning situations that take place in the normal flow of work "leave out all the snobbery," that the kind of know-how acquired through informal workplace learning is already specialized, that is, finely attuned to the scholars' specialist field and working style.

The Significance of Professional Identity

The sociocultural context of formal ICT courses could be experienced as too far removed from the everyday practice of science and research. Some researchers stated they opposed formal ICT courses "as a matter of principle" (junior researcher, literature, woman). Within their own work communities, researchers slowly move from novices and apprentices to the role of experts and senior scholars. Attending courses was experienced as difficult by senior scholars, especially professors, because they require an identity switch from the role of expert and teacher to that of a novice and student. Furthermore, training courses were by some experienced as social situations that involve a real risk of public humiliation, of "losing face," having one's ignorance about ICT come out in the open. Social learning strategies such as learning within collaborative work, incidental learning by observing others and by asking for help[9] could be artfully adjusted by all parties to minimize threats to professional identity.

The avoidance of threats to professional identity also partly explains the reluctance of researchers to turn to official PC support staff when they needed help in solving work task related, rather than infrastructure level, ICT problems. They presumed, or had experienced, that IT professionals have a different perspective on computing and that they speak in a different language. When asked about the role of IT support staff in learning, some researchers narrated how they had failed to describe their problems using "the correct IT terminology" (senior researcher, nursing science, female), or how they had felt stupid because they had not understood the advice they had received:

> We once had quite an amusing situation, we just didn't understand one another at all. I phoned PC support and this bloke asked me, what program am I using, and I said Word, no no not that programme, something else. We just couldn't get on the same wavelength at all so he said he would come over and have a look. So he came over and it turned out that one of us was on the moon and the other was on earth. We just didn't understand each other. In any case, he made the changes, but he couldn't explain it to me. I have to say this is an extreme example. I do have some good experiences as well. (Junior researcher, literature, female)

The communication between researchers and IT support staff could fail because of lack of shared context. When researchers had problems with applications related to administrative work, they liked to turn to office staff for help. Asking office staff to help on applications where staff was assumed to be more knowledgeable did not pose similar problems regarding shared context. Office staff was attuned to scholars' professional identity and tasks, and faculty and staff were both familiar with the department's practices and language. In some departments, it was in fact part of the work of office staff to help with ICT tasks. At some departments, researchers could delegate tasks such as setting up home pages or database searches to office staff. Due to office staff's regular working hours, it was also often easier for researchers to get in touch with them than to wait for an opportunity to ask a colleague.

SUMMARY AND CONCLUSIONS

This article looked at the contextual issues surrounding the growth of ICT expertise. The findings lend support to earlier findings showing how the way work communities perceive and assimilate ICT is largely determined by the work practices and social and cultural traditions of those communities. ICT clearly meant different things in different disciplines and in different specialist communities even within the same disciplines. Specialist communities could have divergent interests and styles of working, consequently, their ways of approaching and using ICT for work tasks varied.

In the light of the findings, the growth of ICT expertise in academic communities is not primarily dependent on the provision and acquisition of formal education and training. Individuals' motivation to learn was also secondary in importance compared to the importance of time resources and social resources for learning. Social relationships within the workplace community, other social ties and networks, field of expertise and professional identity, the nature of work tasks and place of work, defined the boundary conditions for learning.

Considerations such as these are rarely foregrounded in, for instance, information society initiatives. These tend to recommend formal courses such as computer driving licenses as a means for providing computing skills, often termed in such contexts as "information society skills," for citizens (Vehviläinen, 1999). In the context of higher education (HE), the central information society initiative in Finland is the National Strategy for Education, Training and Research in the Information Society Ministry of Education, 1999, which proposes the introduction of standard computing skills testing systems to guarantee that teachers in all levels possess the relevant IT skills. The strategy is based on the assumption that offering standardized formal courses based on predefined standardized learning requirements is the best way for developing HE teachers' IT competencies.

The drive towards the institutionalization and standardization of learning requirements, course contents, and skills assessments is based on the notion that there exists a given, universally useful, and uniform set of ICT knowledge and skills. The basic assumption underlying the proposition of offering standardized courses and training is that the necessary IT competencies are essentially the same for every teacher and scholar, regardless of work tasks and specialist field. ICT applications are understood as entities having invariant inherent properties and functions.

In the light of this study, ICT applications are not the same for everyone, rather, the nature of a certain application, its uses and usefulness, its strengths and weaknesses, are highly context dependent. The nature of a scholar's specialist field and work tasks in fact defines what "expertise" is in a specific context. Hence, there can be no ICT expertise that is not linked with domains of work, concrete work tasks, and types of problems to which information technology is applied.

The fact that ICT competence is something that evolves with experience gained in practice, and in the context of performing concrete work tasks, explains why the know-how provided by ICT training courses is not necessarily easily exportable from one sociocultural context to another. This implies that serious questions need to be asked about the educational strategies that do not consider the importance of the social and cultural context. If ICT expertise is primarily a dimension of practical action, "knowing enacted in practice" (Orlikowski, 2002), and a social resource, it is not measurable in a context-independent manner. In fact, it may not be fruitful to look at ICT expertise primarily as something possessed by individuals. ICT applications, in addition to the knowledge, skills, and attitudes related to them, can be seen as something that are developed collaboratively in specialized user cultures and communities.

ICT is only partly "already designed," perhaps more importantly, the character and uses of specific applications evolve in (sub)cultural communities and practices. In efforts to develop ICT expertise, mutual confidence and trust, a shared language and reciprocity have a crucial role to play. The findings reached in this study encourage further studies into informal workplace learning: into learning in natural settings, in concrete work tasks, and through peer-to-peer instruction. More research is needed into how to consciously design workplaces as optimal learning environments.

NOTES

1. The study was undertaken as a part of a larger project, "Information Technology, Media and Cultural Interpretations," funded by the Academy of Finland as part of the Research Program of Media Culture.

2. In this article, I do not elaborate on Lave's and Wenger's community of practice (CoP) concept (see Wenger, 1998; Hara & Kling, 2002; Orlikowski, 2002; Nardi, Whittaker, & Schwartz, 2002) but look at the entangled web of issues surrounding the development of ICT expertise.

3. Earlier papers on the project have looked at field differences in the production and use of networked resources (Talja & Maula, 2003; Talja, Savolainen, & Maula, 2004; Fry & Talja, 2007) and field differences in types of collaboration in document seeking, searching, and filtering (Talja, 2003).

4. The interviews were conducted by the author and MSc Hanni Maula.

5. In the light of the detailed questions we presented about learning processes in connection with various ICT applications, there were no significant differences in patterns of learning between ICT applications. Therefore, although information and communication technology is a broad field of diverse and differently used applications, ranging from homepages and academic mailing lists to spreadsheets and Powerpoint, I discuss ICT here in general terms.

6. This indicates that it is often quite difficult for people to recognize the depth and extent of their own expertise. For instance, researchers who had thought they were not particularly competent users recounted having gone on training courses only to discover that they were capable of dealing with the issues covered by the course by themselves. The growth ICT expertise is a long process that is partly invisible to the learner. We keep learning new things in our everyday use of computers without consciously thinking about learning. We see new things, make mental notes about them, and pick up clues that might be useful to us later. The participants who had the longest experience with ICT often remarked they thought courses irrelevant because they had grown to trust the learning by doing and learning through trial and error methods.

7. We may distinguish between two basic types of ICT problems: problems at infrastructure level and problems at program level. The latter comprise problems and questions such as 'where can I find this function?' Problems and questions at infrastructure level concern for instance the properties of computers, installation of programs and network connections.

8. A distinction is routinely made between weak and strong social ties. Strong ties, such as those between immediate colleagues, family members, and friends, are characterized by more continuous contact and reciprocity in sharing services, assistance, and information (Garton, Haythornthwaite, & Wellman, 1997). Weak ties are usually less regular, for example relations with members of the workplace community with whom one has no direct cooperation, and relatives and acquaintances (*ibid.*). Granovetter (1973) refers to the strength of weak ties, with which he means that those relations that are less close will often yield a larger amount of novel information from a wide range of areas of life.

9. Twidale and Ruhleder (2004) succinctly term such incidental and spontaneous help-seeking and help-giving instances as "over the shoulder learning."

REFERENCES

Becher, T. (1989). *Academic tribes and territories: Intellectual enquiry and the cultures of disciplines*. Milton Keynes: The Society for Research into Higher Education & Open University.

Brown, J. S., & Duguid, P. (2000). *The social life of information*. Boston, MA: Harvard Business School Press.

Cox, A. (2005). What are communities of practice? A comparative review of four seminal works. *Journal of Information Science, 31*, 527–540.

Davenport, E., & Hall, H. (2002). Organizational knowledge and communities of practice. In: B. Cronin (Ed.), *Annual Review of Information Science and Technology* (Vol. 36, pp. 171–219). Medford, NJ: Information Today.

Eastin, M. S., & LaRose, R. (2000). Internet Self-efficacy and the Psychology of the Digital Divide. *Journal of Computer Mediated Communication, 6*(1). Available at: http://www.ascusc.org/jcmc/vol6/issue1/eastin.html

Fry, J., & Talja, S. (2007). The Intellectual and Social Organization of Academic Fields and the Shaping of Digital Resources. *Journal of Information Science, 33*(2), 115–133.

Garton, L., Haythornthwaite, C., & Wellman, B. (1997). Studying Online Social Networks. *Journal of Computer-Mediated Communication, 3*(1). Available at: http://www.ascusc. orgjcmcvol3issue1garton.html

Granovetter, M. S. (1973). The strength of weak ties. *American Journal of Sociology, 78*, 1360–1380.

Halttunen, K. (2004). *Two information retrieval environments: Their design and evaluation*. Doctoral dissertation. Tampere: University of Tampere. Available at http://acta.uta.fi/pdf/951-44-6009-X.pdf

Håpnes, T., & Sörensen, K. H. (1995). Competition and collaboration in male shaping of computing: A study of Norwegian hacker culture. In: K. Grint & R. Gill (Eds), *The gender–technology relation: Contemporary theory and research*. London and Bristol: Taylor & Francis.

Hara, N. (2007). IT support for communities of practice: How public defenders learn about winning and losing in court. *Journal of the American Society for Information Science & Technology, 58*(1), 76–87.

Hara, N., & Kling, R. (2002). *IT supports for communities of practice: An empirically-based framework*. Bloomington: University of Indiana, Center for Social Informatics, CSI Working Paper No. WP-02-02. Available at: http://www.slis.indiana.edu/CSI/papers.htm (accessed 29 May, 2002).

Hargittai, E. (2002). Second-Level Digital Divide: Differences in People's Online Skills. *First Monday, 7*(4). Available at: http://firstmonday.org/issues/issue7_4/hargittai/index.html

Jerabek, J. A., Meyer, L. S., & Kordinak, T. (2001). "Library anxiety" and "computer anxiety:" Measures, validity, and research implications. *Library & Information Science Research, 23*, 277–289.

Kay, R. H. (1993). An exploration of theoretical and practical foundations for assessing attitudes toward computers: The computer attitude measure (CAM). *Computers in Human Behavior, 9*, 371–386.

Lave, J. (1988). *Cognition in practice: Mind, mathematics and culture in everyday life.* Cambridge: Cambridge University Press.

Lave, J., & Wenger, E. (1991). *Situated learning: Legitimate peripheral participation.* Cambridge: Cambridge University Press.

Lie, M. (1998). *Computer dialogues: Technology, gender and change.* Dragvoll: Senter for kvinneforskning, Norges teknisk-naturvetenskaplige universitet.

Lyman, P. (1995). Is using a computer like driving a car, reading a book, or solving a problem? The computer as machine, text, and culture. In: M. A. Shields (Ed.), *Work and technology in higher education: The social construction of academic computing* (pp. 19–36). Hillsdale, NJ: Lawrence Erlbaum Associates.

Massey-Burzio, V. (1999). The rush to technology: A view from humanists. *Library Trends, 47*, 620–639.

Ministry of Education. (1999). *Education, training and research in the information society: A national strategy for 2000–2004.* Available at: http://www.minedu.fi/julkaisut/information/englishU/index.html

Munro, M. C., Huff, S. L., Marcolin, B. L., & Compeau, D. R. (1997). Understanding and measuring user competence. *Information & Management, 33*, 45–57.

Nardi, B. A., & Miller, J. R. (1991). Twinkling lights and nested loops: Distributed problem solving and spreadsheet development. *International Journal of Man–Machine Studies, 34*, 161–184.

Nardi, B. A., Whittaker, S., & Schwartz, H. (2002). NetWORKers and their activity in intensional networks. *Computer Supported Cooperative Work, 11*, 205–242.

Noble, G., & Lupton, D. (1998). Consuming work: Computers, subjectivity and appropriation in the university workplace. *The Sociological Review, 46*, 803–827.

Orlikowski, W. (2002). Knowing in practice: Enacting a collective capability in distributed organizing. *Organization Science, 13*, 249–273.

Orr, J. (1996). *Talking about machines: An ethnography of a modern job.* Ithaca, NY: IRL Press.

Sharrock, W., & Button, G. (1997). Engineering investigations: Practical sociological reasoning in the work of engineers. In: G. C. Bowker, S. L. Star, W. Turner & L. Gasser (Eds), *Social science, technical systems, and cooperative work* (pp. 79–104). Mahwah, NJ: Lawrence Erlbaum Associates.

Silverman, D. (1985). *Qualitative methodology and sociology: Describing the social world.* Aldershot: Gower.

Star, S. L., & Ruhleder, K. (1996). Steps toward an ecology of infrastructure: Design and access for large information spaces. *Information Systems Research, 7*, 111–134.

Talja, S. (2003). Information sharing in academic communities: Types and levels of collaboration in information seeking and use. *New Review of Information Behavior Research, 3*, 143–159.

Talja, S. (2005). The social and discursive construction of computing skills. *Journal of the American Society for Information Science and Technology, 56*, 13–22.

Talja, S., & Maula, H. (2003). Reasons for the use and non-use of electronic journals and databases: A domain analytic study in four scholarly disciplines. *Journal of Documentation, 59*, 673–691.

Talja, S., Savolainen, R., & Maula, H. (2004). Field differences in the use and perceived usefulness of scholarly mailing lists. *Information Research, 10*. http://informationr.net/ir/10-1/paper200.html

Twidale, M. (2005). Over-the-shoulder-learning: Supporting brief informal learning. *Computer Supported Cooperative Work, 14*, 505–547.

Twidale, M., & Ruhleder, K. (2004). Over-the-shoulder learning in a distance education environment. In: C. Haythorntwaite & M. M. Kazmer (Eds), *Learning, culture and community in online education: Research and practice* (pp. 177–194). NY: Peter Lang.

Tyre, M. J., & Orlikowski, W. (1994). Windows of opportunity: Temporal patterns of technological adaptation in organization. *Organization Science, 5*, 98–118.

Vann, K., & Bowker, G. C. (2001). Instrumentalizing the truth of practice. *Social Epistemology, 15*, 247–262.

Vehviläinen, M. (1997). *Gender, expertise and information technology.* Tampere: University of Tampere, Department of Computer Science.

Vehviläinen, M. (1999). Naisten tietotekniikkaryhmä: yhteisöllisestä ja paikallisesta kansalaisuudesta [Women's information technology group: Communal and local citizenship]. In: P. Eriksson & M. Vehviläinen (Eds), *Tietoyhteiskunta seisakkeella: teknologia, strategiat ja paikalliset tulkinnat [The information society in a stop: Technology, strategies, and local interpretations]* (pp. 187–202). Jyväskylä: SoPhi.

Wenger, E. (1998). *Communities of practice.* Cambridge: Cambridge University Press.

Ylijoki, O.-H., & Mäntylä, H. (2003). Conflicting time perspectives in academic work. *Time & Society, 12*, 55–78.

ABOUT THE AUTHORS

Ari-Veikko Anttiroiko is a docent and acting professor in the Department of Regional Studies, University of Tampere, Finland. He has conducted and directed several research projects, including The Future of Electronic Services in Local Government and the Local Governance in the Information Society financed by the Academy of Finland. He has worked as an expert in several national and international e-government projects. His academic contributions include in a nutshell nearly 30 monographs, about 40 articles, and some 20 conference papers. He has memberships in several scientific organizations and editorial boards.

Eeva-Liisa Eskola, MA, has held the positions of research assistant/researcher/assistant lecturer at the Department of Information Studies, Åbo Akademi University 1997–2002. Her present position is that of an information specialist at Library at the Turku University of Applied Sciences (since 1999). Her research interest is information behavior in educational contexts. Her dissertation topic is students' information behavior in a changing learning environment.

Turid Hedlund is assistant professor in Information Systems at the Swedish School of Economics and Business Administration in Helsinki, Finland. She has an MA in economics with specialization in information systems and has earned her PhD at the University of Tampere in information science. Her research interests are information retrieval, scientific communication, and open access publishing.

Maija-Leena Huotari, PhD, is Professor of Information Studies in the Department of Finnish, Information Studies and Logopedics, and Dean of the Faculty of Humanities at the University of Oulu, Finland. She holds a BA in economics from Vaasa University, Finland, an MSc. in social sciences from the University of Tampere, Finland, and a PhD in social sciences from the University of Sheffield, UK. Her current research interests include strategic management of organizational information and knowledge, information behavior and practices, and health information management.

Mirja Iivonen, PhD, is the Director of Tampere University Library, and a docent of information studies at the University of Oulu, where she earlier worked as a professor of Information Studies and as the Head of the department. She has published several articles both internationally and in Finland, and presented numerous papers in international scientific conferences. She is a member on the Editorial Board of Library & Information Science Research. She has worked as a visiting scholar at the Universities of Rutgers and Maryland, both in the United States, and has had positions of trust in IFLA (International Federation of Library Associations and Institutions). She is involved in the activities of the Network of Finnish university libraries and the chair of the consortium group of the National Electronic Library. Her main research interests include academic libraries, their role and new tasks, as well as management and leadership issues.

Arja Juntunen, Licentiate of Humanities, is the Head of Services at the Kuopio University Library. She has graduated from the University of Oulu. In her licentiate thesis, she discussed the 18th century Finnish self-educated writers. She has worked in several libraries, both public and academic. She has published papers on distance learning and library management.

Vesa Kautto, PhD, is the former Director of the Oulu University Library. He served as an acting Professor of Information Science at the University of Oulu during 1988–1998. During 1971–1983, he was the Director of the Tampere University of Technology Library. He has also served as board member of the Finnish Council for Scientific Information, chair and board member of the Automation Unit of Finnish Research Libraries, and chair of the Finnish Subject Headings Project. His research interests include information literacy, library administration, and classification. He received his PhD from the Department of Information Studies at the University of Oulu in 2004.

Terttu Kortelainen, PhD, lecturer of Information Studies at the University of Oulu, where she received her PhD in 1999. Her research interests are in informetric research, in the evaluation of libraries, and study of digital libraries. Her publications consist of two text books, and articles on bibliometrics, as well as articles on the study projects of the department concerning usability evaluation of Web services.

Harriet Lönnqvist received her PhD from the Department of Information Studies at the University of Tampere in 2003. She received a Licenciate of Philosophy degree in history from Åbo Akademi University in 1978 and a Master of Librarianship degree from University of Wales (College of Librarianship Wales, Aberystwyth) in 1982. In 1980–1987, she held vacancies at Helsinki University of Technology and NORDINFO, the Nordic Council for Scientific Information. During 1987–1988 she conducted a NORDINFO-funded research project on humanities scholars' information seeking behaviour in all Nordic countries, Denmark, Finland, Iceland, Norway, and Sweden. During 1988–1993, she served as a senior assistant professor at the Department of Information Studies in Åbo Akademi University. Harriet has published mostly in the field of information seeking research.

Ilkka Mäkinen, PhD, is senior lecturer at the Department of Information Studies at the University of Tampere. He received his doctorate in Information Studies at the same university in 1997. He leads the Research Group on Library History at the Department. He has published books and articles on Finnish library and information history and history of reading, e.g., in *Libraries and Culture*. He is active in the Nordic-Baltic-Russian research network on the history of books, libraries, and reading (HIBOLIRE). His present interests include history of reading, the role of public libraries in the welfare state, and the fates of books, libraries and archives during the Second World War.

Päivi Rasinkangas, MA, has worked as a lecturer and a researcher at the Department of Information Studies, University of Oulu, and as a project secretary in the joint development project of northern Finnish libraries. At the moment, she is an Assistant Director at the Oulu City Library – Regional Central Library, but also working on her licentiate thesis focused on the diffusion and the implementation of the evaluation methods in public libraries.

Annikki Roos is head of information services at The National Public Health Institute in Helsinki, Finland. She has an MA in social sciences from the University of Tampere and is a doctoral student at the Swedish School of Economics and Business Administration in Helsinki, Finland.

Jarmo Saarti, PhD, is the Director of Kuopio University Library. He has graduated from the University of Jyväskylä (MA) and from the University of Oulu (Lic. of Soc. Sci., PhD). He has studied and published papers mainly on the content representation of fiction, as well as, on the information society and the libraries' role in it. At the present he also is interested in information literacy and issues on management. He continues his studies in Jyväskylä on literature and is specialized on the translations of the Chinese works in Finnish. He is a member of the IFLA University and Research Libraries section.

Reijo Savolainen is a professor at the Department of Information Studies, University of Tampere, Finland. His current research interests are information needs and seeking in the context of everyday life, in particular, the role of the Internet in information seeking. He is also interested in conceptual and methodological questions of information seeking and use. Savolainen has about 80 publications in the field of information and library studies. For details, see http://www.uta.fi/~liresa/.

Sanna Talja, PhD, is Senior Lecturer at the Department of Information Studies at the University of Tampere. She teaches in the areas of knowledge organization and knowledge management. She received her PhD in Information Science at the University of Tampere in 1998. Dr. Talja's work focuses on the interaction between new technologies and scholarly communities' information and collaboration practices. She is interested in theories, approaches, and empirical studies related to the use and shaping of ICTs in scholarly communities. She has written and co-edited four books, and contributed articles to a number of journals, including *Journal of the American Society for Information Science and Technology*, *Journal of Documentation*, *Information Processing and Management*, *Library and Information Science Research*, *Information Research*, and *Library Quarterly*.

Kimmo Tuominen works as a head of Reference and Archival Services at the Library of Finnish parliament. He received his PhD from the Department of

Information Studies, University of Tampere in 2001. His research interests include information seeking, participatory digital libraries, knowledge organization, and methodological approaches in library and information science. Before joining the Library of Parliament, Tuominen was the director of the Arts Faculty Library at the University of Helsinki.

Timo Turja works as a chief information specialist at the Library of Finnish parliament. After earning licentiate's degree in political sciences at the University of Helsinki he has studied political theory as a Fulbright scholar at Drew University (NJ). Currently, he is writing a doctoral dissertation on the Finnish parliamentary culture.

Gunilla Widén-Wulff is acting professor at the Department of Information Studies, Åbo Akademi University, and Docent at University of Tampere, Information Studies. She received her PhD (2001) in information science, business information cultures, from Åbo Akademi University, Finland. Her research fields include information management in organizations, and she has published articles and papers especially on aspects on organizational learning, social capital, networks, and knowledge sharing in different kinds of groups and organizations. During the winter of 2004–2005, she was a visiting researcher at School of Computing, Napier University, Edinburgh.

AUTHOR INDEX

287

SET UP A CONTINUATION ORDER TODAY!

Did you know that you can set up a continuation order on all Elsevier-JAI series and have each new volume sent directly to you upon publication? For details on how to set up a **continuation order**, contact your nearest regional sales office listed below.

To view related series in Library & Information Science, please visit:

www.elsevier.com/libraryscience

The Americas
Customer Service Department
11830 Westline Industrial Drive
St. Louis, MO 63146
USA
US customers:
Tel: +1 800 545 2522 (Toll-free number)
Fax: +1 800 535 9935
For Customers outside US:
Tel: +1 800 460 3110 (Toll-free number).
Fax: +1 314 453 7095
usbkinfo@elsevier.com

Europe, Middle East & Africa
Customer Service Department
Linacre House
Jordan Hill
Oxford OX2 8DP
UK
Tel: +44 (0) 1865 474140
Fax: +44 (0) 1865 474141
eurobkinfo@elsevier.com

Japan
Customer Service Department
2F Higashi Azabu, 1 Chome Bldg
1-9-15 Higashi Azabu, Minato-ku
Tokyo 106-0044
Japan
Tel: +81 3 3589 6370
Fax: +81 3 3589 6371
books@elsevierjapan.com

APAC
Customer Service Department
3 Killiney Road #08-01
Winsland House I
Singapore 239519
Tel: +65 6349 0222
Fax: +65 6733 1510
asiainfo@elsevier.com

Australia & New Zealand
Customer Service Department
30-52 Smidmore Street
Marrickville, New South Wales 2204
Australia
Tel: +61 (02) 9517 8999
Fax: +61 (02) 9517 2249
service@elsevier.com.au

30% Discount for Authors on All Books!

A 30% discount is available to Elsevier book and journal contributors on all books *(except multi-volume reference works)*.

To claim your discount, full payment is required with your order, which must be sent directly to the publisher at the nearest regional sales office above.